Growing Old, Staying Young

Also by Christopher Hallowell:

People of the Bayou

Growing Old, Staying Young

Christopher Hallowell

William Morrow and Company, Inc.

New York

Library of Congress Cataloging in Publication Data

Hallowell, Christopher.
Growing old, staying young.

Includes index.
1. Aged—United States—Life skills guides.
2. Aging—United States—Psychological aspects.
3. Aged—United States—Care and hygiene. I. Title.
HQ1064.U5H195 1985 305.2′6 85-13732
ISBN 0-688-04839-0

Printed in the United States of America

First Edition

1 2 3 4 5 6 7 8 9 10

BOOK DESIGN BY ANN GOLD

For my mother
who never realized the
force she was behind this book

Acknowledgments

*T*hough the idea for this book did not crystallize until three years ago, the seeds were planted long before as I watched my parents and various relatives gradually slip into old age, a bewildering period during which they experienced increasing poor health and helplessness. They were victims, as so many elderly are, of social attitudes toward aging, of discouragement, of tightening finances, of poor nutrition and of a lack of mental and physical stimulation. Not everyone joins this stereotype, of course. I wondered how some elderly people preserved their enthusiasm for life. This book is partially an exploration of that curiosity.

Many people have made this book possible. Scientists interrupted their experiments to talk to me. People just becoming aware of their own aging struggled to articulate their fears. Elderly people took the time to recollect the changes they encountered. Others provided me with valuable information by the care they took to avoid talking about their own aging. Even children contributed by expressing their often predictable attitude toward aging; growing old to so many of them means only wrinkles, sickness and death.

Inevitably, a handful of people stand out for the time and thought and observations that they gave me. In no order of preference I am indebted to: Dr. Vincent J. Cristofalo, director of the Center for the Study of Aging at the University of Pennsylvania; Dr. Peter Davies of Albert Einstein College of Medicine; Dr. Arthur K. Balin of Rockefeller University; Dr. Edward J. Masoro of the University of Texas at San Antonio;

7

Dr. Robert Sapolsky of the Salk Institute; Dr. Robert N. Butler, chairman of the Department of Geriatrics and Adult Development at Mount Sinai Medical Center in New York; Dr. Arthur Ship; Dr. David J. Wolf; Dr. David Zakin; and to Harvey Ginsberg, my editor, who so enthusiastically responded to the initial idea for this book and who has since then diligently commented upon several versions of the manuscript.

I am also grateful to Hal Bowser, Dr. Rhodes Adler and to my wife, Willa, for their invaluable criticism, suggestions and unrelenting support.

—Christopher Hallowell

New York
1985

Contents

Do not go gentle into that good night,
Old age should burn and rave at close of day;
Rage, rage against the dying of the light.
—Dylan Thomas

Preface

My father died quite casually
one cold January night. He was tough. He had survived three
heart attacks, followed by two strokes. When he came home
from the hospital after the second stroke, he looked scared.
No wonder. The left side of his face slumped. His speech was
slurred. He could not raise his left arm above his chest. Worse,
his mind did not work right. I remember asking him a mundane question about physical therapy that he was unable to
understand. As he slouched in his chair, the realization of loss
lit his eyes. They shone with a peculiar light that I can inter-
pret only as a bewildered scream for help.

But within two months my father had regained most of his
old capacities. He played tennis. He read the newspaper from
the first to the last page every day. He drank two whiskeys every
evening before dinner and two martinis every Sunday before
lunch. Still, there seemed to be something missing. He stared
into space a lot; not thinking, just staring.

One night a year and a half later, in 1979, he came down
with the flu. I was away at work on a book but was told later
that he did not appear very sick—just groggy and listless, with
a slight fever and loss of appetite. He went to bed early that
night but woke up a few hours later with a cough that brought
up phlegm. He was having difficulty breathing. My mother
called the doctor, who was at his bedside within ten minutes.
He listened to my father's chest through a stethoscope for about
thirty seconds and called an ambulance. Somewhere along the
dark snow-swept road to the hospital, my father stopped

breathing. He was seventy-three years old. The doctors said he died from "water in the lungs." The death certificate lists pneumonia.

My mother and my father lived together for thirty-five years in a marriage that had survived, like many marriages, in the familiarity of habituation and in seesaws of guilt, dependence and the fear of being left alone. My mother's reaction to her husband's death was one of total calm. She called the relatives, replied to the condolences and did the shopping. Driving back from the supermarket one day, she went through a red light at an intersection and hit a car broadside. There were no injuries but from that point on my mother's mind seemed to collapse. She could not remember the day of the week, the name of the month, or what appointments she had made. Her handwriting turned garbled and jerky. She could no longer add numbers; she forgot how to brew coffee. She left the stove on. My sister took her to a neurologist who diagnosed her as having Alzheimer's disease. We realized, upon reflection, that our mother's mind had been deteriorating for some time. But the meshing of personal interactions that three and a half decades of living with another person provides had concealed the changes. In recent years, we recalled, my father had guided her through every step of every day, reminding her to do this, telling her again and again what day of the week it was. He probably wondered how this collapse could be taking place before his very eyes.

Caring for my mother had to have been a wearying task. My father may have sensed the exhaustion that the future would bring. I have often wondered if he took the opportunity of a mild case of the flu to die, to walk away from a life in which he had never been very happy with himself, foreseeing, perhaps, the additional sadness and turmoil that my mother's condition was sure to bring upon both of them.

My mother was moved into an institution four years ago. There was no way that she could remain alone in a rambling old farmhouse, unable to drive, to cook, to remember how to change a light bulb or how to write a check. The caretakers that she initially had either took advantage of her failing mind and stole from her, or she, in her increasing paranoia, treated them so poorly that they quit.

The institution is an attractive place with graceful grounds, wide corridors and friendly personnel. But the residents do not fare well there, perhaps not so much because they have been separated from their belongings, family, friends and familiar surroundings as because there is no motivation to keep up, to exercise mind and body and to eat the right food. My sister and I saw our mother's mind deteriorate month by month. By last spring, she could no longer walk and was restricted to a wheelchair. Her ability to speak was beginning to go and she was having difficulty eating. Her mind floated between the present and events she had experienced and people she had known years ago. Sometimes, she told us, she had had conversations with people who had gone out of her life decades earlier. My mother was well along on the devastating trip that Alzheimer's disease takes its passengers on.

Growing Old, Staying Young

Introduction:
The Hope

*A*ging. Everyone has stories about what it does to others or to themselves. We too easily assume that the process carries us inevitably toward physical incapacitation, mental incompetence, social rejection, loneliness and poverty. As evidence, we see elderly people every day who sit hunched up on park benches, in bus station waiting rooms and in senior-citizen centers. They stare vacantly and passively at the death they feel closing in around them. Go into any nursing home and you see hundreds of them. Gnarled hands grip the arms of wheelchairs, skinny legs dangle uselessly to the floor.

But aging has another side, one that does not necessarily lead to crippling and devastation. The other side of aging is the subject of this book. While not all the diseases and frailties that accompany the passage of years can be avoided, the pain and damage of many of them can be alleviated. Alzheimer's disease is one of the few exceptions. Cancer in some forms is another; these can creep up on us no matter how well we take care of ourselves. Yet we have far more control over our aging than we thought possible even five years ago. Americans are beginning to realize the potential grace, even the elegance, of being old. Within us, we harbor an image of the ideal old—a sharp-boned, quick-minded, glistening-eyed soul whose compassion, wisdom and independence of thought beckon and caress us. It is the grandparent image—someone much wiser than we who spoils us when we are good and scolds us by ignoring us when we are bad. Not everyone has or had such grandpar-

19

ents, but the image remains strong, perpetuated in children's stories, in films, in art and in history. We want to see the real gray-haired George Washington crossing the Delaware, the real Giuseppe coaxing Pinocchios into good people. We want to see Mr. Chips on every park bench.

As idealistic as these tales are, something happening in this country is coloring their messages with an edge of possibility. A gradual transformation is arising; the elderly are taking a role in their destiny, not only by joining lobbying groups but also by fighting the negative stereotype that a short time ago aging was given in our society.

This change did not occur overnight. It began in many of today's elderly in their younger years, when they adopted attitudes and hopes to fight the drawbacks associated with being old. The elegant elderly of today took care of themselves yesterday. They were not people who merely retired at sixty-five. They asked themselves what they would retire to. They have treated life as an ongoing experience and experiment.

Younger people, those in their forties and fifties, are following this lead in increasing numbers. The boom in exercise and the concern about proper diet and health are just indications. People are switching careers in mid-life, fearful of getting stuck in a rut. People are moving out of large cities to seek calmer, less stressful existences in small cities and rural towns.

But the greatest impetus to aging well are the models that have sprung up. Politics aside, there's Ronald Reagan. Seventy-four years old at the beginning of his second term, he carried himself well physically. His gaffes and misstatements of fact seemed caused not so much by age as by enthusiasm for whatever program he was trying to push. During his re-election campaign, he rolled along on a cloud, apparently enjoying himself immensely. Such behavior is not thought characteristic of the elderly.

There are many others. Willem de Kooning, the abstract expressionist, is painting furiously at the age of eighty. Armand Hammer, at eighty-six, is not only chairman of the Occidental Petroleum Company, but a mediator between the U.S. and Soviet governments. Maggie Kuhn, now seventy-eight, founded the Gray Panthers, a lobbying organization for the rights of the elderly, after she was forced to retire from her job at seventy. "My wrinkles are a badge of distinction," she says. "I earned them." And there is a host of actors and actresses—Bob Hope, George Burns, Helen Hayes and Katharine Hepburn, to name but a few—who are still professionally active in their seventies and eighties.

Historical figures also contribute to the awakening acknowledgment that the elderly are a force whose persistence and purpose can serve as an inspiration to younger people. Archimedes invented the mirror when he was seventy-five; Cato learned Greek when he was eighty; Sophocles wrote *Oedipus Rex* at seventy, *Oedipus at Colonus* at eighty-nine, and died at ninety; and Goethe completed the second part of *Faust* at eighty-three. And these people lived when the average life expectancy was less than forty years. People can do extraordinary things at extraordinary ages. Today, business executives in their eighties are still going strong, as are teachers, musicians and farmers. Extraordinary feats by the elderly are becoming so commonplace that they do not even merit the publicity that they would have received a decade ago. When seventy-year-old Jack Halbeisen flew a motorized kite coast to coast and back again in 1984, the first person ever to have done so, *The New York Times* acknowledged the accomplishment with a notation less than two column inches long.

Numbers are favoring the elderly. While the total population of the country is expected to increase by a bit over 30 percent through the year 2050, the Bureau of the Census projects that the over-fifty-five population will increase by 113 percent during that period. By 2050, one out of every three people will be over fifty-five. People over seventy-five are the fastest growing segment of our population. In 1982, only five percent of the population was older than seventy-five. By 2030, more than 10 percent will be over this age, a higher proportion than today's sixty-five-plus population.

This phenomenon is not due to the lengthening of the human life span. Gerontologists have long thought that to be maximally between one hundred and ten and one hundred and fifteen years. The oldest person on earth whose age has been authenticated is a one-hundred-and-nineteen-year-old Japanese man who, according to the *Guinness Book of World Records*, says the best way to lead a long life is "not to worry" and to leave things to "God, the Sun and Buddha." All those claiming to be older have been unmasked. The Swedish government, perhaps the most conscientious in following up longevity claims, has never been able to verify an age of over one hundred and ten years.

The increase in life expectancy* is due to the benefits of medical technology, preventive medicine, improved sanitation, better diet and, most recently, to regular exercise. At the turn of the century, life expectancy in the United States, was about forty-seven years. It has crept up each decade to its present 74.6 years or, more precisely, 70.9 years for men and 78.2 years for women. By 2050, life expectancy is projected to be just under seventy-six years for men and just under eighty-three years for women.

Death rates for those over sixty-five have diminished since 1940 from about 72 to 53 per thousand. One of the major reasons is the decrease in deaths from heart attack and stroke, though heart disease remains the nation's prime killer. In 1968, 270 Americans out of 100,000 died of heart disease. Since then, the numbers have crept down. In 1980, the death rate was 202; in 1981, 195; and in 1982, 191. Even so, 555,000 Americans died of heart disease in 1982.

Researchers strongly suspect that this decline has to do with the way we are treating ourselves. Though teenagers may smoke, the middle-aged and the elderly are quitting. Older people are also paying more attention to what they eat. And innumerable studies have confirmed the benefits of regular exercise for the cardiovascular system and as a way of lowering cholesterol.

The result is a dramatic shift in the look of survival curves, which are to a gerontologist what profit charts are to a businessman. A survival curve plots the percentage of a population that survives as time goes by. In 1900, only 30 percent of the population lived to be seventy years old. In 1980, 60 percent lived to this age. Alex Comfort, who is a reputable gerontologist though he is better known as the author of *The Joy of Sex,* has noted that survival curves are gradually taking on a rectangular shape as a greater percentage of the population lives into old age. What this may mean is that a dream of ger-

---

*Life expectancy is the average length of life that an individual can expect to live; life span is the maximum length of life that we as members of a species can expect to live.

ontologists is coming true: that people are living to a ripe old age because the chronic diseases so typical of the elderly are being compressed into the few years before death. But not all gerontologists agree. The dissenters say that the percentage of chronic disease among the elderly is as great as ever but that modern technology can keep these people alive longer. Advocates of this view place the need for health-care planning for the increasing numbers of people suffering from heart conditions, arthritis and impaired vision and hearing as our highest priority.

According to the National Center for Health Statistics, about half the elderly in America suffer from one or more chronic conditions, arthritis and hypertension being the most common. Most of these people have to change their way of life to some extent because of the diseases. Just as the rate of heart disease and stroke have diminished because people are beginning to take better care of themselves, the ravages of other diseases could be lessened. The ten most prevalent chronic conditions are, in order, arthritis, hypertension, deafness, heart conditions, sinusitis, poor vision, orthopedic problems, atherosclerosis, diabetes and varicose veins. The severity of six of these—arthritis, hypertension, heart conditions, orthopedic problems, atherosclerosis and diabetes—could be reduced through preventive measures. Stretching exercises can, for example, help relieve osteoarthritis. A low-fat diet, dieting and exercise can reduce high blood pressure and alleviate many heart conditions. Osteoporosis, a leading bone ailment, can be largely prevented by increasing calcium in the diet, by reducing alcohol intake and by exercising during one's younger years. And adult-onset diabetes has been strongly associated with being overweight.

As we age, a lot can be done about how we age, though there is no remedy for aging itself. This book will explore the inevitability of aging in both the worst and the best of cases. Though we can now to some extent control the state we are in when we turn sixty-five, the means of transportation to that state still remain elusive. It is not even known, for example, why women live longer than men; why Ronald Reagan still has all his hair; why some neurotransmitters—the brain's chemical messengers—diminish with age; why our immune systems slide downhill as we get older and then, when we reach our mid-eighties or early nineties, suddenly rebound and get stronger, at least in the case of resistance to cancer.

Gerontologists—those who study the aging process—are pioneers exploring one of the last strongholds of life's secrets. Only during the last few years has the specialty attracted medical students in numbers. Now, gerontology, together with geriatrics—the care of the elderly—is a hot new field, and medical schools around the country are strengthening their teaching in these areas. As the number of the elderly grows, gerontologists hope to decipher some of the codes that govern the aging process. The prominent gerontologist Vincent J. Cristofalo is investigating the cell to try to figure out why it ceases some of its crucial functions after a certain point. His search is just the opposite of that of cancer researchers, who search for the mechanisms that lead cells to uncontrolled proliferation. The keys may be duplicates.

Other scientists that we will meet are trying to find out how external forces influence the cell's and, ultimately, the body's behavior. Some wonder if aging is influenced by hormones. If so, it means that the seat of hormonal activity in the brain acts as a clock, tick-tocking the years away and adjusting the flow of hormones to conform to the number of years that have passed. One hormone, dubbed the death hormone, increases as we grow older and blocks the influence of thyroid hormone, which is crucial to the proper functioning of the metabolism. If an antidote to the death hormone exists, death may be postponed for many years. Another hormone, one that discourages death, decreases with time. Called dehydroepiandrosterone, or DHEA for short, it appears to have a profound influence on the immune system. If a way can be found so that its derivatives can be given in proper doses to sufferers of such chronic diseases as diabetes, the extent of its benefits may be enormous.

Understanding the process of aging, just what goes on inside our bodies and minds to change a young person into an old one, is complex for two principal reasons: First, it involves not one physiological system but every system and, second, because the precipitating agent—the something or somethings in our bodies that begin all the changes—has yet to be discovered. So we are left with a lot of theories as to why and how we age. Many are mentioned in this book, particularly in

Chapters 4 and 5. Most possess an intrinsic fascination not just because they are clues in a grand detective story but because each contains within itself theories about life and death. Understandably, these theories are complex, but their essence can be summed up in two statements. First, though the ultimate cause of aging is unknown, scientists are gradually intertwining the separate mechanisms that contribute to aging to create a detailed picture of the process. Second, though we can do nothing about the process, researchers are beginning to see how adjustments in the way we live will alter the rate of our aging and increase our capacity for a happy and healthy life well into old age.

Here are a few examples. While some scientists are sifting through the body's chemicals, others are looking at how we treat that body. The effects of diet on longevity is a burgeoning research field. For decades it has been known that if you give laboratory animals less food, they live longer. Why this is so is just beginning to be understood and has enormous implications for human longevity, especially in light of the fact that people who live the longest *do* consume less food than others.

The effect of nutrition has been largely ignored. What is known about vitamins and minerals is based largely on theory and controversial experiments. Even the traditional view of carbohydrates, fats and proteins is now coming under attack. But knowledge of human nutrition is so young that it is still fickle. One month we are warned to keep away from oily fish such as mackerel and salmon, which are high in cholesterol. A few months later, we are told that this same oil contains a substance that may both reduce the protein deposits that make arthritis more severe and clog organs, including the heart. Reaching valid conclusions from the deluge of information that is beginning to flow from nutritionists' laboratories is impossible. Better wait awhile and stick to what is known, i.e., do not overeat, and limit your intake of cholesterol and foods containing saturated fats.

No matter what the physical mechanisms of aging are and no matter what you eat or how little you eat, successful aging depends as much on attitude as on physiology. Psychologists are discovering firm links between stress and disease. They are also finding, though, that some people have learned to cope with stress and that others even thrive on it. Their principal finding is that you can exert some mental control over health and thus indirectly over longevity. So subtle are the internal mechanisms of aging—the inner workings of cells, the flow of hormones and the functioning of the brain—that they are beyond our influence. But we can have some effect on how we think and what we think, and we do have the power to make ourselves happy or unhappy.

Some people just ignore the graying hair, the slowing body, the lack of stamina. They just keep on going, gradually adjusting their life-style to conform to the physical and mental changes brought on by aging. Others try to deal with these changes, at least initially, through camouflage—cosmetic surgery or cosmetics. Beyond the visible one, the effects of these latter measures on health are unknown. It could well be, though, that the apparent rejuvenation that results from a face-lift might boost a person's self-esteem enough to ward off some of the diseases that the elderly are prone to. However, cosmetic surgery and cosmetics are only superficial ways of avoiding the pitfalls of aging. Aging cannot be fooled; wrinkles are sure to break through the foundations and creams or the tightened skin. Only attitude can stave off the negative effects of retirement, disease, the loss of spouse and friends, the increasing inability to get around, the supposed mental incompetence, the possible loss of self-esteem and the loneliness. Study after study and interview after interview with those who are happy and relatively healthy in their later years come up with the same conclusions—aging must be prepared for. Those who ignore its approach or who let it sneak up are going to be thrown off balance.

We prepare for almost everything in life except aging. A toddler is taught to share and cooperate in preparation for independence from adults. School teaches skills necessary for later life. Sports instill the spirit of cooperation and competition. Only those who are facing aging with uncertainty are left to fend for themselves.

The word "preparation" perhaps implies too much consciousness. The key to successful aging is *involvement.* People who age the best tend to be involved in various interests; they are involved with people; they are curious and they are flexible. For some, these are natural inclinations, and those who possess these traits are fortunate. Other people can learn these traits, not easily, but it can be done. They must develop interests outside their occupations; they must force themselves not to be isolated, a tendency that males are prone to in this society and one possible reason why females live longer. They must whet their curiosity and let their mind go on a few rampages of imagination. They must exercise and expand all their capacities.

As inevitable as aging is, it is a continuing process, the outcome of which is far more susceptible to our control than we have ever before envisioned.

Chapter 1

Making the Best of the Inevitable

*P*aul Charlotte is fifty. Each morning he charges into his office for a daily marathon of business negotiations. He meets colleagues and adversaries alike with a crunching handshake and a piercing though not un-friendly stare. He makes decisions from the gut and tends not to deliberate. If one of the decisions is bad, he shrugs and goes on. Not many are bad. Success has placed him in the executive vice presidency of a major advertising firm, a business known for fast turnover of its personnel, and those who get turned over land in the street.

Charlotte (not his real name) looks the picture of New York corporate success. Head and shoulders thrust forward, he strides rather than walks, often consuming a five-inch-long cigar with oral caresses as he goes. No midriff pudge, he's lean and hard. His suits are well-tailored, but not showy. His shoes are of supple leather. His face, still firm with only a slight droop around the jowls, is clean-looking and of healthy complexion.

Though his hair is trimmed close, it still has body. It is light brown with reddish overtones but the reddish effect is tempered by scattered flecks of gray and the hair around the temples is a nice clean white. The color scheme is calculated. Every few weeks Charlotte "colors" his hair, as he calls the process. Hiding most of the gray hair is crucial to the future of his professional life, or so he thinks. "Look, gray hair is almost like being fat. If you're overweight, people may not bother to find the real you underneath. It's the same with gray hair; it means you're old."

Charlotte told me this one day in his office that overlooks the jumble of similar offices that make up midtown Manhattan. Charlotte's office has pink walls. It is an uncluttered, efficient space, suggesting the same crispness as its occupant. On one end of a handsomely veneered file cabinet is a photograph of his seventeen-year-old daughter playing tennis. On the other end is a photograph of a dozen or so of the firm's employees who ran in a New York City Marathon. Charlotte is among them, his gray hair sparkling under a cap. Six months later his hair was a different color.

"Unless you are number one, unless you are very secure," he continued, twisting his cigar around in his mouth, "there is something about gray hair that is looked upon as a negative. I didn't want to be perceived as just another gray old person. I don't want to take that chance. I am not about to take a chance on anything limiting my potential to grow professionally and I am going to do what I have to in order to make it in the world I have decided that I want to make it in."

The decision to change hair color came precipitously. In mid-1983, the firm was in the throes of being sold to a holding company. Personnel changes were rumored. Heads were expected to roll. At the same time, Charlotte made a business trip to Europe and happened to see some photographs of himself. The combination of the expected firings and Charlotte's fear that gray equals old moved him to search for a new self-image.

Early graying and early death run in his family. His father died of a heart attack at sixty-eight. Charlotte turned gray in his thirties. Yet, even after this happened, he never saw himself as gray. Now, he's up by six in the morning and runs three to five miles before work. (On weekends, he runs eight miles each day. He has run in several New York City Marathons, the first when he was thirty-nine.) By eight, he's in his office, arriving with a lined pad in his attaché case, the first page neatly filled with the day's agenda. His office hours are taken up with decisions—on client relations, on acquiring new accounts, on finances, and on promotional strategies. Evenings are for family and entertaining. But Charlotte makes even this time sound like it has an element of work in it. With perverse pride, he does not like the idea of relaxing. His idea of a vacation abroad is to hop from one historic and cultural place to another. He does not expect to live past seventy. "I go faster than most people," he says, "so I have to assume that my machine is going to wear out sooner. Besides, I don't see life past seventy being very enjoyable."

The first time Charlotte had his hair colored, his dreams were realized. "All of a sudden, everyone saw me differently. They asked me what had happened, why I looked so good. They didn't realize I had colored my hair; they just thought the difference was because I had gotten a short hair cut." The second time was not so happy. The formula was off. Charlotte's hair came out bright red and people stared at him. He felt like a bruised tomato. Now, everyone in the firm knows that he dyes his hair. But he is viewed in a much better light, he says, and the formula is down so pat that there will be no more mistakes. The holding company bought the firm. Charlotte and his new hair were asked to stay.

It is a sad fact that in America aging is a risk-laden journey. For many, it is a time of shriveling up in a disappointed heap. A seven-billion-dollar-a-year cosmetics industry helps people believe that they can stave off the visible signs of old age, a multimillion-dollar-a-year exercise industry operates toward the same, though medically sounder, end. While the population of the country ages, the business of keeping people from looking and acting old is in its youth. Many of its customers share Paul Charlotte's belief about the social attitudes that led him to dye his hair.

The advertising industry fosters these attitudes. Advertisers still call upon youth to display products, and the industry uses most of its resources to sway younger people. TV commercials typecast older people as quirky comics or providers of grandfatherly advice. Center stage is still reserved for sleek bodies, smashing hair-dos and fast cars.

The study of animal behavior can teach us much about our own behavior. Where resources are limited, those who cannot fend for themselves suffer because the stronger and the younger push them aside. The weak and the weakening must forage for themselves and, in all probability, fall victim to a predator.

While we pride ourselves on belonging to a civilized society, we too shoulder the elderly aside. It is ironic that many primitive human societies revere their old people and seek out their counsel. We should and could do the same. Have you ever noticed the Ageless Ones? You see them on occasion. R. Buckminster Fuller, the designer, was one example. Margaret Mead, the anthropologist, was another. Fuller, at eighty, could lecture to a crowd without notes for five hours straight, stopping only when his listeners were so exhausted by the seeds of the ideas that he had sowed in their minds that they could not absorb any more information. For these people, their chronological age is irrelevant; their love of life has imparted to them a sense of agelessness. But that impression is just that—an impression. R. Buckminster Fuller and Margaret Mead have died, of course, but there are thousands of others with the same spirit to succeed them. What is special about such people is that they just keep on going despite inconveniences. Undoubtedly more and more people will become this way as the country's population gets older and as we come to grips with the idea that aging does not have to lead to enfeeblement and decrepitude.

Now, most people hide from getting old and for a time, anyway, enjoy their private fountain of youth in the form of night creams and weight-lifting sessions and trust that the infirmities of age will stay away until next year or the year after or the year after that. The process of aging, though, is happening to you as you read these words, no matter how old you are. Our bodies begin their journey toward old age from the minute we are born. But it is not until we are in our mid-thirties that the telltale signs of aging reveal themselves, whether they be gray hair, a thickening waistline, stiffening joints, dropping the butter dish or forgetting a lunch meeting. Never mind that we have been forgetting those meetings all along. At a certain point the added years and yet one more incident of mental or physical lapse jolt us into admitting that age has crept up.

Early Aging

How do our bodies begin the aging process? When? Some of the early signs are obvious. Looking in a mirror one morning in our thirties, we see a single white hair half-hidden behind the tens of thousand of dark ones. Reactions to it are as varied as people. Charlotte's effort to conceal his gray hair is just one response. A young woman exclaimed to me, "I just couldn't believe this white thing was in my hair. Then I thought, 'Oh, well, at least there won't be any more.' " Dozens of people have the same reaction.

But for some, the first gray commands extraordinary attention. Its arrival marks an irrefutable crossing from youth to adulthood. The lucky first few get a terrific pampering, their darker partners often combed aside to permit the world's gaze to fall upon this symbol of the adult world.

Gerontologists do not become at all excited about gray hair. "It seems a fair approximation," one writes, "that at fifty years of age, fifty percent of the people are at least fifty percent gray, irrespective of sex or hair color." Hair turns gray because of a decline in the density and activity of melanocytes—cells in the skin and in hair roots that manufacture the dark pigment melanin, which determines skin and hair color. Genes dictate the abundance of these cells. Blacks have more melanocytes, for example, than whites, brunets more in their hair roots than blonds. As a rule, beginning around the age of thirty, 10 to 20 percent of the hair's melanocytes either die or become inactive during each ensuing decade. President Reagan's dark thatch is a physiological impossibility. Naturally, he dyes his hair. What is incredible is that he has so much to dye.

Why is it primarily the hair on our heads that turns gray? Gerontologists theorize that melanocytes in this hair cease to function earlier because it grows faster here than anywhere else on the body, making the melanocytes work harder producing enough pigment to keep pace. Melanocytes in the slower-growing hair of other parts of the body lead far more casual lives and thus survive longer, a characteristic that pops up again and again in the aging process. Stress and longevity, as will be discussed later, do not always make good companions.

The Skin, the Years, and the Sun

One of the main jobs of a melanocyte is to help protect the skin from the sun's ultraviolet light. That is why people get tan; the more hours a light-skinned person spends under the sun, the more melanin the cells secrete and the darker the skin becomes. But as a person gets older, he better be careful for two reasons. First, a lot of his melanocytes will have died off, leaving fewer to protect him. And second, without this protection, the sun burns, rather than tans.

Something happens, too, that is potentially far more serious than a sunburn. In the early 1970s, Drs. Ronald Hart and Richard Setlow performed some experiments at the Oak Ridge National Laboratory that suggest what happens to old skin and young skin when both are exposed to ultraviolet light. (Though sunlight is less than five percent ultraviolet and much of that is absorbed by the ozone layer, enough gets through to affect us.) Old cells, and even young ones that are not protected by abundant melanin, go berserk when bombarded by this kind of radiation, their chromosomes breaking into fragments as the cells divide. Skin cancer is the all-too-frequent result. A study by the National Cancer Institute removed any shadow of doubt of the connection between skin cancer and sun exposure. People in sunny Dallas–Fort Worth had over twice as great a chance of getting skin cancer as those in St. Paul–Minneapolis, far to the north.

Most skin cancer is relatively harmless because it is slow-moving and can be detected early. The cancer strikes most frequently in those areas commonly exposed to the sun, such as the arms, neck, face and scalp (if you are bald). An indication that skin cancer may be developing is the appearance of a small, smooth nodule with edges that look as though they are flowing outward. As the nodule grows, it develops a crusted ulcer in its center. This type of growth is known as basal-cell carcinoma. It develops slowly, invades only cells right under the skin's surface and rarely spreads to distant sites. The prognosis is excellent if the nodules are removed early.

Another sign of skin cancer is the development of rough spots on the skin. These are known as solar keratoses. You see them sometimes on the faces or arms of elderly farmers or other people who spend a lot of time outdoors. They can grow to ungainly proportions, lunar landscapes nestled into a soft cheek or forearm. From this unappealing but harmless state, they can change into squamous-cell carcinomas, far more dangerous than basal-cell because they can spread to nearby lymph nodes and then through the body, though this happens in less than two percent of all cases. An existing mole cannot change into either of these types of skin cancer.

Most skin cancers can be avoided by having any suspicious

spots examined by a dermatologist. If they look precancerous, they can be removed by using liquid nitrogen to freeze them off, a knife to cut them off or an electric needle to burn them away. All these procedures are virtually painless with local anesthesia.

Not all skin cancers are so easy to control. Malignant melanoma is an extremely dangerous kind of cancer because it moves much faster than basal or squamous cancers. It is fatal to 50 percent of those who get it and the incidence rate is currently doubling every ten to fifteen years as the once-youthful and sun-adoring leisure class begins to age. Right now, 17,500 people have it. One out of every 250 people in this country are destined to get it. Danger signs are the sudden formation of odd-shaped moles. If an existing mole begins to grow rapidly or change color from black to purple, have a dermatologist look at it.

Dermatologists and cosmetic surgeons say that sun worshipers by day may glow in the evening but carry around shriveled faces for the rest of their lives. Not only does ultraviolet light affect a skin cell's genetic material, it also tends to harden and thicken and dry out the skin's upper layer, the epidermis. The skin can recover from such ravages until the mid-twenties before beginning to take on a permanent leathery look. After thirty, the sunbather's skin loses its suppleness and elasticity. It begins to sag in some places and to pucker up in others. When this happens the temptation all too often is to keep right on gazing at the sun, especially if it has made you more beautiful or handsome in the past. Some people often turn to the sun as others turn to cosmetics to cover up wrinkles, blemishes, acne or other imperfections. Unfortunately, the sun is not so accommodating as cosmetics.

Dr. Earl W. Brauer, an associate professor of clinical dermatology at New York University School of Medicine and an officer with a well-known cosmetics firm that he does not wish himself identified with for reasons that will become apparent in Chapter 3, offered me this hypothetical anecdote as a way of emphasizing what sunlight does to our skin: "If I were given a set of identical twins, let's say females, though it makes no difference, and I told one of them that she could lead a normal life, and the other one that she could go outdoors only after four in the afternoon and only if she was wearing a sunscreen, you wouldn't see much difference between them after ten years. Even after twenty years, there would be little difference. But by age thirty, the differences would be very pronounced. There would be no doubt in your mind that the twin leading the normal life was five or six years older than the other one. At fifty, the twin leading the normal life would almost look like the other's mother."

Wrinkles—Marks of Time and Experience

Wrinkling is inevitable *even if* we avoid the sun, though the process is considerably slower. By the age of twenty-five we may see our face smiling back at us in a mirror and suddenly notice that our mouth is adorned with fine lines above and below the lips and that our eyes have a complex network of "crow's feet" spreading out from them. Even if these changes are not visible by the mid-thirties, they are nevertheless taking place. The skin secretes less oil and its childhood resilience is being gradually replaced by the flaccidity that comes with adulthood. Smoking, diet, sun, lack of exercise and urban pollutants take their toll. Gravity does, too. After a certain number of years, the skin just cannot support the underlying facial tissue. It begins to sag.

Skin cells nestle in collagen, a cushiony protein that gives bounce and fullness to young faces. Collagen is present throughout the body and is one of the principal ingredients of such connective tissues as tendons and ligaments. If it were boiled long enough, it would turn into something resembling gelatin. During childhood and youth, the protein aligns itself in fibers bunched together and parallel to each other. The arrangement gives it strength and elasticity. Another protein, elastin, helps, but it makes up only two percent of the skin's dry weight compared to collagen's 70 to 80 percent.

One reason that skin loses its elasticity as we age is that collagen and elastin fibers hook up with neighbors a couple of ranks over, thus lessening their linear tensile strength and disrupting the passage of nutrients and wastes. This cross-linking, as it is called, is how animal skin is rendered into leather; foreign ingredients (formerly tannin) in a solution allowed to soak their way into a skin will change it into leather by causing its collagen to cross-link. No wonder an old skin, particularly an old salt's skin, looks like leather.

One of the latest innovations in cosmetic surgery is to inject cow-skin collagen, purified and ground up, under the facial skin to soften major wrinkles and acne scars. It works, at least for a while—a protein cushion that puffs up the face in the right places. But alas, its wonders exhaust themselves after about a year. At around $300 per collagen treatment, the cost of fudging wrinkles must be weighed against their possible merits.

While our collagen is collapsing, epidermal cells replace themselves at an increasingly slower rate and make more mistakes as they go along. In the 1960s, the gerontologist Leonard Hayflick discovered that a population of lung cells taken from an aborted human embryo will double about fifty times before dying out. The finding reinforced the theory that aging is due to the eventual failure of each cell to continue dividing. Hayflick also discovered something even more tantalizing. He found that if he took cells from successively older people, they would divide fewer and fewer times, depending upon the age of the donor. He also noticed that these cells looked older when he peered at them through a microscope; the older the cell, the larger it was with more fluid between its membrane and nucleus. It would seem that cells "know" how old they are, an idea that Hayflick stunningly verified by letting human embryonic lung cells divide twenty times and then freezing them in liquid nitrogen. After thawing them out, he watched to see what would happen. The population doubled thirty more times and died. And if the freezing took place after ten divisions, the cells doubled forty more times. Someone is counting. Baffled gerontologists and biologists have dubbed the phenomenon "the Hayflick limit." Though Hayflick's pioneering work is still respected, the limit has been exceeded in numerous experiments, as will be discussed in Chapter 4.

Balding—A Meaningless Presage

Balding is another early sign of aging. Like graying, the phenomenon is so benign that gerontologists are not very interested in it. It stirs enough interest in those it affects, however, to keep dubious health faddists in business selling agents that will supposedly make hair miraculously reappear. It also provides some business for cosmetic surgeons who can transplant tufts of hair from the forever hirsute back of the scalp to the shining dome.

Men bald far more frequently than women because genes for baldness are dominant in males but recessive in females. The actual process involves the death of hair follicles over many parts of the body, the exceptions (in men) being in the ears and nose and on the back, places that are apt to get hairier with age. Before scalp hair falls out, beginning above the temples and continuing to the top of the head in the sequence termed male-pattern baldness, it changes into finer stuff, much like the hair on a child's forearm. This dramatic transformation, which begins anywhere between the ages of twenty and forty, is influenced by a decrease in androgens (male sex hormones, the principal one being testosterone) that many, but not all, males experience as they get older.

We are constantly shedding and regrowing hair. Men in their thirties may be alarmed to look in the bathtub drain after a shower and see a formidable array of hairs trapped there. That is the strongest evidence that the balding process has commenced. Though virtually all men except President Reagan experience this loss, not all become bald. At a certain point, the process can come to a halt. Whether this occurs depends very much on heredity.

Changing Bones

Gravity is responsible for a number of the more obvious changes that age brings upon us. It gives us jowls, yes, and makes our eyelids droop and our neck muscles sag. It also makes our ears "grow." Though ears would not seem to weigh much, it's enough for gravity to work wonders with. The lobe's fatty tissue begins to lengthen in our mid-twenties when average ear length is something over two-and-one-half inches. Fifty years later, our lobes will have gained half an inch.

But gravity and age wreak their greatest havoc with our bones. Indeed, the skull is the only bone mass that does not have to contend with the effects of gravity. The results, while not obviously apparent, are certainly baffling if you assumed that your hat size would always remain the same once you reached adulthood. Skulls do not stop growing until well into old age. The circumference of a sixty-five-year-old's head, for example, will be about two percent greater than it was when he was twenty years old. Indeed, the last skull sutures, the "cracks" on top of the skull that allow a fetus's head to change shape to ease its struggle down the birth canal, do not entirely close until we reach the age of eighty.

Most of the bones in the rest of the body are affected by the pressure of the tissue, organs and bones that bear down upon them. We usually do not feel our bones changing within us except under special conditions. One of these is osteoarthritis, a disease of the joints caused by the gradual wearing away of the cartilage between them because of pitting and cracking with age. Cartilage acts as a cushion and without a cushion, bone ends come against each other. That can be painful and accounts for the billions of aching joints that roll out of bed each morning and the trillions of fingers with swollen and ill-shaped joints. The pain tends to become more severe as the day wears on and the joints are used, particularly the large joints that support weight. The bones try to repair the damage by making new bone at their ends but that only makes the situation worse. The only really effective traditional treatment is aspirin or the like. The medical community is beginning to realize that gentle stretching exercises like swimming tend to stabilize the situation. A corollary is that regular exercise such as swimming, bicycling or rowing—exercises that stretch and strengthen muscles—may dissuade the disease from striking in the first place.

Exercise can also discourage back pain, a complaint that grows more common with the passing of the years. It is hard to pinpoint the exact cause of lower-back pain, which is where most of the problems occur, because of the complicated intertwining of nerve, bone and muscle down there. Even so, it is safe to say that we would not suffer so much lower-back pain if more attention were paid to keeping our back and abdominal muscles in shape and our weight down. Being overweight is a prime cause of back problems. Another is the sedentary existences many of us lead. Sitting at a desk in an office hour after hour, day after day, concentrates a lot of pressure on the lower vertebrae and the surrounding muscles. As a way of getting the weight off the lower spine, some health-training programs suggest that companies install high desks behind which workers stand rather than sit.

One of the most fascinating but horrifying bone ailments that affect people as they grow older is osteoporosis. This is a disease in which bones become more porous and consequently weaker as they age. This happens to some extent to everyone. On the average, an eighty-year-old woman will have 25 percent less bone mass than a thirty-year-old woman, and an eighty-year-old man over 10 percent less than a thirty-year-old man. When 30 percent or more of bone mass is gone, the loss is labeled osteoporosis. Some 15 million people in America suffer from it, most of them postmenopausal women. The affliction in its severest form can be seen in the telltale configuration of the upper back into what the medical profession terms a dowager's hump. While it may have been true in the last century that wealthy widows—sedentary, helpless and waited upon— were most likely to suffer from osteoporosis, today it is the uneducated and the unexercised who are the victims. In any case, dowager's hump is caused by the collapse of the upper vertebrae into wedge shapes, their narrower ends pointing toward the chest. The upper back bulges outward, forcing the head forward and creating the impression that the neck has vanished. As a result, a person can shrink by one-and-one-half inches. If the disease is permitted to continue, the lower vertebrae begin to compact, frequently with considerable pain. At this time, the sufferer can suddenly shrink by two-and-one-half additional inches until the point is reached where the bottom of the rib cage comes to rest on the pelvis. No more shrinkage can occur for now the victim is literally a stack of bones. Broken hips and wrists are other common effects of osteoporosis.

The disease's primary cause is a continuous drain of calcium from the bones. One way to think of the skeleton is as a bank into which calcium is deposited until the skeleton is largely mature sometime in the third decade of life. After skeletal maturity, no more calcium can be deposited in the bank. The body then begins to make withdrawals from the skeleton to meet its needs. The person who deposited the most calcium during his early years will run out of the mineral at a slower rate as he ages. The way to counteract the inevitable loss is for everyone to consume a lot more milk and other calcium-rich foods than he or she does during the first thirty years. Osteoporosis experts think that everyone should consume at least 1000 milligrams of calcium per day rather than the typical 400 because, as people age, they absorb less calcium from the food they eat. Postmenopausal women are advised to consume even more, about 1500 mgs. per day. One thousand milligrams is the approximate equivalent of six six-ounce glasses of milk. There are other ways, however, of getting calcium. A small yogurt has about 200 mgs., a cup of almonds, 230; an ounce of Swiss cheese, 270; three ounces of sardines with bones, 370; a cup of turnip greens, 265. Most dark green vegetables are a good source of calcium but some such as spinach, chard, parsley and beet greens contain oxalic acid, which inhibits the absorption of calcium. You can also get calcium by taking calcium supplements although the body does not absorb the mineral from this source as readily as it does from foods. If you take supplements, be sure to choose ones that contain more than 40 percent calcium per tablet.

That the disease principally strikes women after menopause has led researchers to believe that the calcium loss is exacerbated by the sudden drop in estrogen levels that comes with menopause. Still, the disease's etiology is shrouded in a certain amount of mystery. Very few Blacks get it, for example. The most susceptible are postmenopausal women of Japanese, Chinese or northwest European ancestry. Blonds and redheads with freckles are also more at risk. Such findings would suggest a genetic predisposition. But then other bits of evidence have surfaced that obviously have nothing to do with genes: Women who have never had children are more likely to get the disease than those who have. And those who smoke are likely to get it more easily than nonsmokers. The relationship between childbearing and osteoporosis is due to an increase in the bone-building hormone calcitonin that accompanies pregnancy. Women who smoke often have an earlier menopause, and smoking blocks calcium absorption.

Estrogen-replacement therapy is one of the most common treatments, but it must be started within ten years of getting the disease and the use of the hormone can lead to uterine cancer. Another, simpler therapy is to lessen the mineral's drainage from bones by increasing calcium consumption through calcium supplements such as pills or by eating high-calcium foods. Small doses of Vitamin D also enhance calcium absorption.

Still another therapy is fluoride, which works well when taken with calcium. Fluoride does the same thing for bones that it does for teeth; it makes them grow and it makes them stronger. Most towns and cities in this country add one part per million of fluoride to their water supply to prevent tooth decay. But balance is needed; too much can be just as damaging as too little. A Texas community that added eight parts per million found that although both tooth decay and the incidence of osteoporosis plummeted, other problems arose. Children wound up with discolored and pitted teeth and the elderly found that they had grown painful bone spurs and that their joints had stiffened. Treatment of osteoporosis with fluoride is still in an experimental stage as scientists try to determine the best and the safest dosage. There are also questions about the structural soundness of bone that has been stimulated to grow as a result of fluoride.

As in most diseases, prevention is a much better cure than the cure itself. The most obvious preventive measure is a high calcium consumption during one's first three decades. But the good this does can be compromised by a poor diet or by a lifestyle that will increase the amount of calcium that the body excretes. Nicotine, coffee and liquor are three examples of substances that increase calcium excretion. A high intake of protein, which is common in Western industrialized countries, also causes increased calcium excretion by the kidneys. Excessive consumption of sodas, which all contain phosphorous, can cause the bones to further lose calcium.

Exercise is consistently the best and least complicated way of preventing osteoporosis, which is why today's dowagers are more unlikely to get it than their ancestors were. Numerous surveys show that the wealthy and the educated in this country are far more apt to exercise regularly than the poor and the uneducated. Studies have also shown what exercise or lack of exercise does to bone mass. Marathon runners, for example, never have a problem with weak bones, even when they are old, according to John F. Aloia, an osteoporosis expert and chairman of the Department of Medicine at Nassau Hospital on Long Island. Tennis players also have large muscle and bone mass.

The best exercises are those that use the muscles connected to the body's larger bones. The key is to put stress on the bones, for it is stress that strengthens them. Since weightlessness places no stress whatsoever on the bones, astronauts may find themselves in trouble. After only a few days in a capsule, they already suffer a calcium drain from their bones, and bone experts fear that the continuation of the drain over months could be one of the greatest problems facing the space program.

Gum Decay, A Silent Disease

Teeth also suffer as we get older, not from tooth decay but from gum decay, or periodontal disease. The enamel that coats and protects our teeth actually gets harder as we age, though it does wear down to some extent. Gum decay entails the gradual receding of the gums, leaving the part of each tooth that is unprotected by enamel exposed to attack by food particles, bacteria and plaque. Given time and free rein, these culprits will eat away at the supporting bone and threaten the existence of the teeth. Almost 40 percent of American males between the ages of forty-five and fifty-four suffer varying degrees of periodontal disease and almost 60 percent of men between sixty-four and seventy-four. Women, curiously, are not afflicted with quite so high a frequency.

The major culprit is plaque, sticky stuff made up of saliva and gum secretions. This goo collects near the gum line and pushes its way under the gums, gradually hardening into tartar as it does so. The increasing accumulations force the gums away from the teeth, leaving room for a further build-up. Eventually, you will have "periodontal pockets" between your teeth where the gum has withdrawn. Having made its way into these pockets, the plaque rots away what gum material remains and eventually attacks the underlying bone. It also lets off an odor and is one of the prime causes of bad breath.

All this could be avoided if people brushed their teeth properly. After physical maturity has ended the childhood predilection to cavities, people tend to relax both their brushing and their visits to dentists. One day, when you are around thirty-five, you see that your toothbrush comes out of your mouth pink after a brushing. You look in the mirror and notice that your gums seem to be growing smaller. More dramatic is the unpleasant experience of feeling an irritation somewhere along your gum line which soon turns into a throbbing pain. What you probably have is gingivitis, the first step on the long road toward periodontal disease.

The only way to stop further encroachment on your gums and teeth is to get to a dentist fast. He will give you a good scaling—removal of the tartar—both on your teeth and under your gums and take a full set of X rays to determine the extent of bone loss. If your gums are in really bad shape, you may be offered a "flap," a minor surgical procedure (though it sounds major) whereby the gums are lifted from the teeth, which are given a good cleaning, then replaced in a more suitable position and sutured. All this can be done in the dentist's chair and you will have a sore mouth for no more than three weeks following. After you get the bill, you will take care of your teeth with neurotic obsession.

If the damage is not too great, your dentist will merely explain how to brush your teeth properly, which is about as embarrassing for an adult as having someone tell you how to tie your shoe laces. Proper care involves brushing along the gum line, both inside and out, rather than just the ends of the teeth. He will also tell you to floss you teeth daily, which is a good activity to pursue as you watch the late evening news, and to come back for a checkup every six months.

Losing Weight Without Trying

Another change that occurs as we get older involves our weight (see Chapter 5 for more information on weight and health). Though it might seem that people get heavier as they age, this is not usually the case. The stockbroker down the street may look plumper with success each year. But when he is in his sixties, he will start losing weight, even without trying to do so, and he will continue losing. Women will start losing weight about ten years later than men and the process will not be so dramatic. One reason is that men have more muscle that atrophies. Between fifty and seventy, for example, the weight of their triceps muscle may diminish by 15 percent. Loss of water, which constitutes just over 60 percent of body mass at age twenty-five but just over 50 percent at age seventy, is also responsible for weight loss. Cell matter decreases by about seven percent and bone mineral by one percent.

Weight loss is not necessarily healthy, particularly for older people, though most people feel that they should be thinner. One theory, discussed in Chapter 5, maintains that elderly people should eat much more than they do in order to get all the essential nutrients. A corollary is that if they can store away some energy in the form of fat, they will have reserves to fall back upon during sickness. However, as a rule, overweight people die earlier than their skinnier peers. There is a lesson here that the nascent field of nutrition is just beginning to come to grips with.

Immunity and Age—A Link to Nutrition

As the preceding information suggests, we age internally much more than externally. If the internal aging changes were as visible as wrinkled skin and graying hair, we would marvel more at the resilience of the human body than we despair of its mortality. One of the most dramatic changes that takes place is in our immune system. With aging, it weakens, leaving us far more vulnerable to disease. Some gerontologists believe that the decrease in the ability of the system to ward off disease is one of the prime causes of aging, not that it causes aging per se, but that it increases the rate of often fatal diseases. Elderly people certainly are far more vulnerable to cancer. Pneumonia and influenza are leading causes of death among the elderly. Some scientists believe that even the increase in heart disease with the years is due to immunity's decreasing strength.

Immunity is provided by cells called lymphocytes. To fight disease, these cells produce antibodies, proteins that attack foreign substances in the body. About one trillion lymphocytes are continuously being formed from cells in our bone marrow. Half of them migrate to the thymus gland where they mature under the influence of thymic hormones and become known as T-cells. From the thymus, they are then sent out to the spleen, tonsils, appendix and the lining of the respiratory and gastrointestinal tracts. Some, also from the thymus, continue circulating in the blood, ready to attack enemies in the form of viruses and bacteria. The other half of the lymphocyte population matures as B-cells in the marrow and take up guard duty in the lymphoid tissue.

Gerontologists are fascinated by the thymus. Until we are about fourteen years old, it fills a cavity behind the breastbone and processes lymphocytes into T-cells. After fourteen, the gland gradually shrinks. By middle age, the thymus is only 10 to 15 percent of its former size. Though the bone marrow produces just as many lymphocytes over the years, the diminished thymus is not able to process them to maturity, leaving the body with millions of immature and useless T-cells in its bloodstream. And those T-cells that do mature do not function as effectively. One result is the dramatic increase not only in the diseases that we are accustomed to seeing the elderly suffer from, but also in autoimmune diseases. These are caused by antibodies that, failing to recognize that the body is a friend and not a foe, attack it. Rheumatoid arthritis, systemic lupus erythematosus and myasthenia gravis are common autoimmune diseases, especially among women, which is ironic because the female immune system may be stronger than the male system. There is some evidence that immune response is influenced by genes on the X chromosomes, which are the sex chromosomes. Because females have two X chromosomes, they theoretically have a double dose of genes for immunity. This may not be as good as it sounds. Double immunity is fine in a woman's younger years, but later it can backfire for reasons no one yet understands. Some studies have indicated that the stronger immunity, in combination with female sex hormones, may allow T-cells to turn dramatically against the body. Even so, women have a longer life expectancy than men, perhaps because of their double immunity.

A recent study of seventeen healthy centenarians found that their immune systems were comparable to those of people at least forty years younger. John S. Thompson, the leader of the research team at the University of Kentucky College of Medicine, is puzzled but notes that diet may play a role in preserving immune strength. He notes that some of the characteristics of weakened immunity in typical elderly people are similar to those of younger malnourished people. Once these people are put on a nutritious diet, their immune response improves. Deficiencies of zinc and iron are closely associated with a weakened system, and the elderly are often deficient in these two minerals.

Other scientists are researching ways to strengthen immunity through injections of animal thymic hormones. In working with children with deficient immune systems, Dr. Alan Goldstein at George Washington University had such success treating a child with the substance called thymosim, one of the thymic hormones, that the child's system began functioning on its own.

Pulmonary Power

While our immune system decreases steadily with age, our ability to take in air goes through various phases before beginning a downward trend in our mid-fifties. An eighty-five-year-old person is able to inhale half the volume of air that a thirty-year-old can. Yet, in this half-century-plus time, actual lung size doubles, principally because the chest cavity gets deeper from back to front, which is why some very old men walk around with the barrel chests of weight lifters. But the increase in size does not help breathing efficiency. The ribs have become too stiff and the chest muscles too weak. Breathing becomes a fast, shallow effort, made more difficult by the fewer alveoli—the myriad tiny air sacs that in younger days gave the lungs their expansive volume.

Fighting Cardiovascular Disease

The capacity of the heart to pump blood at eighty years dwindles to half what it could accomplish at twenty, even though the pulse rate of old and young people at rest is about the same. The difference becomes most pronounced in response to physical stress such as exercise or illness. When an older person's heart is exerted, it simply does not contract as well or as fast as a younger person's. The problem is made worse by changes in the vascular system. As blood vessels lose their elasticity and become clogged with plaque, the heart must work harder to pump blood through them. Its muscle cells increase in size in order to do this. Though the enlarged cells may give the heart increased strength, the thickened walls, particularly of the left ventricle, which pumps blood to the body, becomes stiffer and less efficient. Although these changes are regarded as part of normal aging, cardiovascular disease is the commonest cause of death in the elderly and in middle-aged men. But cardiovascular disease is not inevitable and thus cannot be considered a norm. Over 714,000 Americans died of the disease in 1982, the latest year that the National Center for Health Statistics has figures for. That is an enormous number but it is 25 percent smaller than in 1968, the year with the most cardiovascular fatalities the United States has ever suffered. While the death rate from heart disease may have decreased because Americans have become more health-conscious, it is also possible that the diminishing death rate reflects not fewer heart attacks but better survival rates.

Cardiovascular disease is a broad term that encompasses heart attacks and strokes, which are both caused by atherosclerosis, better known as hardening of the arteries. Atherosclerosis* refers to a process by which plaques—fatty deposits formed in large part by cholesterol and calcium—clog the arteries that supply the tissues of the body with oxygen. These deposits result in a decrease in the diameter of an artery. The tissues downstream from the plaques, which, in the case of the heart, are muscle cells, are deprived of oxygen and are killed, or, in medical jargon, infarcted.

Why plaque accumulates on artery walls is unknown. One theory suggests that the immune system plays a perverse role. Plaque tends to build up at points of irritation, and one typical place of irritation is where an artery divides. Blood constantly rushing against the inside of the fork may cause excessive wear and tear. Another possible source of irritation is the chemicals in cigarette smoke that get into the blood via the lungs. Wherever the arterial lining is damaged, the immune system goes into action. Ironically, the repair job that follows can cause us to die. To patch over the diseased place, the immune system will use cholesterol, fats, cellular materials and calcium, causing the artery to get smaller and smaller and thereby reducing the flow of blood.

All the debate about whether cholesterol does or does not cause atherosclerosis—and thus heart attack and stroke—seems to be settling in the dust as a result of the findings of a ten-

---

*Atherosclerosis is one kind of arteriosclerosis, a group of diseases characterized by thickening of the arterial wall and loss of elasticity. Most doctors use the two names interchangeably.

year study spearheaded by the National Heart, Lung and Blood Institute on 3800 middle-aged men with high cholesterol levels. The conclusion is that cholesterol levels have an enormous impact on whether or not a person is in danger of getting a heart attack. The higher the cholesterol in the bloodstream, the greater the danger. One of the highlights of the study was that for every one percent reduction in cholesterol in the blood, there is a two percent less chance of a heart attack.

Yet, oddly, cholesterol is crucial. It is important for making the membranes that contain our cells and it is the building block for many hormones. Its levels rise dramatically according to the amount of saturated fats, mostly animal fats, that we eat. In the liver, where it is manufactured as a semiliquid waxy-looking substance, it combines with proteins and is released into the bloodstream. One particular combination of protein and cholesterol, called low-density lipoprotein (LDL) worries scientists and doctors because it appears to be responsible for artherosclerosis. Another combination of protein and cholesterol makes scientists and doctors much happier. This is called high-density lipoprotein (HDL). Its role is much less certain. People who exercise a lot tend to have higher levels of HDL and run a lower risk of suffering heart attacks. But it is unknown whether it is the exercise or the increased HDL that lowers the risk.

As people age, their blood pressure tends to rise, an increase that is undoubtedly abetted by atherosclerosis. Between the ages of fifty and eighty, the systolic blood pressure (the higher number of your blood pressure and a measure of the force with which your blood goes through an artery) typically rises by twenty to thirty millimeters of mercury. The diastolic pressure (the lower number and a measure of pressure when an artery is relaxed between contractions of the heart) also tends to rise. It has been well documented that these increases are dangerous and that the higher the blood pressure, the greater the risk of cardiovascular disease. Despite this knowledge, doctors are not clear about what should be regarded as normal blood pressure in the elderly and at what level treatment should be initiated to bring it down.

The case is much clearer for what constitutes high blood pressure in younger people. One famous study conducted by the Pooling Project Research Group, a project that pooled the findings of five longitudinal studies* of heart disease in middle-aged men, showed the drastic dangers of high blood pressure. When systolic pressure is less than 120, the chances are that only two men out of every 1000 in a group of forty- to forty-four-year-olds will have coronary artery disease, a more precise name for the kind of atherosclerosis that causes a heart attack. But if the systolic pressure of men in this same age group is over 150, 47 out of every 1000, almost twenty-four times as many, will show symptoms of the disease.

The study also showed that coronary artery disease seems to be an inescapable part of aging for both men and women. Men in the sixty- to sixty-four-year-old bracket, even those with systolic blood pressures under 120, had a greater than five percent chance of having the disease. Those with systolic blood pressure greater than 150 had around a 15 percent chance.

Does this mean that there is no way of decreasing our chances of succumbing to an eventual heart attack? One way of helping ourselves is to eat right. The indications are that genetic predisposition is a genuine factor in having an excess amount of LDL in the bloodstream. Give those genes a chance, and they will cause a heart attack. But if you give them as little cholesterol as possible, they will have nothing to work with. The best way to do that is to eat food low in cholesterol and avoid saturated fats—fats that stay hard at room temperature. These mostly come from animals but they include some plant fats such as coconut oil and palm oil, which increase the levels of cholesterol in your blood no matter how low your cholesterol is.

The American Heart Association recommends a daily intake of no more than 300 milligrams of cholesterol, with no more than 30 percent of your daily calories made up of fats. No more than 10 percent of these fats should be saturated. Many experts think this is too high and suggest cutting daily cholesterol consumption in half. Whichever figure is better, the American public has a long way to go. In 1984 the average daily consumption amounted to 500 milligrams.

You can reduce this amount substantially by keeping away from fatty and high-cholesterol foods. The ones to stay away

---

*A longitudinal study follows a group of individuals during a number of years to trace changes over time. A cross-sectional study makes a one-time comparison of the same characteristics in a sample group.

from, according to Jane E. Brody, medical reporter for *The New York Times* and author of *Jane Brody's Nutrition Book*, are organ meats like liver and kidneys, egg yolks (the whites are all right), and such fish as sardines (even though they are a good source of calcium) and shrimp. Red meats tend to have more cholesterol than white meats. Most shellfish have low cholesterol despite numerous reports to the contrary. A three-ounce serving of lobster, for example, contains about the same amount of cholesterol as a three-ounce lean hamburger patty. Stay away from fatty sausages, chicken skin, marbled steaks, butter, fried foods and constant nibbling on cookies and cakes. But a couple of glasses of wine a day or one cocktail of hard liquor may lower your cholesterol. No one knows why.

Diabetes—The Unknown Epidemic

Too much cholesterol is not the only way you can increase the risk of plaque formation. A chronic elevation of blood sugar can do it, too. This is known as diabetes mellitus, a common disease among the elderly because, as they grow older, people have an increasingly difficult time handling sugar. The phenomenon is so characteristic of aging that the National Institute on Aging has proposed that the measurement of glucose in the blood be adjusted for age. Otherwise, so many elderly people would be classified as having diabetes that the number of diabetics would go off the charts.

There are two different kinds of diabetes among the 12 million people who have been diagnosed as having the disease, a deadly serious illness that has become one of the nation's top ten killers. It *is* the leading cause of blindness. The majority of people with the disease (over 10 million) have adult-onset, or Type II, diabetes, ordinarily diagnosed after age thirty-five. It affects women more than men and many of those with it are overweight. The other two million sufferers have juvenile-onset, or Type I, diabetes, which is usually diagnosed in childhood or adolescence. Why an increasing number of people get diabetes as they age is not known. Heredity plays an important role. If one twin gets adult-onset diabetes, there is a 95 percent chance that the other will get it as well.

The disease can be disastrous. Because it increases the rate at which atherosclerosis develops, diabetics are in greater danger of having heart attacks and strokes and of not being able to maintain a good blood supply to the lower legs and feet. Sometimes the circulation to these areas is so poor that they must be amputated. Even if the blood-sugar level is controlled, circulation problems will probably develop. Treatment *can* alleviate some of the other common symptoms, among them blindness, nerve damage and kidney failure.

Since the disease is more common in overweight people, it should come as no surprise that the first way doctors try to get the blood sugar under control in adult-onset diabetes is by prescribing a diet and daily exercise program. But these do not always work. Both take perseverance and, too often, diabetics, as do we all, skip an exercise session or take one more slice of chocolate cake. In cases where the patient's discipline falters, the alternative treatment is oral medication, specifically sulfonylureas. The third step is to prescribe insulin injections.

The Changing Brain

As mentioned earlier, atherosclerosis can also attack the brain. One popular theory for why the brain ages maintains that plaque formation starves it of its high oxygen needs. Twenty-five percent of the oxygen carried by the blood goes to the brain and 15 percent of the heart's output of blood flows there as well. And if that volume of nutrient- and oxygen-laden blood cannot get to the brain's myriad folds and crannies, the brain's powers begin to wane. The relationship between the brain's ability to function and the blood that travels to it is a complex one. One of the characteristics of aging for most of us is that the amount of blood flowing to the brain diminishes with the passing of years. Half as much blood goes to the brain of a fifty-year-old as to the brain of a ten-year-old. But this difference is not nearly so frightening as it sounds because most of the reduction occurs between ages ten and thirty. And no one ever accused a thirty-year-old of being senile. After thirty, the decrease is very gradual. Some fortunate people show no decrease at all. One study found that extraordinarily healthy people in their seventies have the cerebral blood flow of people in their twenties and thirties.

The most dramatic and unfortunate way that atherosclerosis can affect the brain is through a stroke. Half a million Americans suffer from strokes every year. Over 160,000 of them die. Atherosclerosis does the same thing to the brain that it does to the heart—it kills part of the organ because all oxygen and nutrition are cut off.

Aside from the effects of cerebro-atherosclerosis, why do so many of the elderly tend to be so forgetful? Why do people forget telephone numbers, names of people they have just met and of places they have just visited? Why do we drop things for no apparent reason or begin to bump into the same chair over and over, one that we have successfully skirted a thousand times before? Does the fact that I have recently taken to running my car up on the curb every time I parallel park have to do with changes taking place in my forty-year-old brain?

The brain does change with age; there is no doubt about it. A longitudinal study begun twenty-one years ago on aging and the mental capacities of 3000 people in Seattle aged twenty-two to eighty-one years old found that mental abilities usually begin to decline between ages sixty-seven and seventy-four. Reasoning, adding numbers, word fluency, comprehension and recalling ideas peaked between thirty-two (for adding numbers) and fifty-three (for comprehension). But typically, it was only the post-eighty group that exhibited mental abilities that were below the middle range of mental performance of young adults.

The oldest but most questionable theory to account for the decrease in the brain's ability to function with increasing age is the dramatic daily die-off of cells. We are born with anywhere between 10 billion and 100 billion neurons or brain cells, as many as we will ever have. During adulthood, around 100,000 of them die every day. The average weight of a man's brain at twenty is around 1450 grams; at eighty, around 1300 grams, a 10 percent decrease. Females' brains are smaller, weighing an average 1300 grams in a twenty-year-old and 1175 in an eighty-year-old. That females are as intelligent as males is one indication that brain size and intelligence have little to do with each other, and people in their eighties and nineties can be every bit as intelligent as those sixty years younger. As logical as it would seem that the death of brain cells would diminish mental functioning, the brain has so much reserve capacity that the loss of some two billion brain cells over a lifetime probably makes no difference at all.

Another prominent, and more plausible, theory for any decrease in the brain's ability to function is that its neurotransmitters, chemicals that carry messages from neuron to neuron, get out of balance, One of these neurotransmitters is called acetylcholine, of great importance in maintaining a memory of recent events. Alzheimer's disease victims have very low levels of acetylcholine. (Much more about this mind-destroying affliction in Chapter 10.) Dopamine is another neurotransmitter whose levels can diminish with aging. The result is the tremor and fixed stare of Parkinson's disease.

Still another theory points to the accumulation of a fatty substance called lipofuscin in neurons. Lipofuscin, which is pigmented and emits bright fluorescence when excited by ultraviolet light, can easily be seen in brain cells beginning at age ten. In lay terms, it is waste material that builds up in the cells as a result of the breakdown of fats, mostly in nondividing cells such as those that make up the brain and the heart. Logic would dictate that a cell gradually filling up with waste products would not function as well as one free of debris. Studies have not yet determined, however, the specific effect of the substance on a cell's day-to-day life.

The plethora of medications that the elderly are given for physical ailments undoubtedly influences mental abilities. Any one of them, or various combinations, can have a disorienting affect and cloud the mind. Too many people are said to be senile when the real problem is the wrong dosage of a drug.

Another reason may be a lack of sleep. The elderly often spend restless nights, sleeping in short spurts and suddenly awakening fully alert. If their immediate environment pushes them toward staying awake all day without napping, it is no wonder that their minds do not work properly. After sixty, the circadian rhythm that makes younger people feel sleepy at night and permits them to sleep the night through begins to falter. One result is that the all-important time of Rapid Eye Movement (REM) sleep declines. This is the dreaming sleep when the body sleeps but the mind, judging from the amount of eye movement, is very active. Nevertheless, it awakens fresh and ready to perform. The elderly do not enjoy so long a holiday from the real world. The late Elliot Weitzman, a pioneer of sleep research at Montefiore Hospital and the Albert Einstein College of Medicine, theorized that the shortened sleep of the elderly is due to changes in the central nervous system. Scientists have found, for example, that laboratory-research animals whose hypothalamuses (a small part of the brain that regulates body temperature and influences the response to hunger, pain, pleasure and sex) have been altered lose their ability to adhere to circadian rhythms of wake-sleep and activity-rest. Instead, their wake-sleep pattern is irregular and fragmented in much the same way that an elderly person's is.

Not only can this phenomenon make an older person so drowsy and unalert during the day that he or she could be thought to be senile, but too little sleep does not bode well for a long life. An American Cancer Society study of one million Americans aged thirty to eighty-five found that the mortality rate for those over seventy who slept only four hours a night was about double that of people who slept 7.5 hours per night. (Ironically, the same statistics applied for people who slept more than ten hours per night, perhaps one reason researchers view the findings with some skepticism.)

The most recent thinking on the relationship between aging and brain function has produced the most stimulating theory of all. It suggests that whatever changes do take place are extremely subtle and it incorporates the notion that society in general too easily assumes that mental abilities decline with age. We become prisoners of our own biases and in doing so compromise our own future as we get older. An eighty-year-old man who constantly misplaces a set of keys is senile; a forty-year-old man who does the same thing is merely forgetful or absentminded. The elderly themselves have latched on to this stereotype by willing their minds to think less efficiently as the years go by. Those elderly people who believe in their ability to think and analyze can do so with nearly the same clarity as someone decades younger.

Recent research indicates that "crystallized intelligence," the mind's ability to make use of what it has learned over its lifetime—what many people would call wisdom—increases with age. Studies have shown, for example, that elderly people can be more adept at arguing a complex issue. This is true for several reasons: First, they have more knowledge to draw upon; second, they have, through practice, become skilled at interweaving bits and pieces of this knowledge into a unified argument. And third, they can present this argument in different guises.

Other studies have shown that verbal abilities tend to hold up in those elderly people who constantly use that facility, just as writers, artists and musicians can excel in their disciplines well into old age because they are constantly honing their skills.

Basic intelligence, the ability to think out our problems, can remain far into old age. Bernard L. Strehler, an eminent gerontologist at the University of Southern California, has come up with a theory about the way our minds process information. An older mind is far more discriminating than a younger one. Youth's mind takes in reams of knowledge; but, since the young mind is largely empty, it finds ample space to store away the information it is given.

We cherish preserving the memory of the first fruit. Details of the first train trip, the first date, the first job, tend to stick. Visions of first times are always lurking, waiting to be called up. But then such experiences become passé. Traveling about the country, going out on a string of dates, signing one contract after another—it happens so often that one blends into another. Only those very special, emotionally charged times are swaddled and caressed and allowed to remain in the memory.

If society looks upon the elderly as being incapable of keeping up, the elderly are hardly going to feel encouraged to try. Besides, this is a fast-paced society in which words and actions fly thick and furious. Many elderly are oriented differently. They are not interested in competing for the sake of winning an argument. They are no longer interested in being the center of attention.

It can be said that it is not the elderly who have changed, but society. Not so long ago, extended families were common. Grandparents were the titular heads of the household; they were listened to and, to a certain extent, obeyed. One of their prerogatives was the dissemination to younger generations of the wisdom that they had filed away over the years. Now, we are not so much interested in wisdom; we are interested in quick facts and a minimum of reflection.

Studies have found that those whose minds have remained lively and clear tend to share certain characteristics. One of them is that they have numerous friends or acquaintances with whom they are in frequent communication. K. Warner Schaie, a psychologist at Pennsylvania State University who led the Seattle longitudinal study, discovered that elderly people who live in families actually increase their mental abilities over a number of years, whereas those who live alone or who have withdrawn from society lose, to some degree, their ability to think.

Another shared trait is flexibility. Gerontologists have long noted that the process of aging brings with it a hardening of attitudes and a need for schedules. Some of this may be due to the insecurity that accompanies frailty and diminished hearing and eyesight. But some of it may also be due to an increasing lack of willingness to try new things. Researchers have recently discovered that those elderly people who are willing to test new ground are those whose minds remain the youngest. It only makes sense, after all; those who are able to adapt to unknown situations must have the mental facilities to learn new rules, meet new people and face unknown situations. In other words, their minds still have to be able to bend. Those who are so rooted to one spot that they cannot adapt to changes would tend to have rigid minds.

A corollary of this is that those who are intellectually active tend to preserve their minds far longer than those who are not. Education has a lot to do with this. Education trains people to think. Those who have never been taught to think will more easily let their minds go blank. Studies have found that the verbal intelligence of involved people increases over the years.

The dictum behind all these traits is the old adage "Use it or lose it." Trite as it is, its truth runs through successful aging from head to toe, from birth to death. If you "use it," you are going to be far more alive in your later years and you may even live longer.

Is Waning Sexuality Just a Myth?

It is no news that the older we get, the less sexual activity we engage in. And study after study has confirmed what we already know. For selected participants of the Baltimore Longitudinal Study on Aging (a study that has examined the aging process in almost 1000 individuals since 1958), the number of "sexual events," as researchers term them, dwindled from 140 per year in the late twenties to less than 20 per year at age seventy.

But some of the elderly men had far more sex than others, and these people also turned out to have higher testosterone levels. Further, the most sexually active men had enjoyed a high amount of sexual activity throughout their lives.

Elderly Don Juans are rare in the general population, though they could be more common if this society did not blush at the thought that the elderly have just as much right to a sex life as the young. A change in attitude will probably and unfortunately be a long time in coming because so few elderly people dare to express themselves sexually.

One reason is that sensations wither as we get older, especially if we do not keep them alive through frequent use. We feel less, see less, hear less, smell less and taste less. Beginning in our adolescence, nerve endings in fingers lose their ability to differentiate between sensations, though women are able to maintain their tactile sense to a greater degree than men. This may be because women traditionally rely more on the sense of touch. Younger people can differentiate warm from cool far more readily than the elderly and are more sensitive to pain.

Eyes, Ears, Nose and Throat—Some Changes Can Be Stopped

Visual sharpness is at its height in a fifteen-year-old and decreases gradually from that age. A forty-year-old can see in the dark only half as well as a twenty-year-old and is apt to suffer from presbyopia, the condition that makes a person increasingly farsighted because of the reluctance of the lens to change shape according to the distance between eye and object. This condition, easily remedied by a visit to an ophthalmologist, forces a middle-aged person to hold a book at arm's length. While presbyopia typically begins in one's forties in a temperate climate, it comes on much earlier in tropical latitudes. No one knows why, but one can theorize that the condition is exacerbated by constant heat.

Cataracts are an eye condition endemic to the aging process. If everyone lived to be one hundred years old, everyone would have cataracts. Some people half that age have them but are not bothered by them. They are the whitish circles you see around the lenses of the eyes. In some people, they do not grow, but in others, the cloudiness creeps over the entire lens. The only remedy is surgical removal. But with the lens gone, there is no means of focusing an image on the retina and it will thus be blurred. Thick convex glasses used to be used to correct the blurring. Some people still wear these but they have two severe shortcomings. One is that they enlarge whatever you may be looking at by about one third its size, making everything seem much closer than it is. The other is that only objects straight ahead will be in focus.

Contact lenses are a huge improvement, but many elderly people cannot get used to putting them in and taking them out. The really exciting news for those who have had or are about to have cataract operations is the possibilities offered by intraocular lenses, plastic lenses that are permanently implanted under the cornea. They imitate the natural lens so well that many people who have had cataract operations do not need glasses at all. The only possible drawback is that no one knows what effect they may eventually have on the eye. For this reason, some ophthalmologists hesitate to insert them into the eyes of relatively young people who have had cataract surgery.

Glaucoma is a common and major eye problem that the elderly suffer. It is a silent, insidious disease, slowly cutting off vision before the victim is even aware of what is happening. The disease is caused by a buildup of fluid within the eye because of the blocking off of passages through which the fluids normally drain. The high pressure causes eventual blindness by destroying the retinal cells and the optic nerve. In rare cases, pressure can build up very quickly and cause extreme pain. This is acute glaucoma. It is unknown why it occurs but stressful events have been tied to it. If an ophthalmologist determines that the condition is caused by a malfunctioning drainage system, an operation can be performed to cut away a bit of the iris, near where fluid drains out, to open up a passage.

Chronic glaucoma, as opposed to the disease in its acute form, is far more common. In this case, the draining mechanism tends to clog slowly. The victim may be aware of changes, such as decreasing peripheral vision or haloes around lights, but may not associate them with glaucoma until it is too late and he is left with tunnel vision. If the condition is discovered in time, symptoms and progression can be quite effectively treated by medication (eye drops) that relieve the pressure. Some ophthalmologists use a laser treatment as a last resort—tiny laser burns that open the clogged drainage canal. Another treatment, experimental though promising, involves the use of ultrasound. The procedure takes fifteen minutes and the success rate is close to 80 percent, says Michael E. Yablonski, a Cornell University researcher who has used the technique at the university's medical college in New York City. After the patient's eye is anesthetized, tiny beams of sound pierce the sclera—the white of the eye—and weaken it. This causes three reactions: It allows liquid to slowly drain through the weakened area; it prompts blood vessels in the eye to increase fluid absorption; and it reduces fluid secretion by cells.

Hearing loss is also endemic to aging. The principal reason is the voluminous loss of microscopic hairs that cover auditory nerve cells in the cochlea, the coiled tube in the inner ear that looks like a snail's shell. When stimulated by sound, these hairs activate the nerve cells that translate the sound into messages that are sent to the brain. It is not known whether this loss is due to aging per se or to general wear and tear on ears by noise pollution, no matter how distant the urban clamor. The result is that, the older you are, the harder it becomes to hear high-frequency sounds like a whistle, a violin or a female voice.

It also gets harder to understand speech, the decline beginning in one's forties. A seventy-year-old can understand about half the words spoken at the normal clip of 175 words per minute. Studies have found that an elderly person with hearing problems understands best when spoken to at around 125 words per minute, or, peculiarly, at the very fast pace of 300 words per minute. The reason may be that listeners are jolted into alertness when they hear such babble and they suddenly understand more, but for only a short time.

Taste and smell, the senses that piggyback on each other, also dwindle with aging. The process begins early; olfactory nerves start to disappear during the first year of life. By old age, almost three quarters of them have vanished. Sense of smell deteriorates to such an extent that someone over fifty can detect only the most pungent odors, like acetic acid. But again, the old adage "use it or lose it" applies. People who use their nose as a means of livelihood, such as perfume sniffing or inspecting meat—where one sniff informs the professional when the animal was killed—are able to maintain their sense of smell well into old age.

Most of us do no better with our taste buds than we do with

our olfactory nerves. At birth, we possess about 250 taste buds per papilla, which are the raised platforms on the tongue, to give us a total of some 10,000 buds. After seventy-five, we have closer to 100 buds per papilla. It is not that we cannot taste at this age but that tastes become distorted, and sweet and sour are the predominant taste sensations that we are left with. A zinc deficiency in the diet may exacerbate the loss of taste.

The voice also ages. After about sixty-five, the collagen that makes up the connective tissue of our vocal cords begins to lose its elasticity. The result of the stiffening is the quavering so noticeable in an elderly person's voice. The many membranous folds momentarily stick in one position before moving to the next. In a younger person, the constant up and down motion of the vocal cords is responsible for smoothness of tone. In men, the voice also gets higher, reedy and raspy-sounding, with age, because of a decrease in the number of vocal-cord folds.

Though aging begins when we are very young and involves the steady lessening of the capabilities of cell, tissue and organ, the body's reserves run high. Even in old age we have plenty of brain cells left to maintain mental alertness. And though the kidneys lose almost one half their filtering capacity between ages twenty and ninety, the remaining nephrons—filtering loops—are able to do the job very adequately. Even so, the elderly find that they have to urinate more frequently because their bladders have shrunk to half the size they once were. Aging does not have to follow the stereotypical pattern that Americans stamp it with—the gloomy vision that persuaded Paul Charlotte that he better conceal his graying hair. Aging has its benefits. Even Charlotte has discovered that. While cells increasingly refuse to duplicate themselves, while bones shrink and while lungs lose their capacity to fill with air, something else happens of enormous importance—we gain experience and wisdom. Dying his hair may have helped Charlotte keep his job, but the knowledge of almost two decades in business management probably helped him even more. When Charlotte was young and inexperienced, he was constantly worried about being beaten to the next promotion. Now Charlotte just shrugs. "Sure, they come out of graduate school and they have their management and marketing models and they can do things that I can't do, but they don't know how to make decisions like I know how to make them. Every year that goes by, I feel that I am more knowledgeable, more worldly and more secure in my own prowess."

One way to look at aging, then, is that it's nature's way of trimming the excess from our bodies. We are left a leaner but more fragile being. How nature goes about trimming the excess is a jigsaw puzzle that keeps gerontologists in laboratories for long hours hovering over microscopes and psychologists puzzling over statistics hoping to find the complex keys that explain how we can age in the best way possible.

Slowing the Clock

Aging is inevitable but we can slow down the process without making undue sacrifice. Some of the effects of aging mentioned in this chapter are ones that change our appearance. Others are of a deeper, more internal nature. Here's a quick look at some steps to take to age more healthily. This is not meant to be medical advice. A doctor should be consulted before making any decisions.

Cholesterol and Fat Intake

Heart disease and stroke are the number one killers in America today. They are caused primarily by atherosclerosis—the buildup of fatty deposits in the arteries, better known as hardening of the arteries. Depending on diet, atherosclerosis can begin in childhood, but change in diet can slow or stem the process in adulthood. Cholesterol and animal fats, all of which are saturated, have been strongly implicated as leading causes of this accumulation, and foods rich in these substances should be avoided. Cholesterol comes only from animal products. Animal fats, which are saturated, meaning that they remain hard at room temperature, raise the cholesterol in your blood. Plant oils are generally unsaturated and thus have little effect on cholesterol, save for two exceptions—coconut oil and palm oil. These two are saturated and thus unhealthy.

The American Heart Association recommends consuming no more than 300 milligrams of cholesterol per day, while no more than 30 percent of the total calories should be from fats. Many heart experts think this is too high. They recommend 150 to 200 milligrams per day and no more than 20 percent of calories from fats. In late 1984, the National Institutes of Health came out with cholesterol risk ratings for different age groups. If your cholesterol level is higher than the following measurements, in milligrams per 100 milliliters of blood serum, for your age group, you should make serious dietary adjustments in consultation with your doctor: age 20 through 29—185 mgs.; age 30 through 39—240; and over 40 years old—260. You will have to go to your doctor to find out what your cholesterol level is.

What foods have the most cholesterol? Generally the darker the meat, the higher the cholesterol, though there are many exceptions. Organ meats like liver and kidney have the highest levels. Hot dogs have a lot. Pork has the least of the commonly consumed meats. Egg yolks are extremely high, though the whites are all right. Dark chicken and turkey meat have more than white meat. Most fish have low levels, even shellfish like lobster and oysters. But there's a lot of cholesterol in shrimp and sardines. Butter and cream, as you might expect, are loaded. But buttermilk and low-fat yogurt are very low. Stay away from rich desserts and snacks, as a general rule.

Osteoporosis

Like cholesterol and animal fat, this insidious and debilitating disease can be avoided. It is by far the most easily preventable of the diseases that strike the elderly. What is it? It is the deterioration of the bones that afflicts some 15 million people in this country, mostly postmenopausal women. The cause is calcium loss, exacerbated by a decline in estrogen after menopause, by smoking, by sedentary living and by a diet not only low in calcium but high in substances that prevent the bones from absorbing whatever calcium might be available. Even though all the bones are affected, the typical symptoms are collapsed vertebrae, which can be excruciating; fractured hips, arms and wrist bones; and decreased height. Osteoporosis victims can shrink by more than three-and-one-half inches.

All this can be avoided with adequate calcium intake and with exercise. The recommended daily calcium intake is 1000 milligrams, or 1500 milligrams for postmenopausal women. One thousand milligrams is in six glasses of milk, a lot to ask an adult to drink. There are, however, other ways to get calcium. A small container of plain yogurt, for example, has around 200 milligrams. Swiss cheese is a good source. Most fish are another good source. Turnip greens, collard greens and kale are high in calcium. But not all greens are good. Spinach, chard, parsley and beet greens contain oxalate, a substance that prevents bones from absorbing calcium.

Exercise is the other key. Stress the bones, as happens in running, bicycling, swimming, dancing and walking, and the bones will get stronger. Bedridden people lose calcium very fast, as do weightless astronauts whose bones are rarely stressed while in space. Exercise and dietary care should be initiated during youth. As one expert in the disease told me: "Everyone should be putting bone in their bone bank for withdrawal during their later years."

Adult-Onset or Type II Diabetes

The complete name for the disease is diabetes mellitus, which in Greek means "sugar siphon," because the urine of an untreated diabetic contains so much glucose that it was feared that the victim was urinating his essence away. There are two types of diabetes. One is known as juvenile-onset, or Type I, which usually strikes during childhood or adolescence. The other, known as adult-onset, or Type II, is ordinarily diagnosed after age thirty-five. Symptoms of both types can consist of an enormous appetite, the frequent need to urinate, an unexplained weight loss, fatigue, weakness, blurred vision, slow healing of cuts and bruises, numbness or cramps in the legs, itchy skin and frequent skin infections. At its worst, the condition can lead to blindness, impotence, heart attack, gangrene, amputation, coma and death.

The great majority of people diagnosed as having Type II diabetes are overweight. Many are obese. Insulin shots are not always prescribed for adult-onset diabetics, whereas they are the usual course of treatment for juvenile-onset diabetics. Successful treatment for those suffering from the adult form of the disease usually consists of strict weight control through dieting and exercise.

Periodontal Disease

It occurs in epidemic form. Though there are various kinds of periodontal disease, the gum separates from the teeth in all of them. The results are catastrophic for the mouth: swollen and tender gums, bleeding, painful abscesses and teeth that spread, loosen and fall out unless the situation is attended to. The destructive process can take years. It is by far the leading cause of tooth loss. Almost 40 percent of people forty-five to fifty-five years old have it and 60 percent of those sixty-five to seventy-five.

Prevention is the best cure. The best prevention is to follow the old adage: "Brush after every meal and visit your dentist once every six months." Food particles and bacteria are the leading causes, both of which can be eliminated by dedicated brushing, yes, but the areas where the gums join the teeth must be included. What's crucial about brushing there is that it rids the mouth of bacterial plaque—a combination of food debris, saliva and gum secretions—which offers a hospitable environment for bacteria and eventual infection.

Once you have the disease, your dentist, after chipping away the tartar—hardened plaque—may tell you to use a water pick, a toothpick or floss to remove the particles that your toothbrush misses. If the deterioration has progressed beyond the point where these preventive measures will do any good, he may cut away some of the destroyed gum tissue. Or he may want to do a "flap," in which the gum is lifted away, the underlying teeth are cleaned and the gum is repositioned and sutured back in place.

Skin and Sun

Long hours baking under the sun is bad for your skin at any age. But if you like the sun, stop for a minute in your mid-twenties and reflect. The sun's direct rays not only dry out your skin and make its collagen, the substance that gives it elasticity, turn brittle, but ultraviolet light also wreaks havoc on the skin cells' DNA, the genetic material within every cell whose duplication is essential in cell division if mutations are to be avoided. The DNA in a child or teenager's skin can repair itself. But as cells grow older, DNA makes increasingly more mistakes trying to duplicate itself. Eventually, it can't. Mutations abound. Mutation is the stuff of cancer, and the association between sun exposure and skin cancer is strong. Most skin cancer is relatively harmless. But one type—malignant melanoma—is fatal in 50 percent of cases. Even if you don't get skin cancer, the effect of all that sun on your skin is going to make your collagen misbehave and you will end up with prunelike and parched skin.

All this can be avoided. The best way is never to expose your skin to sun without wearing a sunscreen rated between 12 and 15. Never mind the stuff with a rating of 3 or 4. It won't do any good. And after you have been in the sun, use a moisturizing cream.

Intelligence and Aging

The brain has far more resilience than other parts of the body in defying old age. Some forms of intellectual activity are much more alive in an eighty-year-old than in a forty-year-old. What we call wisdom—the accumulation of years and years of learning, observation, intuition and emotion—is very much alive and well and growing. The elderly can be more adept than younger people at verbally communicating their knowledge, of being able to weave together all the bits and pieces of the accumulated past into a comprehensive concept or thesis or of approaching an argument from a number of angles.

Some mental capacities, however, peak at a relatively early age. Studies have found that the ability to add numbers begins declining in the early thirties, to reason in the late thirties, and the ability to perceive spatial relationships in the mid-forties. To some extent this means the older you get, the more difficult it is to learn new things, which is why a child can learn a foreign language with so much more ease than an adult. And new technology and aging do not get on well together. A young person just learning how to use a home computer can become facile on it more quickly than an elderly one.

Yet it is impossible to find a meaningful decline in mental functioning in the general population before age sixty. The most rapid decline takes place between the late sixties and early seventies. But it is heartening to keep in mind that only after eighty do mental abilities fall below the average mental performance of younger people. Yet becoming senile is one of the greatest fears we have of growing older. The idea that senility is inevitable is entirely wrong. Forgetfulness in a thirty-five-year-old is due to absentmindedness, anxiety, pressure or any number of other reasons. Forgetfulness in an eighty-year-old is put down to senility. If the elderly want to break this vicious circle, they must stand up for themselves. They cannot allow themselves to fall victim to the impatience of youth, who assume that anyone with gray hair and stooped shoulders is senile.

There are a number of steps to be taken to keep the mind alert:

First, keep yourself involved socially. Keep up friendships or at least make an effort to meet people. You can do this by taking courses, doing volunteer work and just by keeping your eyes open for opportunities that will put you in contact with others. Do not withdraw. Studies have shown that elderly people who live in large families fare better mentally than those who live alone.

Second, keep your mind stimulated. You can enroll in adult-education classes that make you think. You can travel through any number of educational organizations that offer discounts. Think of retirement as an opportunity to do what you have always wanted to do.

Third, continue to get physical exercise. The evidence is strong that exercise slows the aging process and lessens the chance of disease. If you can keep yourself in good shape physically, your mind will probably be more active.

Fourth, be flexible. Rigidity is a precursor of a deadened intelligence and spirit. Be open to new experiences, new types of people and new places.

All of these steps require motivation. It is motivation that stretches the mind and allows it to grow well into old age.

Chapter 2

An "Old Man's" Vigor

Claude Pepper looks like everyone's grandfather, but no one's grandpa. He does not seem the type to take a kid to the circus or dandle a tot on his knee. Pepper makes people jump by just turning his head in their direction. He barks, too. But the eighty-five-year-old Democratic congressman from Florida has no intention of being mean. When he discovers that his growls have on occasion sent a staff member to the bathroom crying, his remorse is such that he will not call upon that person for several days, undertaking his or her perhaps mundane duties himself. And he does not look mean. Age has given him a benign, quizzical appearance, as if he does not quite know what to expect from his fellow human beings. He may cultivate the image.

Despite his perpetually puzzled look, few people accomplish more; and he probably walks at least five miles a day, if you count up the trips he makes from his office to the floor of the House of Representatives to the chambers of his Rules Committee to the office of the Subcommittee on Health and Long Term Care, to the various rallies, speeches and civic events about town. However, he by no means restricts his activities to Washington. He is in Miami much of the time and he frequently flies about the country by himself, no aides tagging along.

On Capitol Hill, he is a tireless lobbyist for bills that will benefit the elderly. He led the 1982 struggle to fight off Reagan-backed efforts to reduce social security benefits. As former chairman of the Select Committee on Aging, he had considerable success, much of it single-handed. Though concessions were made, social security survives largely intact. His other legislative efforts have included a bill that eliminated mandatory retirement for federal employees; another that resulted in the formation of the National Cancer Institute; a resolution that helped create the World Health Organization; and a series of bills that resulted in the formation of the National Institutes of Health.

He gets up at 6:30 each morning and is at work by 8. His days are a nonstop series of meetings, telephone conversations, speeches and trips to the House floor. Younger government employees constantly seek him out for advice. His office receives an average of ten requests a day from the media for interviews. He is a man who finds it difficult to say no.

His age gives him the physical appearance of a stereotypical old man. His hands are red-splotched and his fingernails have turned yellow. He has a slightly hunched upper back, which might indicate the beginnings of osteoporosis, and his neck has all but disappeared. His nose is red, veined and very large. (This leads some people to assume that he is a drinker, but his consumption of alcohol is limited to the demi-carafe of white wine he has every day with his lunch in the House dining room.) He wears two hearing aids, thick trifocals, a pacemaker and a synthetic heart valve. Despite all the accoutrements of age, Pepper tries to ignore their causes. One of the reasons he can do this is because his mind and attitude have stayed young. "The Lord blessed me with a good temperament," he is fond of saying. "I don't think of the future; I think about today."

His aides jump when he turns his watery eyes on them because they correctly anticipate that they are about to be addressed with a question or a demand that will put their expertise on the line. Pepper knows exactly what kind of information he wants from them if he is preparing a speech or a bill. They either know it or they don't know it. If they don't, they get a terse command in Pepper's southern drawl: "Well, find it out for me." When Pepper calls a meeting of his staff, most of whom are in their thirties, to discuss an upcoming speech that "we" are going to make, there is no discussion at all. Pepper rattles off the ingredients needed, a warning that if the ingredients are not found, "it might be embarrassing for us," and a dismissal.

It might be easier to work for the congressman if he ranted

and raved and threatened to fire. The difficulty of working for an eighty-five-year-old man is that his physical appearance— from liver spots to hearing aids to stiff-jointed walk—creates a charged empathy. People want to help. Why, look at his body falling apart bit by bit. Yet the constant rediscovery that his mind is sharp and clear, "brilliant" say some of his aides, adds up to feelings of guilt and awe that urge them to greater efforts on his behalf. His staff, many of whom have worked for him for years, adore him and hover about in total homage.

Three aides bend over Pepper's cluttered desk in Room 2239 of the Rayburn Building, watching attentively as the congressman reads some legislation. The office is large and rectangular, with 16-foot ceilings. Every inch of the considerable wall space is crammed with the congressman's mementos. He has served with eight administrations and there are dozens of autographed photographs of Pepper with every President except Ronald Reagan. The majority are of him with Franklin D. Roosevelt, his mentor, whose New Deal is the foundation of his political beliefs. The only photograph that shows Pepper in a relaxed pose is one with Jimmy Carter. They are both sitting, looking as if they are swapping stories. In the others, Pepper is all attentive, looking into each presidential face with a sort of innocent "teach me" expression.

Another aide comes in to tell him that so-and-so is on the phone. I am sitting in a chair in the corner, merely a casually observed observer. So-and-so is evidently a frequent caller. "Doggone it," Pepper barks, "sometimes I think that man doesn't seem to understand that I am a congressman who has to get some work done." The conversation is brief.

Yet another aide comes in with a label that Pepper is supposed to wear on his jacket while he attends a vigil for Soviet Jewry on the Capitol steps. The label bears the name of a Soviet Jew who has been denied an exit visa.

"What's that?" he drawls without really looking at it.

"This, Senator,* is a label for you to wear to the vigil."

---

*Pepper served as a senator from 1936 to 1951, when he was defeated in a reelection bid. He returned to Washington in 1963 as a congressman, but many people still address him as "Senator."

"Yes, yes, that's right," Pepper answers, returning to the papers on his desk.

"Now, Senator," persists the aide patiently, "do you want me to put it on your right lapel or your left lapel?"

"What? Oh, never mind. Leave it right here on the desk and put it on me later."

"Yes, sir. I'll leave it right here and I'll be sure you have it when you go."

Pepper seems irritated by minutiae. He is a man with so many projects, so many hopes, that he barely tolerates whatever interferes with them. But detail as much as grandiose legislative action is the stuff of politics. Pepper knows it. A few minutes later, he is in his outer office inviting his staff to the vigil. There's a flurry. Who's coming? Who's staying? How many can sit into the congressman's worn Lincoln Town Car parked in the basement garage? Details, details. Pepper points to six people. "You, you, you, you, you, you. Come on." Then he stops. "Where's that label? We can't forget that. It wouldn't look right."

Down in the garage, the aide designated to drive (Pepper usually drives himself but his staff says he goes too fast) hesitatingly asks Pepper if there is a street leading past the Capitol's west side, near the steps overlooking the Reflecting Pool and the Washington Monument, where the vigil is to be held. The congressman is getting agitated; it's late. He sarcastically replies, "Not unless they built one in the last two minutes. Come on, man, we'll be late." Just as he gets in the car, his label falls off and flutters to the ground. I pick it up and hand it to him. He looks at me as though I am doing the most absurd thing he has ever seen. "Well, put it on me. Don't give it to me."

Because there is no street near the west side of the Capitol, the closest place to park is along the base of the east side, which means that the entourage must walk through the Capitol. It is the height of the summer tourist season, and tour buses are disgorging passengers near the huge structure. Pepper and his youthful aides scramble from the car and, Pepper in the lead, make their way toward the arch under the big stairs where congressmen always pose for snapshots with their constituents. There should be an entrance under there, but the group finds only a dead end and has to back out. Pepper heads toward another arch under the stair complex; another dead end. He starts mumbling to himself. His staff members, like cubs behind an angry bear, increase their distance from him. None dares bolt ahead to find a door. Finally, Pepper finds one. All the tourists looked like they were ascending the main stairs to the House and Senate visitors' galleries but the foyer inside this door is crammed with them. Pepper barges into their midst. Some of them gasp. They recognize him. "Isn't that Claude Pepper?" one of them asks excitedly. "He was just on the cover of *Time*." The crowd suddenly hushes and all eyes turn toward Pepper and company. Pepper ignores them. "Excuse me, excuse me," he exclaims as he churns through, spreading his arms and hands in front of him as he goes, as if he were swimming. He makes his way to a guard and asks directions to the west steps. By this time the audience has quieted down to enjoy the show. When they realize that he, the elder statesman who was just on the cover of *Time*, is lost, some of them giggle. I never knew whether the giggles turned to general mirth. Pepper was halfway down the next corridor and his aides were trotting after him.

Eventually, we get to the west steps and Pepper joins a group of congressmen standing behind a podium while a series of speakers condemn Soviet treatment of Jews. The sun is blazing. It is a mercilessly hot mid-July day. All the other congressmen are almost certainly younger and look fitter and trimmer. Pepper stands with them under the sun for almost an hour. He must be miserable. I think. I worry about him, but when the vigil breaks up and a young woman television reporter from a Florida station rushes up to ask for an interview, he looks pleased, as if such an honor rarely comes his way, and says, "Why, of course."

Pepper's oratory has carried him far. But in my observation of him today, I have not heard him bubble forth with silvery words. Now I hear them. When the camera begins rolling, he opens his mouth and the honey flows. "We do not control our people's destiny . . ." and "Whoever chooses to leave may do so . . ." are statements made with an eloquence not expected on a hot day under a cruel sun that has bombarded an old man's balding head. Where did the poise come from? It was sitting inside him all the time, just waiting for a camera and microphone to propel it into action.

After the television crew packs up, Pepper turns to me. "Isn't this beautiful here? You don't see this side of the Capitol much.

Mildred and I used to come here some evenings and watch the sun set." Mildred is his beloved wife, lost to cancer in 1979. He talks about her as if she is still very much alive. "Mildred said . . .", Mildred told me . . ." Mildred, Mildred, the only person in Pepper's life who could make him slow down, who could make him relax just a little. The walls of his office carry dozens of photographs of her: Mildred skiing in Germany, Mildred on an elephant in Sri Lanka, Mildred meeting British royalty. Mildred's death plunged her husband into a depression which he could pull himself out of only by immersing himself in work. He hasn't stopped yet and he has no plans to. "Growing old doesn't bother me," he says. "I just keep thinking about what has to be done." If he's lucky, he takes two weeks off every summer to play golf in North Carolina with friends. But it is hard to envision this man without some legislation in his mind.

Pepper's table in the House dining room is one of the larger ones. Ten people sit at it, wondering whether to order lunch from the attentive waitresses or wait for the congressman to arrive. Pepper is on the floor voting on a bill, and delays are frequent there. His guests decide to order. They consist of a couple with their teenage daughter from Pepper's congressional district; three summer interns, college students from the South working in the Subcommittee on Health and Long Term Care office; three staff aides; and me. Pepper arrives twenty minutes later and as soon as he is seated, a waitress sets down his demi-carafe of wine, a plate of graham crackers and a bowl of minestrone. Pepper starts every meal with soup and crackers, even breakfast. He tries to play host, asking his guests if they have everything they want, if the service is all right. But the concern is lackadaisical, the questions asked in a monotone. I ask him about a health insurance bill that he is about to introduce. He hems and haws with an uncertainty that tells me he does not have the bill's details on the tip of his tongue. He turns to an aide and directs him to tell "Mr. Bookman," as he has nicknamed me, the pertinent statistics. The aide obliges, spewing out dazzling clusters of numbers, reams of abbreviated technical names, and jargon-supported calculations for why the bill has so many merits. After a while he cuts the aide short, turns to me and exclaims excitedly, "What that means is that we can have a plan that lets people be fully insured without having to worry about any deductible and they can get their medical care wherever they please." It sounds much more sensible this way. But what impresses me is that Pepper has translated all the technical information into lay language that voters can grasp.

A buzzer sounds. Ten minutes to a vote. By this time, Pepper has finished his soup and begins wolfing down lunch—knockwurst with boiled cabbage. He grabs a bottle of catsup but the bottle is new and the catsup won't come out. He turns to an aide for help.

Five minutes to the vote. He asks the teenage girl if she wants to go to the floor and vote for him. He flashes his plastic voting card and gives it to her. She giggles with delight. "I'm kidding," he says, but his face never cracks a smile. His humor seems to be all internal. "I'll go with you and make sure you vote the way I want. I guess we won't get caught." I was wrong. Claude Pepper *can* be a grandpa. But not too often.

He can be a father, too. Back in his office, Pepper offers some paternal farewell words to Arthur Teele, a young black man from Tallahassee, who had recently resigned as the head of the Urban Mass Transportation Administration to return to Florida and practice law. Pepper is concerned about Teele's future. They sit in two black leather upholstered chairs in the corner of his office. "Now, Arthur," Pepper says, "have you made any good legal connections in Miami?" Teele mentions a firm that has approached him about a job. Pepper does not approve. "Arthur, you have a wonderful opportunity now. Get with a good firm. Now's the time to make your money." That is just what Pepper did when he lost his Senate seat: He went back to Florida and made a fortune practicing law before he returned to Washington.

Pepper gives a few more minutes of advice before drawing the meeting to a close. He has to give a talk to a group of high school students from Connecticut. Teele hesitates for a moment before going and says, "Senator, do you remember you said you would send me an autographed copy of you on the cover of *Time*? Well, I never got it. I was just wondering if you could get one for me before I leave." Pepper is upset. He apologizes profusely and promises to bring one to a party for Teele that evening.

* * *

Pepper is late for his speech to the high school students, and that means he might be late for a special meeting of his Rules Committee that he has called later on to introduce its members to Edward Teller, the physicist. As we rush to the room where he is to give the speech, he tells me that he met Teller in California the previous week and was impressed, so he asked him to stop by.

One of Pepper's aides is waiting for him at the door of the room where the fifty or so students have been sitting for half an hour. She asks Pepper who should introduce him but he brushes her aside, rushes past several teachers who have stretched out their hands to him, and onto the podium. "Hello, I'm Claude Pepper. I'm sorry I'm late and I won't be able to talk long . . ." Pepper launches into a monologue about his accomplishments, his visions and the New Deal. The students fidget. They are disappointed; he's not connecting. A few doze off.

Twenty minutes later, Pepper is out the door, I at his heels. I ask him if he ever cancels appointments when his schedule gets too cluttered. He ignores me and churns down the corridors of the Rayburn building. I assume that he is on his way to the Rules Committee, which meets in the Capitol, but he seems to be heading toward his office. I guess that he is returning to collect some papers. But to ask where he is going is out of the question.

The Rayburn Building's monotonous layout makes it a confusing place. It consists of four sections: two wide rectangles parallel to each other joined by two thinner rectangles, also parallel to each other. From the air, the building looks like a squat capital H with two cross bars instead of one. The two cross bars contain elevator banks. Only the elevators of one bank stop at the mezzanine from which one can get to the Capitol via an underground passage.

By this time, I am sure that Pepper is going back to his office, which is just at the end of the next corridor. Suddenly he freezes and begins turning his head from left to right as if looking for a landmark. I realize that he must be lost and a disquieting sensation arises in me. I feel an elation. At last, I think, here is a sign of this old man's age; he cannot even find his way back to the same office that he has been occupying for the past twenty years. Then I feel depressed in my realization that I, too, am a victim of this society's prejudice against aging and the aged. I decide to help him out and point to the next corridor, telling him that his office is just down there. He looks at me as if I were mad. Then he starts cursing under his breath while he goes up to some numbers and arrows painted on the wall. He turns and hastens down a corridor that leads away from his office. It flashes through my mind that the day may have just been too much for him. But now he seems to know where he is going and he soon comes to an elevator bank. Beside one elevator, I see a sign that reads "To Capitol." Despite my freshly revealed prejudice, I am relieved. He didn't get lost, after all. He just had a short lapse trying to find the right elevators. It could have happened to anyone.

As the doors close to take him on the next leg of his journey to the Rules Committee (closed to the press and public), he answers my questions. "Sometimes I just have to say no. It's not because of my age and strength, you know. It's a matter of time. Sometimes, there's just no time."

Chapter 3
Rearranging Nature

*P*eople deal with aging in different ways. Some, like Claude Pepper, just keep going, like a marathon runner who ignores the fatigue that is wracking his body. I doubt if the congressman is one to look at himself in the mirror every morning and moan and groan about his wrinkles. Other people try to rearrange the aging process so that they appear much younger than they really are. Upon awakening they sit down at their vanity table for the daily ritual of covering up the damage that the years have brought. Others opt for a longer-term solution: They undergo plastic surgery to have their wrinkles stretched out and their flab removed.

Cutting Away the Signs of Aging

Almost 500,000 people underwent cosmetic surgery in 1984, according to the American Society of Plastic and Reconstructive Surgeons. These operations were performed by surgeons certified by the American Board of Plastic Surgery.* Many more procedures were done by noncertified doctors. "The public just recently has recognized that plastic surgery offers another

*The American Society of Plastic and Reconstructive Surgeons is a national organization based in Chicago that promotes plastic surgery through educational programs. It has a referral service for people looking for competent plastic surgeons. To become a member of ASPRS, a plastic surgeon must be certified by the American Board of Plastic Surgery by passing written and oral examinations by the board.

76

means to further improve an individual's self-image," says Dr. John A. Coin, president of ASPRS. The specialty does not restrict itself to cosmetic surgery. Most plastic surgery is reconstructive and includes the repair of injured hands, cleft lips and palates, microsurgery and the removal of tumors. Breast augmentation is the most popular form of plastic surgery. In 1984, 95,000 of these operations were done. Cosmetic surgery also includes procedures to lift drooping eyelids (the second most popular procedure), reshape noses, transplant hair, contour bodies and remove acne scars and wrinkles through dermabrasion or chemical peels.

Face-lifts are by far the most expensive procedure. If you decide on a face-lift with eyelid surgery and a chemical peel, too, to get rid of those fine wrinkles above the upper lip, you have to be prepared to spend around $7000, of which insurance will not pay one cent. Women have long submitted themselves to these procedures, but men are joining them in increasing numbers. Everyone who makes the decision to have a face-lift does so knowing full well that wear and tear and gravity will eventually undo a surgeon's work, no matter how skilled he is. The effects of a face-lift last an average of only five years before the skin resumes its baggy and wrinkled shape. Though a face can be lifted any number of times, the successive stretching of the skin renders it paper thin and fragile. And people who are inclined toward this type of surgery are rarely satisfied with just one face-lift. When wrinkles reappear, enthusiasts simply make a return visit to their plastic surgeon to "tidy up," as the industry jargon terms it. By the tenth face-lift, the skin is stretched so tight and has lost so much body that it resembles parchment on a drumhead. What was once a face with texture enriched by time and experience becomes an ageless apparition, albeit one with few wrinkles.

The recuperation time, i.e., the time required after a face-lift before one feels sufficiently healed to appear in public, may be two months. Complications are possible—hemorrhaging during the operation is one; a severed nerve resulting in permanent damage is another. Why would anyone want to undergo such surgery? Despite warnings by plastic surgeons of both the dangers and the short-term effects, there is an illusion of permanence that comes from the knowledge that pieces of excess skin and globules of fat have been removed. One thing is certain about cosmetic surgery: The so-called miracles that plastic surgeons can achieve do not have to be flaunted on TV commercials the way night creams are. Word of mouth and sight of eye are much better advertisements.

I met Deborah (not her real name), a painter and former professional actress, a week before she had a face-lift. By prearrangement, I would be watching the procedure. I was amazed at how young she looked when she greeted me at the door of her Greenwich Village apartment; in her mid-forties, I guessed. Over her shoulder, I could see some of her abstract paintings of curved shapes as smooth as the cheeks of her own face. When she told me that she was sixty-seven, I was flabbergasted. Why did she want a face-lift? Her reasons tell why a lot of people undergo what can be a painful and embarrassing experience.

Deborah has always been close to the theater world whose people are not known for their modesty. She left school at fifteen in order to act, and she acted for the next twenty years on the stage and in nightclubs. Her first husband was a well-known television actor. To many of Deborah's friends, getting a face-lift is just something you do when you get older. "When more than half your friends have it done, it gets to you," she told me. "Half the time I am angry at myself for having made the decision. Am I vain? I ask myself why I shouldn't have wrinkles and gray hair and still be accepted. The other half of the time, I am excited. I have friends who are euphoric about their face-lifts and others who can't wait to have them done."

Deborah reflected for a moment and then said more quietly, "My real problem is that I am getting old. If I felt that society accepted me with my wrinkles, I might not get a face-lift. I'm caught up in the uncertainty of where I, as an older person, can fit into this society and how it accepts me. Old people are treated terribly and I am angry about it.

"Still," she added, "I feel lured. I'm attracted to the idea that I can look younger."

Deborah's five-year-old granddaughter gave her the final push toward having the operation. "She looked up at me one day and said, 'Grandma, you're going to die soon because you have so many wrinkles.' It was a real hit."

Deborah made an appointment with Dr. Arthur Ship, a prominent New York plastic surgeon who was also the president of the American Society of Maxillo-Facial Surgeons. The reason she chose him is that he had given a face-lift to one of her best friends and "she looked fabulous," she said. Dr. Ship told Deborah he would try to do the same for her. He would do the job—a complete face-lift, tightening both eyelids and a chemical peel over her upper lip—for around $8000.

"I hope my face-lift will be a dream, a nice present to myself, a fantasy that really does come true," Deborah said plaintively as I left her.

The next time I saw her she was on her back in Dr. Ship's office, giggly, nervous and in pain. So jittery had she been on the bus en route that she had tried to calm herself down by doing muscle-flexing exercises but had succeeded only in giving herself charley horses. The sedatives she had been administered had not yet taken effect. Her head, which lay on a tiny pillow on a narrow table under the lights, was raised up and as free of the rest of her body as humanly possible, given the presence of her neck. Dr. Ship, a middle-aged man with warm, sparkling eyes and full of quick energy, was shaving around her ears and plastering some gooey stuff on her hair. Then he took two locks on her temples and put them in rubber bands so they stuck up like antennae. His actions suddenly transformed Deborah into a little girl, making me wonder again why she felt that she had to submit to this ordeal.

What follows is a description of a face-lift, including tightening both eyelids, largely copied from my notes during the operation: A lot of preoperative preparation and banter takes place. Flora, Dr. Ship's nurse, a solid woman who can be warmhearted and ferocious in successive breaths, gruffly tells the doctor to get his surgical mask away from the instruments that she is carefully arranging on a trolley near Deborah's head. Flora and Dr. Ship's relationship strikes me as one that has evolved over the years into a bickering dependency and a competitive friendship. The doctor asks her where the shoe-coverings are. She patronizingly says that she will get him a pair. He frets and says in an irritated voice, "No, no. Just *tell* me where they are." More banter between the doctor and Flora about surgical techniques. Flora wonders if it is better to begin with the eyes or with the face. Dr. Ship hushes her and says that they will begin with the eyes. Then he turns to me and says proudly that 30 to 40 percent of cosmetic surgery is done in a hospital with two or three surgeons present. He is one of an increasing number of plastic surgeons who do the work in their office.

The operation begins at 9:45 A.M. After stitching a towel to Deborah's hairline, which has been locally anesthetized, Dr. Ship outlines cut marks on the eyelids with a grease pencil and gives her more anesthesia—a quick-acting form for the eyes. Later, he will give her a longer-acting form for the rest of her face. The needle burrows under the skin like a mole under a lawn. The anesthesia, Dr. Ships informs me, will make her skin and muscles tingle before going numb. For the next few hours, she will feel no pain as her face is cut into, the fat removed, the skin stretched and the excess cut off, and the wound stitched up. All she will feel is a lot of pushing and pulling.

After numbness has set in, Dr. Ship begins cutting, placing strips of eyelid skin and globules of fat on a piece of gauze that rests on Deborah's chest. Then he cuts under the lower lid and pulls the skin back. I am reminded of skinning rabbits when I was a boy. Flora presses down the exposed muscle tissue with gauze so that the fat pops up. It is yellow and looks just like chicken fat. Dr. Ship snips it away. From time to time, he picks up an instrument that looks like an ice pick with a plastic handle and cauterizes a blood vessel to stop the bleeding. Smoke and an acrid smell arise. But there is very little blood.

When the doctor can find no more fat, he begins stitching. He's an acrobat. The needle, followed by a length of fragile black thread, flashes toward the wounds, pulls the flaps of skin together and is drawn up by the scissors before flashing down again. In forty-five minutes, the first eye is finished. The bruise marks have not yet set in. When I look at both of Deborah's eyes, I can see that the skin around the one that has just been completed is younger-looking, less wrinkled and puffy.

An hour and a half later, with two eyes done, Dr. Ship begins the actual face-lift. Every once in a while, Flora asks Deborah, "How are you doing, baby?" Deborah is out of it, but keeping her spirits up. "Surviving," she answers once, "but I don't know how spoiled ladies go through this."

"They just want to be put to sleep," says the doctor. "But this is safer." He begins outlining with grease pencil the work he must do on Deborah's face, starting on one side—a line around the front of the ear, another from the middle of the ear across the cheek to the nose, and another from the nose to the side of the chin. He will not cut along these two latter lines; they are for guidance. Remarkably, he only cuts around the front and back of her ears. Then he lifts the cheek skin, snipping, cutting and probing as he goes, so that soon I can see the entire flayed cheek—rosy muscles, dark veins and yellow fat.

Dr. Ship is proud of his technique in this part of the operation. He stops to explain to me that, after removing the fat, he must pull and stitch both the muscle and the skin, not the skin alone, to the area behind the ear. This relatively new refinement of pulling up the underlying muscle results in a longer-lasting face-lift.

The doctor peers into the cave he has created and begins extracting pieces of fat. When he is finished, he pulls and stitches the muscles to an area behind the top and the bottom of the ear. Hair will grow over the scars, hiding any evidence of the incredible procedure taking place before me. As a result of pulling and stitching the muscle, the cheek skin now covers about half Deborah's ear when it is laid out flat. Dr. Ship trims the excess, a strip three quarters of an inch wide in some places. The new edge falls exactly in line with the cut he previously made along the front of the ear. No scar will form here because the two areas of skin are not pulling against each other.

The other side of Deborah's face goes equally smoothly except for one delay, attributable mainly to Dr. Ship's desire for perfection. The principal nerve that controls sensation in the lower cheek arches to the surface of the muscle tissue about midpoint across the cheek before burying itself in deep tissue again. It's a place that plastic surgeons like to steer clear of. If the nerve, known as the seventh facial nerve, is damaged, the face will sag on the side where the injury occurred. The repercussions for both patient and doctor could be enormous. What both tantalizes and frustrates plastic surgeons is that the nerve is often surrounded by nice globules of fat where it comes close to the surface, and plastic surgeons do not like excess fat. The doctor is tempted to take a poke at the fat around the nerve. He keeps lifting up the cheek skin to look and then drops it and pokes somewhere else. Then he lifts it up again. Flora is watching him. She has been through this before. Finally, he turns to me and exclaims, "See that fat in there? Oh, I'd love to take that out."

Flora jumps at him. "Uh-uh, don't gild the lily. She looks beautiful already."

"Flora's right," Dr. Ship sighs, and begins stitching the muscle to the area in back of the ear.

The chemical peel above the upper lip, the last part of the operation, is anticlimactic, a smear of white paste on the mustache area that takes the epidermis right off with a second-degree burn. By 1:30 the operation is complete, and Deborah's head is wrapped in about twenty feet of gauze. She looks as though she has just been knocked out with punches to the eyes. They resemble two purple dishes. She says she feels like she has been beaten. She looks it.

I saw Deborah again about two months after the operation. She looked at me expectantly as soon as she opened the door of her apartment; then disappointment darkened her eyes. She immediately sensed that I was not amazed at the change. While the skin on her face was tighter, the operation had not returned Deborah to her youth. Her eyes looked tired and her upper lip was red. She said that only one person, a friend, had shown any real enthusiasm about the change. "I am very upset that more people don't exclaim," she said sadly. "I don't feel very positive about myself right now."

The last two months had not been kind to her. Her left eyebrow drooped, though it was fast regaining its shape. This, according to Dr. Ship, is an occasional reaction of the main nerve near the eyes to the pushing and pulling experienced during the course of the operation. Deborah was scared and confused despite numerous reassurances by the doctor that the drooping would heal itself. It is the second most common complication in plastic surgery, the first being bruising or nicking a nerve in the neck. "Look," Dr. Ship explained, "in heart surgery, there are never any complaints because if there are complications, the patient isn't around to complain. Plastic-surgery patients don't run that risk, but complications are inevitable. It's the real world."

The specific cause of Deborah's other complaint was never discovered—an allergy that made her upper lip red and the stitches behind her ears feel as though they were bursting. The

allergy came on suddenly, about two weeks after the operation, when she returned to her studio for the first time. "I made
myself a nice lunch; I was so happy to be back there again.
But within an hour, I could feel my eyes throbbing and the
skin tightening up." She had never had an allergy before. She
thought it was caused by paint chemicals. No one knew if it
would disappear. In the meantime, she moped in her apartment as the healing process continued.

Was she glad she had the operation? "I have a feeling I *will*
be glad," she answered, "when I stop feeling so rotten. When
you feel rotten, you ask yourself why you did that to yourself.
But deep down, I guess I feel that it will work itself out."

Four months later, Deborah's face was back to normal. She
looked younger than she had when she began her ordeal, but
not decades younger. She could arch her eyebrows to her heart's
content. Dr. Ship had been right. And she was back in her studio every day with no allergic reactions. But the miracle she
hoped for had never happened. "I'm glad I went through with
it," she said simply and finally, "but I'll never do it again. From
now on, I guess I will just have to age gracefully."

Covering Up the Signs of Age

"Age-controlling creme," "collagen complex," "hydrolyzed
elastin," "cellular recovery complex," "linoleic acid," "soluable
protein," "nutrient-rich formula"—the current catchwords of
the cosmetics industry. The use of cosmetics is another way to
hide the effects of aging. Millions of women and thousands of
men depend upon them, and, as in the case of cosmetic surgery, the effect for those over thirty-five is a return to younger
days, albeit, in the case of cosmetics, for only a few hours. In
fact, foundations, creams and blushes cover the subtler signs
of aging more effectively than a face-lift at a fraction of the
cost. But it's back to the vanity table the next morning.

The people who run cosmetics companies know their de-
mographics. Lines are beginning to wrinkle around the eyes
of the post-World War II baby-boomers; their pores are getting bigger; and the skin around their jaws is beginning to
loosen up. Until five or so years ago, the emphasis of advertising was on enhancing beauty. But times have changed. Today
the emphasis is on preserving what beauty remains, a beauty

that is beginning to wrinkle and sag. How do you convince people that cosmetics will preserve and even rejuvenate, two pretty sophisticated concepts that smack of immortality? You turn to science and sprinkle advertisements with scientific-sounding terminology. Science, after all, is *the* authority these days; what it says will happen, will happen, so the belief goes.

That customers are willing to pay $6.5 billion per year for cosmetics products,* many of which are supposed to make people look younger, is evidence that the industry is doing an excellent job assuring people that its moisturizers and creams really can do something about aging. Dermatologists do not agree with all the claims. "There's a lot of garbage on the market," says Manhattan dermatologist Milton Reisch, "but the manufacturers are very clever about their advertising. If you read it carefully, they never say that their cosmetics will retard aging. They only suggest it."

Dr. Peter Burk, chief of dermatology at Montefiore Hospital in New York, has devoted a great deal of time to telling people that they should not believe the claims of the cosmetic companies. "The whole thing is hype. The industry is making claims that are just wildly absurd. I feel that I am a voice in the wilderness. No matter what you say to people, it seems to make no difference. Women and, increasingly, men think that they need these products to be acceptable. I find the trend bizarre."

Even those who work in the industry agree. One of them is Dr. Earl W. Brauer, a clinical dermatology professor at New York University Medical Center and an officer with a major cosmetics firm that spends millions each year advertising its age-retarding cosmetics in the pages of *Vogue, Glamour* and *Cosmopolitan.* Dr. Brauer does not think such products are necessary. "The best way to moisturize your body is to sit in a bathtub of warm water for fifteen minutes every day and then smear petroleum jelly over your body," he says. For obvious reasons, Dr. Brauer does not wish the name of the firm he works for

---

*This figure is an approximation based on 1983 retail sales of cosmetics and skin preparations as reported in *Product Marketing*'s 37th Annual Consumer Expenditure Study. Cosmetics include such products as makeup preparations, lipsticks, eye makeup and nail products. Skin preparations include face creams, moisturizers, body lotions and suntan lotions.

identified. Other dermatologists mention an application of Crisco as serving the same purpose as many moisturizers. Lanolin and mineral oil are fine, too. "No one wants to put such stuff on their bodies," continues Dr. Brauer, "because it would mess up the bedclothes. So what do the cosmetics companies do? They make a product that is aesthetically pleasing and doesn't mess up the bedclothes because it is so light in texture, and they package it attractively."

The success of the cosmetics industry's age-concealing cosmetics is based on a fundamental of physiology—that moisture can be retained in the outermost skin layer, the stratum corneum, if a proper barrier is provided to prevent its escape. The trapping of moisture ensures that the outer skin will remain slightly swollen, thus concealing fine wrinkles and enlarged pores. There is no profit, of course, in advising people to sit in a bathtub and then smear petroleum jelly over themselves. Yet the most expensive moisturizers accomplish little more. Some do contain glycerin, which attracts additional moisture to the skin from the surrounding air.

What about claims that certain cosmetics will rejuvenate the skin or help repair the skin or that by using them you will enable the skin to absorb such substances as protein or collagen? "None of the ingredients do any more than penetrate the outer skin layer," says Dr. Burk. "If a company claims that use of its cosmetic rejuvenates the skin, it is probably because it is a mild irritant. Anything irritating to the skin will cause an increase in cell turnover."

Improving skin tone, another common claim, is almost pure fancy. Skin quality is dictated by the dermis, the lower layer of skin. If cosmetics could actually do what their manufacturers claim, they would have to penetrate to this layer. But Dr. Burk points out that for the most part this is impossible. "Proteins are too big to get through the skin," he says. "Some substances like cortisone can penetrate but only with difficulty. So the role of cosmetics is restricted to the stratum corneum."

Are cosmetics safe? Given that there are some 25,000 products on the market that contain around 4000 ingredients, perhaps more, the surprising answer is a qualified "yes," despite the fact that the U.S. Food and Drug Administration tests only internally taken drugs, and cosmetics are not made to be ingested.

Each manufacturer does put its products through numerous tests, of which the Draize test is one. Animal lovers have protested because it involves using cosmetics on animals, sometimes in their eyes, to see if bad reactions occur. Effective testing methods are obviously a question of dollars and cents. A cosmetics company is obligated, if not morally then financially, to make sure its products are safe. One lawsuit decided against a manufacturer could put it out of business.

By far the most common complaint that dermatologists hear from users is that cosmetics cause skin irritations. Such charges are difficult to prove, for allergic reactions may not appear for days after a cosmetic is applied. Some do not show up until years later. And the task of discovering which of a product's thousands of ingredients is harmful is often an impossible one.

If cosmetics do not actually rejuvenate and repair cells, they can still be used to cover up the effects of aging. In fact, their overapplication creates much the same effect as too many face-lifts. The same sort of mono-finish is evidently a look that at least one major cosmetics firm, Estée Lauder, cherishes. A few years ago, after an article on aging that I wrote appeared in a large-circulation magazine, the people at Estée Lauder inquired if I would be interested in writing a press release that would contribute to a publicity campaign to introduce their latest product, Night Repair. In the lavishly furnished corporate offices on the thirty-ninth floor of the General Motors building overlooking New York's Central Park, the top personnel of the public relations department told me that I was being called upon to write what publicity people like to call a "feature." This was to be on the nature of sleep. I was informed, correctly, that cells are more active during sleep. Hence, if you give your face a bit of encouragement with Night Repair, your face will look all the more refreshed when you awaken. The subject intrigued me, especially after I was told that I was not expected to push the wonders of Night Repair.

I was even more intrigued, which is not to say attracted, by the faces of my assignors. There were four of them, all women, two edging into what I imagined was their sixties, one in her forties, and a younger woman. But I could not guess these ages by looking at their faces. All were made up as ultrafeminine ghosts, their faces so covered by creams, blushes and powders that individual features as well as age differences were lost. As mouths voiced the serious business of publicizing Night Repair to appeal to the most sophisticated consumer, I looked for character in those faces. I could find none. I looked for humor, thinking that perhaps cosmetics-company employees might find some amusement in their efforts. No humor. Nor could I find signs of boredom, interest, anger, or delight, the casual signs of life that flicker across the faces of ordinary mortals.

Most people do not want to sacrifice facial character in order to conceal the lines and wrinkles inevitable in the aging process. Many adapt to their wrinkles and crinkles and wear each as a battle scar. A friend of mine who is a middle-aged Zen Buddhist defined these feelings eloquently: "When I was little, I often had fantasies about leaping ahead in time. I would try to imagine what it was like to see my face when my hair was turning gray. The pleasure of imagining that disappears when you reach your thirties and forties. You don't like to conjure up an image of yourself as you think you will be in your sixties. There doesn't seem to be anything attractive about it. At the same time, part of the dignity of living is showing signs of having lived, of having expressed your life, and part of that expression is the lines in your face."

Chapter 4
Inside Aging

Immortality and the Cell

What makes us get old? What makes Claude Pepper look like an old man though he has the energy of a young man? Whatever it is, it has a lot to do with his cells, the myriad microscopic bodies that make up our tissues, organs, and even the characteristics of our offspring. Each of our approximately one trillion cells is an entity that can live by itself, ingesting and digesting food, growing and duplicating. Though the size, shape and function of cells vary enormously, their structures are similar. They consist of an outer membrane, or skin, which contains the cytoplasm, a gelatinlike substance in which internal organs, or organelles, as they are commonly called, are suspended. Different organelles control a cell's metabolism—the processes involved in maintaining it, such as ingestion of nutrients and excretion of wastes. The most crucial organelle is the nucleus, for within this inner body lies a cell's DNA, the genetic material that is duplicated during division, the most important function that a cell will ever carry out. Unfailing duplication not only ensures that a skin cell, for example, will always perform the functions of a skin cell, and a muscle cell the functions of a muscle cell, but also the passing of traits to the next generation.

Trying to understand cells is a big part of gerontological research. The science of cell biology—peering into cells to see what makes them tick—demands attention to detail. The problem is not that cells are so tiny; after all, electron micros-

88

copy can enlarge them to look like science-fiction monsters. It is that they are so complex and that so much remains to be discovered about their interrelationships.

Cell biologists must adhere to precise research standards if they want to understand how cells live and die. They must faithfully record all substances that they add to cultures. They have to be able to determine exactly where reactions occur. That these people have to be so orderly and disciplined in their sterile laboratories may be one reason why they appear to be more comfortable surrounded by a mess, out of their labs, than other people might. The sight of routine disorder like papers askew on a desk and a half-filled coffee cup must be a mighty welcome back to the ordinary world. Vincent J. Cristofalo's office at the Wistar Institute at the University of Pennsylvania looks as though it has been ransacked. It is a tiny nook tucked away from a nearby kingdom of gleaming labs, so small that one cannot turn around in it without brushing a wall decoration or an overflowing shelf stuffed with journals and books, or without stepping on the volumes and the article reprints that litter the floor. It looks like the office of a man whose mind disregards the details of life in favor of those of the cell.

The walls of this cubicle are dotted with photographs of sailing boats, yachting being one of Cristofalo's passions. Another is his six small daughters whose faces compete with the boats for wall space. Not so nicely represented are his many accreditations—framed degrees, certificates and honors. They all hang at crazy angles as if they were put up as decorations that no one would or should take seriously. Cristofalo also likes to sprinkle corny humor about this messy place with such printed notices as "You think you've got problems, I'm so far behind, tomorrow is gone even before I get there."

Such an office does not seem appropriate for a man whom colleagues acknowledge as the leading figure in understanding how a cell gets old. He has written more than one hundred sixty papers on the subject and is the director of the Center for the Study of Aging, another University of Pennsylvania research arm. He has received twenty-five awards and honors for his work. In 1983, he received the Brookdale Award, the most prestigious in the field of gerontology.

And his most recent work—exploring cells in hopes of uncovering their potential for immortality—is one of the most exciting areas of gerontological research today. One cold winter day, Cristofalo found space for the two of us in his cubbyhole and told me what he is doing. "I am looking for a trigger mechanism. What shuts old cells off could easily be the same thing that turns cells on in both cancer and atherosclerosis."

But Cristofalo is not a man obsessed with discovering the key to immortality. He does not even care about immortality beyond learning how a cell's on-off switch works. "I see myself as understanding how the watch works. I don't care what time it is," he tells me, rocking back and forth in his desk chair, his interlaced fingers supporting the back of his head.

His attempt to understand how a cell ages is not new to gerontological research. Gerontologists have explored the interiors of cells for years on the assumption that the secret of aging must lie within. Now, with the advent of such technological aids as electron microscopy, improved growing mediums, computerized cell counters and sophisticated methods of analyzing a cell's chemical makeup, the venerable theory that the body's destiny is directed by the life and death of its cells is once again in the forefront of explorations into aging.

Alexis Carrel at the Rockefeller Institute (now Rockefeller University) was the first modern researcher to investigate how cells age. His experiments suggested that cells could be immortal. Begun in 1911 with chicken heart fibroblasts (connective tissue cells that make collagen), they acted as a catalyst for succeeding years of gerontological research. His laboratory populations of these cells divided at such a prolific rate that he constantly had to throw some of the excess down the drain. In 1945, thirty-four years after Carrel began his experiments and a year after his death, the cells were still dividing. Carrel's colleagues at Rockefeller University threw the whole mess down the drain, certain that if the experiment were not halted the population would expand forever.

The halting of the experiment culminated years of sharp controversy over Carrel's findings, for no other scientist had been able to get the same results. Nevertheless, he had such an established reputation that his work was generally accepted. The experiments suggested that if cell populations were well nourished and encountered no stress, they would live indefinitely. If this were indeed so, then aging must be due either to malnourishment or other forms of stress or to reasons un-related to the life of a cell.*

The theoretical immortality of cell populations enjoyed con-siderable favor into the 1950s, helped along by the discovery in 1951 that cancer cells taken from a woman named Hen-rietta Lacks appeared to be immortal, too, when cultured and allowed to divide. HeLa cells, as the descendants of these orig-inal cells are called, now populate countless laboratories across the country. But Leonard Hayflick, who was a predecessor of Vincent Cristofalo at the Wistar Institute, questioned the growing belief that all cells, if properly nurtured, are immor-tal. In the 1950s and '60s, while working on a method of de-tecting tumor viruses, Hayflick discovered that a population of human fibroblasts would double only fifty times before dying out. Why? He seemed to be doing everything that Carrel had done. He put the cells into a vial with food; he let the cells divide until the vial was full. Then he poured out half the con-tents, let it fill again, and so on. Hayflick noticed that the more times the population doubled, the more slowly it did so. The cells also changed; some of their chromosomes were incom-plete or broken; the fatty substance lipofuscin had accumu-lated in some of them; and the way they divided was a more labored process than in younger cells.

The difference between Hayflick's mortal cells and Carrel's immortal ones may have been due to a difference in their lab-oratory techniques, one that affected gerontological research for years. Carrel had fed his cells nutrients consisting of chicken embryos. Scientists eventually realized that the nutrients may have contained at least some live chicken-heart fibroblasts. Every time the culture was fed, then, it may have received a dose of fresh cells. No one knows if this theory is valid. However, im-mortality in cells, with the exception of cancer and sex cells, has never been observed since.

Though improved growing techniques have extended the

---

*While some cell populations appear to be immortal, individual cells, with the exception of cancer cells and sex cells (sperm and eggs) are not. Cells divide, their descendants divide and a population grows. But within the population, older cells constantly die, which is why some 50 million cells die within us every second to be replaced by 50 million young ones.

"Hayflick limit" of fifty population doublings to seventy to eighty doublings, most cells appear to have a limited life span. It is Cristofalo's mission to find out why. In the process, he could well discover why cancer and sex cells are the exceptions. "It's a trigger mechanism," he repeats over and over again while talking about his work, a note of excitement mixed with desperation in his voice. He is a detective hot on the trail of the final evidence—the switch that turns cells on or off depending upon circumstances.

Though Cristofalo is getting closer to finding the answer, he acknowledges that gerontologists have a long way to go before discovering the key to immortality. But it could turn up in the bottom of the next petri dish. A caveat: "We are not going to invent a pill for immortality," he says firmly. "People think that understanding the aging process is similar to the effort that was made to get to the moon. It's much harder. Getting a man to the moon was not a question of discovery. The laws of motion had been known for centuries and we knew what the escape velocity had to be. Here we are looking at some very fundamental processes in the cell which fail with aging and we are just learning about them. Even if we do discover a cell's trigger, the knowledge is not going to help people in nursing homes today.

"But," he muses, "it might help their grandchildren."

Just how close is Cristofalo? He and his assistants have observed that aging cells appear to go through all the preparations for division that younger cells do but then stop just short of the replication of their DNA. The replication of DNA—a momentous event for a cell—requires the increase of a substance called thymidine triphosphate, a building block of DNA, and the activity of an enzyme called thymidine kinase. Both old and young cells fill up with thymidine triphosphate. If all were right, this substance would be shared among two cells in the immediate future. But in an old cell, the replication never proceeds, leaving it large, bloated and sterile at the end of its life.

Another reason that old cells are larger than young ones is that they contain many more lysosomes—bag-like organelles that are thought to digest foreign substances that enter a cell. They also have the capacity to kill the entire cell with their enzymes, sometimes a necessary part of life. A tadpole, for example, must get rid of its tail before it changes into a frog. Lysosomes will do the job. It was because of the proliferation of lysosomes that Cristofalo happened upon a discovery that took him a step closer to understanding a cell's life-extension possibilities. He wanted to study the lysosomes but to do so he had to chemically stabilize them. The most effective chemical for this is a naturally occurring hormone called hydrocortisone. Cristofalo added this to the growing medium. The result was far more dramatic than he had anticipated. While the lysosomes became more stable, the cells jumped into action. Suddenly, the younger populations started to divide and did not stop until they had extended their life span by 40 percent.

Cristofalo therefore believes that hormones have something to do with stimulating a cell to divide by blocking its shut-off signal. He and his investigative team are working on how this occurs. Clues are beginning to accumulate. Cells are ordinarily very discriminating about the substances they allow to enter them and influence their behavior. However, steroid hormones—a class of hormone derived from cholesterol that includes the sex hormones and some stress hormones—enjoy unrestricted entry. Once inside, they bind to specific receptors, prompting a cell into action. Hydrocortisone, one of the steroid hormones, evidently causes cells to produce another hormone called autocrine growth factor, which makes cells increase their rate of division. Other hormones undoubtedly direct cells in as-yet-unknown ways.

Cristofalo rocks back and forth in his desk chair and looks around at the clutter in his office. "The switches just go crazy," he murmurs. "Sometimes they turn off and sometimes they turn on. In old age, they get turned off. But in cancer and atherosclerosis, they get turned on. Whatever is going on, it's a question of finding the trigger."

The Ubiquitous Hormone's Role in Aging

Just as hormones might trigger some cells to turn on or off, they might also trigger entire organs, or in some cases the entire organism. A massive release of corticoid hormones, for example, kills Pacific salmon just after they spawn. And adolescence begins with what Caleb Finch, a gerontologist at the Andrus Gerontology Research Center at the University of California at Los Angeles terms an "endocrine cascade." Finch is one of the leaders in developing a theory that credits our hormones and neurotransmitters with aging us. He wonders if each of us carries around a clock in our hypothalamus, the region of the brain that controls both the secretion of many of our hormones and the functions of the pituitary gland, which dangles from it on a stalk. The job of the hypothalamus is to release substances that tell the pituitary to make hormones that will go to specific organs. Dopamine is one of the substances. When released by the hypothalamus, dopamine travels to the pituitary, prompting it, among other things, to secrete hormones and enzymes that stimulate the ovaries to secrete estrogen.

The female reproductive cycle is largely under the control of estrogen, one of the leading female sex hormones. Finch has found that a decrease in dopamine secretion in a female rat leads to the loss of its reproductive ability. No dopamine, no estrogen, no reproductive cycle. But when he gave L-dopa, a synthetic compound that converts to dopamine inside the body, to middle-aged female rats whose reproductive capacities had long since ended, their cycles suddenly sprang to life.

A deficiency of dopamine, it should be noted, causes the tremors and uncanny muscular rigidity of Parkinson's disease, symptoms that can be alleviated by doses of L-dopa. While the drug has extended the lives of mice, the same has not been true with humans.

Dopamine is only one of many substances secreted by the hypothalamus. It is Finch's hunch that, with aging, the hypothalamus's ability to relay these substances begins to wane. Not enough is sent or the wrong message is given so the pituitary directs the pancreas, the adrenal glands, the sex organs or the thymus to secrete insufficient or overabundant amounts of hormones. The hypothalamus might be the master switch box of aging, slowly reducing the amount of current that it provides to the rest of the body.

Hormones may even halt the action of individual cells, thus performing a function just the *opposite* of that speculated upon by Cristofalo. This does not mean that Cristofalo is on the wrong track; rather it is an indication of the power of hormones— they may well turn cells on under some circumstances and turn them off under others. Hormones influence a cell's life by one of two routes, via receptors either on the cell's outer membrane or in the cytoplasm. The hormones that take the latter route include the sex hormones and other steroids like hydrocortisone.

Receptors for steroid hormones are ubiquitous in most cells, but only some cells have receptors for other hormones. Because steroid hormones and their receptors are so common, the welcome or rejection that cells give these hormones have been well studied. The number of receptors inside the cell drops off sharply with age. The ones that remain are able to receive incoming hormones, but the overall effect is that hormones cannot exert their influence on an older cell as effectively as on a younger one. Like people, older cells become less accommodating of outside influences.

Testosterone is the leading male sex hormone and, of course, a steroid. The connection between its levels and sexual activity is tenuous at best. But it does appear that there is a connection. If testosterone levels fall too low, libido and sexual desire wane. If they are too high, excessive muscular development and hairiness result. Any number of studies have concluded that testosterone levels begin falling off at around twenty-five, but S. Mitchell Harman, a gerontologist specializing in endocrinal studies at the Gerontology Research Center in Baltimore, disputes the finding that testosterone always decreases. He found that the hormone slightly increased in a sample of seventy-six men aged from twenty-five to ninety who were participants in the Baltimore Longitudinal Study of Aging. Part of the reason may be that the great majority of men selected for the study were in exceptional health and most were well-educated and financially comfortable. High stress levels, which tend to decrease testosterone production, were not typical of the group. Most participants in similar studies that measure hormone levels have been drawn from hospital outpatient clinics, customarily frequented by a less fortunate and perhaps less healthy clientele.

Harman's most interesting finding was that the elderly men with the highest testosterone levels tended to be more sexually active. "We don't know why this is so," he says, but cautions that "there are so many unknowns in the study of the endocrine system that what appears to make sense initially may have no bearing on the matter in the final analysis." That the most sexually active older men tended to have had frequent sex during their younger years is one major clue. The receptor sites in a cell that receive testosterone are made up of protein. Protein synthesis ordinarily diminishes with age. But continued sexual activity stimulates the making of proteins that form testosterone receptor sites, according to Estelle Ramey, a physiologist at Georgetown University School of Medicine, thus enabling millions of cells to keep up their contribution to a man's sex life and to influence his emotions and libido. "Think of it," suggests Ramey, "as locks that get all clogged up if they are not being continually used." Even though good health and low stress may encourage a youthful production of testosterone into old age, it may not benefit a man's sex life or his desire unless sexual activity has been important to him all along, thus enabling him to "exercise" his cells' testosterone receptors.

A similar kind of thing happens to women and lends further strength to the "use it or lose it" adage. A common medical finding is that the genitalia of some postmenopausal women atrophy—the vagina shrinks, its walls thin and lose their elasticity and natural lubricants diminish, making intercourse painful. But women who keep up a relatively active sex life after menopause tend not to suffer such misfortune. Why? One theory is that continuous sexual activity stimulates the production of hormones which in turn has a salubrious effect on the sex organs. Another theory is that ongoing sex stimulates cell receptors to more efficiently use whatever estrogen is available.

Hormones are complex juices. Even if the amount of some diminish with the passing years, the effect that that has on the body may be indirect; the decrease, for example, may permit another hormone to assume a supremacy unimagined during younger years. Consider the case of dehydroepiandrosterone, or DHEA for short, a mysterious hormone that some researchers are not sure is really a hormone. It has fascinated endocrinologists since 1934 when it was first isolated from urine and found not only to be crucial to the development of sex hormones but also to be a derivative of cholesterol. Since then, it has become vital to the manufacture of synthetic hormones and birth control pills, an industry based largely in Mexico where a species of yam yields up the raw material from which DHEA is manufactured.

Responsibility for a method of birth control may be the least of DHEA's glories. Life-extension buffs have called it an anti-aging drug that promises to confer immortality on all who take it. Processed in a laboratory, the substance looks like bleached flour. While one substance can hardly be expected to control such a complex process as aging, DHEA does possess some remarkable properties. Researchers were initially intrigued because the amount circulating in the body decreases markedly with age, far more so than with other hormones. A sixty-year-old has only five to 20 percent of that of a twenty-year-old. Of greater fascination and significance is that many of the diseases of aging, such as cancer, heart disease, osteoporosis, diabetes and atherosclerosis increase at the same time that the level of DHEA decreases. Could there be a connection? The answer, in light of recent research, appears to be "yes," especially when some tantalizing findings about cancer are considered. Women with breast cancer consistently have lower levels of DHEA than those without the disease. Researchers have even ascertained that those with the disease had lower levels *before* they got the cancer. DHEA could be a preventive and healing agent of undreamed of benefits.

A Hungarian researcher, Jiri Sonka, was the first scientist to proffer an explanation for DHEA's role. Noting that degenerative diseases appeared to increase with the decline of DHEA, he theorized that the substance might inhibit the activity of an abundant enzyme called glucose-6 phosphate-dehydrogenase, commonly known as G6PD, which is essential for the synthesis of nucleic acids, fats and steroids. Without the normal functioning of this enzyme, the growth of new cells is diminished. DHEA levels, in their ability to influence G6PD, would thus be of enormous importance to the entire body.

Other scientists think that DHEA's functions are even more sophisticated. Both DHEA and cortisol, another hormone, are produced in the adrenal glands, the principal site of steroid hormone production. Cortisol promotes metabolism, not always a good thing. If, as Sonka suggested, DHEA slows down metabolism because of its influence over G6PD, then the aging process, with its decline of DHEA, should leave cortisol unchecked, permitting the increased metabolism that results in the rampant cell growth associated with cancer, atherosclerosis (plaque consists of cellular material) and obesity.

If DHEA could control obesity by inhibiting cell growth, it should also have an influence on diabetes since elderly obese people run a high risk of getting Type II (adult-onset) diabetes. Further, it has been discovered that high cortisol levels promote diabetes. To explore the theoretical benefits of DHEA, Norman Applesweig, a biochemist and an authority on steroids, formed his own company, Progenics, Inc. In 1983, the company filed patent applications for the use of the hormone and its derivatives as a new form of diabetes therapy. Scientists at the Lilly Research Laboratories had already shown that DHEA could control weight gain in mice that had been genetically manipulated to be obese. And Progenics' own research indicates that DHEA will reduce blood-sugar levels in diabetic mice to near normal.

Preliminary tests on human diabetics are encouraging. In one study that Progenics sponsored in Italy, six Type II diabetics whose blood-sugar levels were abnormally high even though they were on oral therapy were given just 10 milligrams of a form of DHEA three times a day. Their blood-sugar levels plummeted.

The hormone may even counterbalance the effects of stress. Cortisol-production increase is one of the physiological responses to stress. The increase leads to a higher risk of diabetes, atherosclerosis, heart disease and cancer, to name but a few of the consequences (see Chapter 7). One explanation is that elevated cortisol production causes the thymus gland to shrink and the thymus is crucial to the immune system. Studies by Applesweig have shown that when laboratory animals placed in stressful situations are given a form of DHEA, their thymus glands do not shrink.

The popular media, encouraged by some optimistic researchers, has touted DHEA as a miracle cure. It may soon turn out that DHEA is not a cure at all. Rather, it may be a preventive that acts by inhibiting the too-rapid metabolism that cortisol promotes. The mechanisms of how the substance works as a preventive, in the case of obesity and diabetes anyway, are close to being understood. What remains to be discovered is the derivatives of DHEA that will best combat these diseases.

Free Radicals—The Enemy Within

As sensible as it should seem that the rise and fall of hormones contribute to aging, this theory, like so many quests for the secret of life, leads the explorer back to the cell. There, gerontologists are focusing on free radicals, the name for fast-moving molecules that have one free electron whizzing around them. Because of their single electron, these molecules try to pair with other molecules. In their search for partners, they may damage a cell. And too many weakened cells can weaken us and encourage the process of aging.

We produce free radicals in the course of normal metabolism. But when their numbers increase, their effects become stronger. The ultraviolet light in the sun can cause them to proliferate and, in the process, create concentrations of pigment called lentigines which in turn create age or "liver" spots on the skin of elderly people. Ozone, petrochemical pollutants, and the breakdown of fat in our bodies can produce free radicals, too. But the most common reason for their presence is the oxygen in the air that we depend upon for life. Air consists of 20 percent oxygen, about 78 percent nitrogen and a bit of argon, carbon dioxide, neon, helium and a few other gases. Though oxygen is absolutely vital to us, its production of free radicals does to our insides just about what it does to a hunk of iron. It "rusts" us enough to cause the accumulation of the fatty pigment lipofuscin. No one knows whether lipofuscin is good or bad for our cells. By the time a person turns eighty, over four percent of each cell in his heart will be solid lipofuscin. Though there is no evidence, it makes sense that such a buildup would have the same effect that a bucket of grease would have if dumped on the engine of your car.

In 1956, Denham Harman, at the University of Nebraska, first came up with the idea that free radicals were a cause of aging. He also hypothesized that they could lead to DNA damage and thus be responsible not only for cancer but for the mutations that fuel evolution. How free radicals form as a result of the oxygen we breathe and how the cells attempt to combat them are illustrative of the war for equilibrium that rages endlessly within our cells. When we breathe, air rushes into our lungs and mixes with blood which transports the oxygen to different parts of the body, where it eventually enters cells. As the cells use oxygen, four complex and successive chemical reactions occur countless times per second. Free radicals can result from any one of the reactions, though the cell protects itself by trying to halt their formation. An enzyme called cytochrome oxidase accompanies oxygen through the cell. It is the job of this enzyme to ensure that oxygen does not escape. Its guardianship, though, is not perfect. At each step, some free radicals do escape and burst into the cell's cytoplasm, sometimes even into its nucleus where DNA is stored.

Ruthless and indiscriminate, free radicals can not only attack DNA and cause mutations, but can also foul up a cell's digestive system and even puncture a cell's outer membrane, killing it and eliminating themselves in the process. But a cell does not passively tolerate such intrusions. It has its own defenses, enzymes—superoxide dismutase and catalase are the most common—that counterattack these molecules.

Not every cell suffers the damage of free radicals. Most cells divide at such a rate that they do not get the chance to do much harm. Ferreting out the mechanisms of free radical damage is a major research area in gerontology today. Arthur K. Balin at Rockefeller University is one of those trying to understand not only what effect free radicals have on the cell but what the cell does to try to defend itself. A short, hefty man with piercing eyes who explains his work by alternating between rapid-fire scientific terminology and colloquialisms, Balin terms lipofuscin "a mess of protein, lipid and carbohydrate, glumped together so that the cell cannot break them down and digest them.

"If you leave butter on the table," he continues, "it turns rancid after a few days because it has been exposed to oxygen. Why doesn't the same thing happen to the fat in our body? Well, maybe it does, but the cells can repair the damage—and to the extent that they can't, oxygen may be contributing to our aging."

Balin's office at Rockefeller University, a luxurious oasis overlooking Manhattan's East River, has the same look as Cristofalo's, his former mentor. It is a mess—journals stacked waist-high on the floor, books spilling out of shelves, desks cluttered

with transparencies, culture dishes, vials and other parapher-
nalia of the adjoining laboratory.

To understand how cells defend themselves against oxygen,
Balin places them in an environment with a greater than normal amount of oxygen to see how their growth and longevity
are affected. "The idea is that stressing the cell just a little more
than usual will put extra demands on its repair system and we
can see what its ability to protect itself is." He has found that
growth of a laboratory cell population varies markedly with the
amount of oxygen it is given. The lower the oxygen, the faster
the growth; the higher the oxygen, the slower the growth.
Oxygen pressure varies greatly throughout our bodies and future research may reveal that those areas that use up oxygen
the fastest because of a higher metabolic rate may age faster.
That adjacent areas of the brain receive very different amounts
of oxygen may account for why certain mental functions remain stable with aging while others decline.

Researchers are on the verge of discovering a connection
between oxygen use and life expectancy. Rats and guinea pigs
that run on treadmills suffer more cell and tissue damage than
sedentary animals, especially if they are deficient in the vitamins C and E. Researchers in California have found that bursts
of free radical production during the exertion cause the damage. Further evidence comes from investigations of the common housefly. R. S. Sohal, a biologist at Southern Methodist
University in Dallas, conducted an experiment to discover
whether metabolic rate influenced aging in the flies. Realizing
that a higher metabolism would produce more free radicals,
he compared the longevity of houseflies at various levels of activity. First, he put a lot of males and a few females in a cage
and let them fly around. As might be expected, all the males
went into a frenzy competing for the few females. Then he put
flies individually into vials so small that they could only walk
but not fly. These flies lived over twice as long as the first group.
Sohal also discovered that lipofuscin levels in the active flies
was much higher than in the sedentary ones.

Where does this leave joggers and swimmers? While the
longer lives of the restricted flies are interesting to consider, it
is safe to assume that people who exercise should keep right
on exercising. The metabolism of people and flies is quite dif-

ferent. Still, the biological basis of human cells and fly cells are the same. Perhaps future research will suggest the ideal amount of exercise that will benefit the heart, tone the muscles and lower cholesterol without damaging cells.

Free radicals have received a lot of interest from the health-food industry. If the body manufactures its own enemies to free radicals such as superoxide dismutase and catalase, it makes sense, on a superficial level anyway, that, if we add free radical scavengers to our diet, we should keep one step ahead of aging. Researchers have come up with a number of free radical scavengers besides superoxide dismutase and catalase. These include vitamins C and E, the element selenium and even the compound known as BHT, which is commonly used as a food preservative. If not much is known about what good they might do, there is very little evidence that they do any harm. Balin is skeptical, however, of beneficial claims of superoxide dismutase, or SOD as it is often called. He points out that it is a protein. When we swallow SOD, the same thing happens to it as happens to a piece of filet mignon. Digestive enzymes attack it and break it down into constituent parts that bring a halt to its scavenging abilities. We might have better luck injecting it, but studies have shown that kidneys excrete it within ten to fifteen minutes. Balin feels quite differently about other free radical scavengers such as vitamins C and E. He takes these on a regular basis in the theoretical belief that they will halt free radical generation in his body.

Some animal experiments have suggested that taking free radical scavengers, or antioxidants, as they are sometimes called, extends life expectancy. Balin again raises a warning finger. The animals in some of the studies got sick from the antioxidants and did not eat regularly as a consequence. It may not have been the scavengers that increased their life expectancy; it may have been that they ate less. More on the effects of diet restriction on life expectancy in the next chapter.

How We Came to Live as Long as We Do

Gerontologists have little argument that, in the final analysis, it is genes that dictate how long we live. Complex genetic influences decree that humans can live between one hundred ten and one hundred fifteen years. Most of us do not live this long because we fall victim to life's misfortunes—accidents, diseases, wars—or because we contribute to our downfall by smoking, eating improperly and not exercising enough. Every species has a designated number of years. A mouse lives no longer than around three and a half years. A rabbit can live fifteen years; a horse, thirty; and an Asian elephant, sixty. The tortoise is the longest-lived animal on record, capable of remaining alive for up to one hundred fifty slow-paced years.

There is no doubt that longevity tends to run in some families just as the risk of heart disease, osteoporosis, cancer or Alzheimer's disease runs in others. Though your family may possess a genetic disposition for, say, heart disease, which was apparently true of the family of Jim Fixx, the author of *The Complete Book of Running*, who died of a massive heart attack despite years of running, this does not mean that you *are* going to die of a heart attack or even suffer a heart attack. But it does mean that you will have to work a little harder to avoid having one. You will have to eat wisely, exercise regularly and do not do something so foolish as to smoke. You should also have frequent medical checkups, a safeguard that Fixx did not take.

What is it in our genes that says that humans can live as long as they do while hamsters generally survive only five years and dogs fifteen? Dr. Richard Cutler, a gerontologist at the Gerontology Research Center, thinks that the evolutionary reason for our long life span may be due to a mere handful of genes. He told me this one day in his office in Baltimore, holding out a cupped hand into which I foolishly glanced, half-hoping I would see a dozen or so genes bouncing around like Mexican jumping beans. And he does not think that humans are necessarily limited to one hundred ten years or so. To Cutler's way of thinking, a species' life span depends upon the outcome of an ongoing battle between forces that retard aging and those that promote it. Two billion years ago in the primordial soup, forms of life much simpler than the simplest cell today had few if any enemies. They lived in the soup for millennia, not knowing that the very food they depended upon would turn out one day to be their greatest enemy. The digestion of this diet broke down carbohydrates into carbon dioxide and water. Over eons, the carbon dioxide, which contained oxygen, accumulated and created the oxygen-rich atmosphere that we breathe today.

Oxygen, a toxin, was life's first enemy. It probably decimated vast populations of slowly evolving proto-organisms. But it also provided energy, and those life forms that were able to protect themselves from it thrived. The principal means of protection was the development of the cell; the outer membrane and the compartamentalization of a cell's internal structures was tantamount to the creation of a fortress whose walls the oxygenated and unfriendly world outside had difficulty penetrating. Since that time, life's defensive weapons have evolved further to include free radical scavengers and cell division. But no defense evolved to combat aging.

If it had not been for one development, a life form could have evolved only so far before age killed it off, to be replaced by another form. Species would not have had a chance to evolve. Sex was the innovation, a means of passing genetic material from generation to generation and, in a sense, thus defeating aging. Packed away in the ovaries and testes, sex cells are far more protected than somatic cells, the ones that make up our tissues and organs. Sex cells have only one objective—to perpetuate the species by joining with a sex cell of the opposite sex—an objective accomplished by endowing us with sexual desire.

This ability does not explain longevity. From a strictly biological point of view, there does not seem to be much point in staying alive after having produced offspring. The genetic material has already been passed on. That, in the case of most species, not much more is left to do in terms of biological success or failure may be one reason why our bodies begin to decline at such an early age, as outlined in Chapter 1.

Members of most species do die shortly after they reproduce or their young can live independently. Nurturing is not even part of their lives. Thousands of insect species die, for example, shortly after laying their eggs. Why are we humans different? The obvious answer is because children grow slowly and need our care, but the real reason runs much deeper.

In the early years of this century, the German biologist Max Rubner found that those species with the shortest life span have the highest metabolic rate. But humans metabolize their food at just about the same rate as deer mice and chipmunks, relatively short-lived creatures. Why, then, are we an exception? According to the late George Sacher, a researcher at the Argonne National Laboratory, animals with high metabolic rates and long life spans have larger brains than those with comparably high rates that live a shorter time. Brain size appears to be one key to human longevity; of all animals, we have the largest brain in relation to body weight.

Our brain size may have evolved largely by accident. Paleontologists can accurately pinpoint the life span of fossil hominids by determining the capacity of the brain case. The bigger the brain case, the longer the life span. Longevity steadily increased from the earliest hominids up to *Homo erectus* or Java Man, a cousin of ours who lived 200,000 years ago and whose life span of around fifty-five years was probably never fulfilled because of disease and malnutrition. Over the next 100,000 years as *Homo erectus* evolved to *Homo sapiens,* life span shot up to its present one hundred ten years, a remarkably short time for such a large change. Present thinking is that a mutation of extraordinary rapidity was responsible since genes usually need millions of years to reach a final point of evolution. Because of the short time involved, the guess is that the mutation involved only a small number of genes, the very ones that I thought Dr. Cutler was offering me over his desk.

Cutler has shown that the longer the life span of a species, the more superoxide dismutase—the major free radical scavenger—its cells have at their disposal. And Ron Hart and Richard Setlow, the two researchers who discovered in the mid-1970s what ultraviolet light did to fibroblast cells, also found that though ultraviolet light damaged the DNA of virtually every species, some species are better able to repair the damage than others. The species that makes repairs most efficiently are the longer-lived ones. Human cells come out far ahead in their capability to make repairs.

A Crucial Cluster of Genes

Yet another clue in the intricate detective story that reveals the reason for our longevity has been contributed by Roy L. Walford, a well-known gerontologist who broke into the popular press in 1983 with *Maximum Life Span,* an optimistic book that, among other things, suggests that we can live far more than onc hundred ten years if we only give our bodies a chance. He hopes that he is giving his that chance by putting it on a firm regime of exercise and calorie restriction and by taking vitamins C and E and other antioxidants such as selenium, cysteine (an amino acid), BHT (the food preservative), and methionine (an organic compound derived from protein).

Walford certainly does not act or look like the usual scientist. He took part in the street riots in Paris in 1968. On one of his Las Vegas gambling sprees, he broke the bank at a casino and got a write-up in the old *Life* magazine. During the Algerian War, he wrote articles for *The Berkeley Free Press*. When I met him in his laboratories in the medical center of the University of California in Los Angeles, he was dressed in a denim shirt, blue jeans and work boots, which he liked to prop up on his desk. He shaves his head every day and wears a mustache whose ends flop down below his chin. At sixty-one, he looks forty-five and is in top physical shape with not an ounce of fat, all of which embarrasses his friend Vincent Cristofalo, who looks his fifty-two years.

"You think he looks forty-five?" Cristofalo asked me with disbelief in his voice. "Well, I don't. I think he looks just his age."

But whatever his other activities may be, Walford is a serious and respected scientist and among the most outspoken about the possibility of life extension. He receives hundreds of thousands of research dollars every year and presides over several laboratories, investigating primarily the role that immunity plays in the aging process. Much of the capacity to fight disease is dependent on the thymus gland, the two-lobed organ behind the breastbone that processes lymphocytes—white blood cells formed in the bone marrow—into T-cells. As noted in Chapter 1, the thymus begins to disintegrate during puberty and continues to shrink through middle age, perhaps due to the dwindling of the hormone DHEA. By old age, its ability to contribute to the body's immune system is a fraction of what it was during childhood.

The key to Walford's thinking about immunity and aging is that though the lymphocytes, bone marrow and thymus are principal actors, the immune system is directed by a gene cluster on our sixth chromosome pair. (Chromosomes are threadlike structures made up of DNA. Genes are fixed at specific locations on each chromosome. Humans have twenty-three pairs.) The location of the genes in question, called the major histocompatibility complex (MHC), was determined by two American scientists, George Snell and Baruj Benacerraf, and a Frenchman, Jean Dausset, all of whom received a Nobel prize in 1980 for their work.

Walford and one of his colleagues suspected that the MHC had a great deal to do with longevity. To test the theory, they manipulated the genetic makeup of fourteen different strains of mice by breeding brother to sister in each strain through so many generations that the mice became genetically identical except for different MHCs. The life expectancy of these almost genetically identical strains raised in the same environment and given the same diet should have been about the same. But some strains lived a relatively long time and some a shorter time, which lends credence to the belief that the MHC must have been the reason for the difference in longevity.

The genes that are responsible for producing SOD and for repairing damaged DNA are also associated with this gene cluster. The circumstantial evidence is strong enough to lead Walford to believe that the genes that mutated 100,000 years ago are part of the MHC. This handful of genes, then, may enable us to fight off disease, to destroy free radicals before they damage our cells and to live as long as we do.

Chapter 5
The Limits of Life

*T*here are many ways to live much longer than we do. Though some are only theoretical, others actually work, at least in animals. Medical technology, improved hygiene and better nutrition have relatively painlessly increased our life expectancy by more than twenty-five years since the turn of the century. But if we want to live longer than seventy-five years, if we want to live to the limits of our life span, we will have to make sacrifices.

We could have our pituitary gland removed. Such drastic experimentation has had rejuvenating effects in animals. The reason is uncertain but lends credence to Dr. Caleb E. Finch's theory that aging is largely controlled by the endocrine system. We would be miserable without our pituitary. It is the master gland that, working in tandem with the hypothalamus, controls the secretion of hormones that dictate growth, sexual development and metabolism. Animals that have had this gland removed can stay alive only if they are given injections of essential hormones. And even then, their bodies do not behave normally. To attempt to prolong a human life by such means would be scientifically interesting but cruelly absurd.

Much of the work on the effects of pituitary removal in laboratory animals has been undertaken by W. Donner Denkla, formerly of Harvard University and more recently with the Alcohol, Drug Abuse and Mental Health Administration. He found that the procedure not only slowed the process of aging but even reversed it in some ways. The supposed reason is that the pituitary secretes a hormone called, with all the objectivity that science can muster, "decreasing consumption of oxygen" hormone. It is commonly called DECO for short. Another name for it, provided by those with a sense for the macabre, is "death hormone." During early adulthood, the pituitary begins to secrete this hormone and to cause us trouble, though we are unaware of it, by blocking the effectiveness of thyroxine, a hormone secreted by the thyroid gland, which helps to govern metabolism. The older we get, the more awry metabolism becomes. Remove the source of DECO and youthful metabolism should continue right into old age. Whether or not this actually happens is a question that Denkla is attempting to answer by purifying the hormone from cattle pituitaries so that he can develop an antidote to it.

At about the same time during one's passage through life that the pituitary begins to manufacture DECO in quantity, another hormone, DHEA (discussed in the last chapter), begins to dry up. Some gerontologists hope that this hormone will turn out to be one of life extension's prime agents. DHEA is so common in the young body that researchers refer to it simply as a "junk hormone." But by old age, just at the time that we are becoming more prone to disease, we do not have much of it. The link between declining levels of DHEA and increasing risk of disease appears irrefutable.

We also might live longer if our body temperature could be lowered below the normal 98.6 degrees. Roy Walford, the UCLA gerontologist, noticed that a species of lizard lived twice as long in the colder climate of New England as it did in Florida. Following up this observation, he raised a fish species in a colder environment than normal and was able to double its life span. But lizards and fish are cold-blooded creatures. Warm-blooded animals are not so easy to deal with. In fact, the only way of doing so would be to tamper with the hypothalamus, which regulates body temperature. Such interference, aside from its dubious morality, would precipitate a host of complications, making temperature reduction as a means of increasing life span, like removal of the pituitary, another exercise in the absurd.

Slightly less drastic but just as imaginative procedures have actually taken place. One of them involved the transplantation of ape testicles into elderly men. Another used goat testicles. Neither had any effect. Another form of rejuvenation therapy injected cells from unborn lamb fetuses. The results were disappointing but the Swiss doctor who used the technique made a fortune.

Yet another therapy, perhaps the most famous, is Gerovital. It was introduced to the world in 1951 by an elusive Rumanian physician, Ana Aslan, who uses it widely in the Geriatric Institute in Bucharest. She claims that Gerovital alleviates the following problems of aging: heart disease, memory loss, wrinkling, gray hair, balding, sexual dysfunction, arthritis and Parkinson's disease. The number of claims is incredible. What is most amazing, though, is that all of them might contain a germ of truth if one believes strongly enough that physical aging is influenced by psychological attitude. The main substance in Gerovital is procaine hydrochloride, the active ingredient in the novocaine your dentist gives you. It not only acts as a local anesthesia; it is also an antidepressant. Those under Dr. Aslan's care, who, incidentally, have included John F. Kennedy, Charles de Gaulle, Mao Ze-dong, Marlene Dietrich and W. Somerset Maugham, claimed that they felt great after her treatments—relaxed, rested, refreshed and rejuvenated. Well, if you feel like that, you are likely to put your worries about memory loss on the back burner; you are less tense so your blood pressure decreases and you sleep well so your wrinkles smooth out, and what are a few gray hairs?

Dr. Aslan has conducted studies on rats in which she reports an over 20 percent increase in life expectancy in those animals given Gerovital. Scientists here and in other Western countries are both intrigued and irritated by these claims, intrigued because there really might be something to the therapy but irritated because Aslan never conducted the double-blind studies (in which half the subjects are given the drug and half a placebo, but it is unknown by both researcher and subject whether the drug or the placebo is being administered) that scientists generally rely upon to test theories and to separate psychological from physical reactions. And in one study in which Aslan claims that the disorders of over 5250 people were alleviated by her drug, she refused to specify the extent of the improvements.

Double-blind studies conducted here and in England hold little hope that the drug can retard aging. But there are some indications that it can alleviate depression. According to a 1982 article in the journal *Geriatrics,* one Duke University study found that Gerovital worked better as an antidepressant than imipramine, a common medication for depression. One theory for this is that procaine hydrochloride inhibits an enzyme called monomine oxidase, which becomes more plentiful with aging and is thought to contribute to depression.

Dr. Aslan is just as much at loggerheads with Western scientists as they with her. She claims that studies conducted here and in England on Gerovital have used a different form of procaine. The procaine in Gerovital, Aslan says, contains small amounts of benzoic acid, which slows the breakdown of the procaine so the body can use it more efficiently. Benzoic acid, in the meantime, changes into p-aminobenzoic acid, better known as PABA, the main ingredient in good sunscreens. PABA is also an antioxidant that helps stop free radicals from damaging cells. When put on the skin, it acts only as an ultraviolet light blocker, not as a free radical scavenger; for that, it must get into the bloodstream.

In the 1960s, a West German pharmaceutical house came out with a life-extension agent called K.H. 3. Its main ingredient is also procaine, although there are a number of additives. K.H. 3 is now sold over-the-counter in seventy countries. While the FDA has not approved the sale of this drug or of Gerovital here, the state of Nevada approved both in 1977. Over-the-counter sales, which began in 1983, are booming despite the complete lack of evidence that the drug retards aging. Double-blind studies have indicated, however, that K.H. 3 and Gerovital do improve concentration, memory, seeing, hearing and coordination, abilities that sometimes wane as we get older. Almost 30 percent of the subjects in one study had improved hearing after taking K.H. 3 for five months. Other studies have found that the drug increases intelligence and vigor and improves emotional stability. Virtually every study has found an increase in psychological functioning which, of course, influences physical functioning. While it is easy to pass off Gerovital and K.H. 3 as pills to fool the gullible, there does seem to be something in them that makes life a little easier for many people. How that ingredient works is the subject of a long-range Australian study now in progress. When all the findings are in, the chances are that the influence that psychology has over physical functioning will be even more firmly established than it now is.

Diet Restriction, a Key to Longevity

Man has probably sought a source of rejuvenation ever since he became aware of aging and the inevitability of death. His success at staving both off has been remarkable (life expectancy during Roman times was, after all, only twenty-two years), but he has not had such good fortune at pinpointing the causes of aging. The mystery of the process has left claims for a cure wide open to droves of charlatans over the centuries. As medical knowledge increases, the quacks are being increasingly drummed out of the field of gerontology, replaced by pioneering scientific researchers of whom Aslan may be one—though her lack of willingness to open her books to scientific scrutiny makes her case difficult to support.

Possibilities for longer lives now crowd the horizon. Recombinant DNA technology (described in Chapter 9 as a means of ferreting out the cause of Alzheimer's disease) stands ready as a vehicle to carry researchers into the heart of a cell's nucleus to discover genes that might control aspects of aging, including the functioning of our immune system. Transplantation of healthy tissue into diseased brains is evolving into a reality, though clinical application still remains in the realm of what-might-be.

If understanding the aging process eludes researchers, one of the principal keys to life extension has been known for some time. Only now are gerontologists acknowledging its existence. All the evidence points to the simple fact that we eat too much. While no gerontologist will be so bold as to say at this point that, if we reduce our daily intake of calories to a certain level, we will increase our life expectancy by so many years, all the inferences have been made and the basic research is continuing.

Rats have been the principal research subjects so far. Scientists are just starting to test the thesis on humans. Researchers working for the U.S. Department of Agriculture Human Nutrition Research Center on Aging at Tufts University are putting volunteers on an exacting diet and restricting them to a hotel where they can be constantly monitored in pleasant surroundings. Unfortunately, it will be years before the results of such experimentation are known.

How close is a rat's aging to a human's? Quite close, thinks Edward J. Masoro, a physiologist at the University of Texas and one of the country's leading researchers on the effects of diet restriction. "It would be very remarkable," he says, "if an animal as complicated as a rat does not age pretty much for the same reasons and by the same mechanisms as humans." But this kind of thinking does not mean that the American Medical Association is going to pounce on calorie restriction as a panacea. Though researchers are agreed on the basic benefits of restriction in lab animals, their findings are clouded with contradictions and confusion. Much remains to be learned about what a lot or a little food does to our bodies.

The possibilities of calorie restriction were first brought to light in 1935 by Clive McCay, a young researcher at Cornell University, though mention of the phenomenon in scientific literature goes back to 1917. By reducing the diet of rats, McCay found that he could extend their life span by as much as 50 percent. Since then, the same kind of experimentation has been repeated many times not only on rats but on mice, on guppies, on fruit flies, and on various microscopic animals and aquatic organisms. The results have always been the same. At first, gerontologists were astonished by the findings. They still are. "The results of these experiments don't make sense," Dr. Nathan Shock, a pioneer researcher in gerontology and a former scientific director of the National Institute on Aging, told me, "Nobody believed them, so they were done over and over again."

A few facts about laboratory rats, the white ones with pink eyes: Average life span among the number of species used ranges between 700 and 900 days, approximately twenty-three to thirty months, meaning that 50 percent of a population survives this length of time. A lab rat that lives 1000 days is a rarity. A month in a rat's life equals about three years in a human's. A six-week-old rat, then, is comparable in age to a four- or five-year-old child (a rat reaches sexual maturity at about ten weeks) and a six-month-old rat is comparable to a young adult of around twenty years.

In an illuminating study, Dr. Masoro used rats that live an average of 700 days when permitted to eat as much as they want of a diet consisting of 21 percent protein, 57 percent carbohydrates (starch and sugars) and 22 percent fat. When a group of these rats was six weeks old, Masoro cut back their diet to 60 percent of what the free-eating animals were getting. The change in average length of life was enormous—1046 days, which was a 49 percent increase. The oldest rat died when it was almost 1300 days old, an 86 percent increase. A person at a comparable age would be one hundred thirty years old.

Rats in another group were allowed to eat as much as they wanted until they were six months old, comparable in human terms to a young adult. Then Masoro reduced their diet to 60 percent of what it had been. The results: The average length of life was 941 days, a 34 percent increase. Again, the oldest rat died when it was just under 1300 days.

These experiments were based on *under*nutrition, not malnutrition. We read about and see the results of malnutrition every day in newspapers and on television. Undernutrition means that while calories are reduced, all the crucial ingredients to well-being are present—vitamins, essential amino acids, fatty acids and minerals. Malnutrition is a severe lack of these ingredients and it can lead to disease and starvation. What happened in Ethiopia in late 1984 and in 1985 was the most dramatic recent example, but malnutrition exists everywhere. The bellies of children swell up horribly. They have skinny arms and legs. Their eyes bulge out and they may suffer mental retardation. But malnutrition is not restricted to developing countries. Have you ever looked into shopping carts as you wait in line at a supermarket checkout counter to see what some people are buying? Too often the goods within are junk food—fried foods, processed foods, sugar-coated foods, fatty foods—America's version of malnutrition that creates fat people with bad skin, dull eyes and the propensity toward diseases like diabetes, heart disease, stroke and possible hyperactivity in children.

Undernutrition is just another way of eating right. Rats that eat less have significantly less serum cholesterol than their better-fed mates. They lose less muscle and bone as they age. They do not get fat. Rats that are allowed to eat as much as they want develop useless fat cells at an early age, useless because the fat within them will not break down when the animal is in need of energy. However, Masoro found that the fat cells of a middle-aged diet-restricted rat are as quick to convert to energy as those of a six-week-old animal and that the cells of these animals also respond more readily to hormones.

The most obvious benefit to eating less, for animals anyway, is a stronger immune system. Most rats develop malignant tumors with time but those whose diets were restricted at six months were much slower to get cancer, even slower, ironically, than those whose diets were cut back when they were six weeks old. Restriction entirely eliminated cancer of the thyroid gland and of the bladder in rats and of the breast and liver in mice, according to studies by Morris H. Ross at the Institute of Cancer Research in Philadelphia. A kink in all this research, though, is that cancer of the adrenal glands seems to be more common, a discrepancy showing that much remains to be learned about the effects of diet restriction. But all in all, restriction appears to result in better health.

A few more examples. Older rats are apt to come down with kidney disease. Masoro found that his diet-restricted rats, even those elderly ones that were thirty months old, showed only minor signs of it. And Robert A. Good at the Sidney Farber Cancer Institute in Boston reports that the immune systems of underfed mice do not develop as many antibodies to their own DNA as those of well-fed ones do, making them less likely to come down with autoimmune diseases. Roy Walford and his colleagues have found that mice whose diets are reduced at a very early age develop stronger immune systems throughout their lives.

Increasingly excited by the correlation between food restriction and longevity, gerontologists are now making a concerted effort to find out just what is going on. So far, they are puzzled. Clive McCay believed that aging begins only after maturity. Therefore, he hypothesized, if you can delay the age of maturity, you can delay the onset of aging. His thinking was correct, at least up to a point. By restricting the caloric intake of rats by 60 percent right after weaning, McCay was able to slow their growth and keep the animals in what he believed was a suspended state between youth and maturity long after fully fed rats had died off.

As fascinating as the prospect of youthful limbo as a result of diet restriction may be, gerontologists now question whether delaying adulthood is really a factor in longevity. Dr. Masoro

found that the difference in the increase in length of life between rats whose diet was reduced at six weeks versus those at
six months, when rats reach physical maturity, was really not
that great, only three or four years in human terms. Masoro
and many other researchers are convinced that the reason for
increased length of life because of food restriction lies in metabolism. One theory of the 1970s that is still adhered to by
some scientists is that eating less food is equivalent to slowing
down the metabolic rate—the speed with which food is turned
into energy. Though Masoro believes that the study of metabolism is the right direction for research to take, he does not
think that the key to longevity is merely slowing down the
metabolic rate by eating less. Some of the long-lived rats in his
laboratory, for example, consume more calories per unit of body
weight than shorter-lived ones. The longer-lived ones thus have
a higher metabolic rate. "But the only way you can tie food
restriction to retarding aging is through metabolic action," he
says, adopting a somewhat baffled tone of voice. "We have no
hard evidence. We are just going on logic."

Logic makes Masoro suspect that reduced free radical action
is the metabolic mechanism at work. "It looks like free radicals
could be the perfect tie," he says. "It could be that food restriction either lessens their generation or somehow alters the
biochemical machinery that protects cells from free radicals. It
seems *so* logical. We are just beginning to do experiments that
we hope will prove or disprove this."

Another possible metabolic tie that Masoro hopes to establish or discard is whether the amount of food eaten influences
the rise and fall of hormones. He has already found that cells
of diet-restricted rats respond better and longer to hormones
than do cells of those rats that are allowed to eat as much as
they want. And finally, Masoro theorizes that fewer calories
might stem the decline in each cell of the turnover of proteins
that accompanies aging.

Problems with America's Nutrition

Children and lab rats are nourished with the same end in
mind—to grow and get strong as fast as possible. Breeders of
rats want to produce and sell as many as they can in the shortest period of time; and for researchers, the faster an animal

grows, the more quickly the results of an experiment will be known. The way to foster growth is to provide a rat with as much food, especially protein, as it wants. "The results are fine," says Masoro, "as long as the rats are used to study acute phenomena like infectious diseases. They are not fine if you're asking questions about aging." Masoro wonders, in his more cynical moments, whether the only significant revelation that he and his colleagues have come up with is that lab rats have traditionally been overfed and suffer shorter lives as a result.

"I think a hell of a lot of people have been set up in the same way that rats have," he declares. "Children have overzealous parents who overfeed them on very rich diets. Supermarkets encourage us to eat all sorts of things that lead to rapid aging. People in affluent societies overeat and age early. In poor societies, the sanitation is so bad that people get diseases or are malnourished and die at an early age."

America's most common nutritional problem is not malnutrition. It is overnutrition. Obesity is a risk that should be treated with the same seriousness as smoking, cholesterol and lack of exercise, concluded a fourteen-member-panel of health experts called together in early 1985 by the National Institutes of Health. Being even five or ten pounds over your desirable weight can be damaging to your health, said Dr. Jules Hirsh of Rockefeller University, the panel's chairman. People 20 percent overweight should reduce under medical supervision. Thirty percent of men and 40 percent of women between the ages of forty and forty-nine are overweight. Sixty million Americans suffer from high blood pressure, a large part of which may be due to poor diet and exacerbated by weight. What one's desirable weight should be is a controversial subject. A long-term study of 750,000 men and women conducted between 1959 and 1972 found that people 30 to 40 percent overweight had a 55 percent greater chance of dying from a heart attack than a person who weighed the proper amount for his or her age and height. And those weighing 40 percent or more over the average were virtually assured of getting a heart attack.

The two statisticians who tabulated the results of the study, Edward A. Lew and Lawrence Garfinkel of the American Cancer Society, found the lowest mortality in those people who either weighed what they should or were 10 to 20 percent below normal. But those more than 25 percent below normal also courted death with a 25 percent higher risk of early mortality than those in the normal weight range. So, if you weigh too much, you are in trouble; if you weigh too little, you are also in trouble, but not in quite as much trouble.

Overeating and cancer are loyal allies, too. The same study found that if you are male and 40 percent overweight, your chances of getting cancer of the rectum or colon are excellent, especially for those who have eaten a low-fiber diet. And an overweight woman stands a good chance of getting cancer of the gall bladder, liver, breasts, cervix, uterus and ovaries.

The statistics that came out of Lew and Garfinkel's computer are not foolproof evidence of the inextricable tie between weight and longevity, though their conclusions make sense when we think of the typically poor health of fat people. But numbers are just numbers and they can be twisted and played with and made to follow biases. Dr. Reubin Andres, clinical director of the Gerontology Research Center at the National Institute on Aging, does not think much of numbers showing that overweight people are apt to die before their time. In an article in a 1980 issue of *The International Journal of Obesity,* he cited sixteen studies which show just the opposite. One suggests that being overweight between thirty-five and forty-four years old is the healthiest way to be. Another indicates that in one's forties, the most dangerous weight is the one you "should be" for that age range. Though one has to scrutinize the numbers that came out of these studies with a calculator and an inquisitive mind, Andres's point is that there is no clear-cut relationship between being overweight and dying.

His news startled almost everyone, certainly dieters and exercise enthusiasts who had been starving or sweating off their fat. How could it be? Dr. Andres comes up with a few plausible suggestions, one that being overweight gives a person a built-in source of energy to call upon during serious illness. But he quickly acknowledges that the matter remains one of the many examples of how the body works in mysterious ways.

In 1983, the Metropolitan Life Insurance Company turned the national obsession with health and dieting again on its head by declaring that new studies of weight and longevity showed that people who were about 10 percent "overweight," that is, 10 percent heavier than the traditional weight tables advised, lived longer. The new tables were derived from the mortality rates of over four million life insurance policyholders in this country. The data suggesting that being slightly overweight increased life expectancy must be interpreted with caution. First, those who purchase life insurance policies tend to make up a special segment of the population. Most of them are males in white-collar jobs who are healthier than most people. Second, only people in good health were included in the data. Third, some of these people were smokers. Smokers tend both to be thinner and to die sooner than nonsmokers, thus statistically skewing the increased life expectancy toward those who are overweight.

Like Lew and Garfinkel's analyses, the Metropolitan's found that people weighing much less or much more than the ideal weight were in trouble. The data also revealed that age and weight are inextricably tied. Such a discovery was not, of course, a discovery at all. We know all too well that the passing years add new pounds, particularly in our bellies, hips, buttocks and thighs. The steady increase continues into the mid-sixties before slackening off for many people. Until then, weight gain often seems relentless, a constant and nagging reminder that the flat bellies and firm thighs of the twenties are only a passing phase of our lives. The health and exercise industries have made millions off our preoccupation with regaining the lithe look of those years. What was new as a result of the Metropolitan Life Insurance Company studies was the realization that weight gain with age is normal, natural and, the advertising industry aside, desirable. In fact, it is unhealthy for people within their proper weight range for their age to reduce too much. A warning, however, to those who would take this information and go on an eating binge: The healthiest places to gain weight are in the buttocks, thighs and hips. A potbelly is bad, caused mostly by poor diet and by lack of exercise and often resulting in heart disease, hypertension, stroke and cancer. Hefty thighs and hips, on the other hand, can be considered a kind of hardy insurance. The fat that collects in those places is the most difficult to remove. It clings as a protective measure to provide the aging and hence less disease-resistant body with a reservoir of energy.

In light of this revised information. Dr. Andres thinks that an average weight gain of around ten pounds each decade is healthy. But he advises that the greater gains are advisable with increasing age. In other words, someone who puts on ten pounds per decade beginning when he is twenty years old may be doing himself a disservice, whereas a fifty-year-old who puts on fifteen pounds per decade may be giving himself a longer life through the protection that his store of fat will give him if illness strikes.

How do you determine your ideal weight under these new guidelines? Dr. Andres has developed a simple method. First, calculate your height in inches and divide by 66. Second, multiply the answer by itself. Third, add 100 to your age and multiply that number by the answer you got in Step Two. The answer is your ideal weight. Here's how a 5'5" forty-five-year-old woman would calculate what she should weigh. First, 5'5" equals 65 inches which, divided by 66, equals .98. Second, .98 × .98 equals .96. Third, the age forty-five plus 100 equals 145; and 145 times .96 equals 139 pounds. This does not mean that the woman's best weight is 139 pounds, no more, no less. Give or take 15 pounds is fine.

Being such a weight depends on a number of factors, including general health, metabolism and the presence or absence of disease. Also primary among the influences are the amount of food consumed and the number of calories worked off over a given period. How the body deals with calories is a mystery. Generally, it is able to achieve a balance between calorie intake and outgo even if it does very little to expend the energy. If a person turns into a glutton and increases his calories by 100,000 over a year, the weight increase might be very small even if he does not exercise. The body appears to be able to burn off excess energy on its own. A 150-pound person who spends eight hours lying down each day resting or sleeping, six hours sitting, two and a half standing, two walking, and the remaining five and a half divided up between eating and doing the things that all of us do everyday burns up an average of 2500 calories. But some people burn much less and others much more. How the body controls its energy consumption is a completely unknown area of nutrition research. About the only concrete findings are: one, that the bigger the meal consumed, the more calories the body will burn off; and two, those people who are in excellent physical shape will burn off calories more easily than those who are not.

There is no question, though, that the less you eat, the less you will gain. But what is the right amount to eat? The answer to that question is unknown. It would seem, though, that we eat far too much in light of information both about the effects of diet restriction in animals and on low caloric intake in certain human societies (discussed in Chapter 6).

The Committee on Dietary Allowances of the National Academy of Sciences' Food and Nutrition Board, the body that tells us how much we should eat to stay healthy—the Recommended Daily Allowance (RDA)—advises a twenty-three- to fifty-year-old man to consume 2300 to 3100 calories per day and a woman in the same age bracket 1600 to 2400. As people grow older, they need fewer calories. The RDA for a man between fifty-one and seventy-five years is between 2000 and 2800, and for a woman, between 1400 and 2200. A teenager on a growth spurt, on the other hand, may require 4000 calories per day, as any parent paying food bills can attest to. That is the approximate equivalent of six hamburgers. While many Americans stay within the guidelines set up by the Food and Nutrition Board, the older people get, the more they go astray. The average caloric consumption for a twenty-five- to thirty-four-year-old man is 2734, for a women of the same age, 1643, right where they should be. But as people get older, their caloric intake begins to dwindle to levels initially near and then below the lower RDA range. While the average RDA for men between fifty-one and seventy-five is 2400 calories, the typical man in the age bracket from fifty-five to sixty-four consumes 2071 calories, and from sixty-five to seventy-four, only 1829,

	Age	Daily Calorie Intake	Range
MALES	23–50	2700	2300–3100
	51–75	2400	2000–2800
	76+	2050	1650–2450
FEMALES	23–50	2000	1600–2400
	51–75	1800	1400–2200
	76+	1600	1200–2000

Recommended daily calorie intake, revised 1980, by the Food and Nutrition Board, National Academy of Sciences-National Research Council.

both far below the RDA. Women also consume many fewer calories than the RDA as they get older. The RDA for a woman between fifty-one and seventy-five is 1800 calories. But those from fifty-five to sixty-four years old typically take in only 1401, and women from sixty-five to seventy-four only 1295 calories.

Study after study has found that the elderly are malnourished principally because of a low or nonexistent intake of vitamins A and B_6, calcium, iron, thiamin, riboflavin and folacin. Nutritionists constantly beseech the elderly to consume more calories on the assumption that if they eat more, the chances are improved that they will take in adequate levels of these and other nutrients. They also tell the elderly that their bodies do not absorb nutrients as easily as younger bodies and that increased calorie intake will ensure fat and energy reserves during sickness. While there is a great deal of truth in these arguments, advising increased calorie consumption in the hope that enough nutrients will be included on the way smacks of rather folksy medicine, similar to telling a child to drink his milk so he will grow big and strong like daddy.

Eating for the elderly is often quite a different matter from what it is for younger people. Younger people generally like to eat. It is a social occasion, at least an excuse for one. Older people often find themselves alone at mealtime and eating alone day after day can dampen the appetite. The elderly also have numerous digestive problems, another appetite squelcher. Twenty-five percent of those over sixty-five complain of digestive disorders, according to one study. Constipation is the leading problem but this is due more to diet than to being old. An excess of animal fats and starch is to blame. Fiber, such as that found in cereals and in vegetables—lettuce is excellent—will alleviate the problem. The elderly also complain that food tastes like cardboard. While the sensation of taste does diminish with the years, the amount of decrease is also diet-related. Recent research has determined that a deficiency in zinc will affect the ability to taste. Zinc is also important for wound healing and may play an important role in keeping up the immune system. The best sources of the mineral are liver, beef, chicken and oysters.

Just as nutritionists and doctors can tell an elderly person to eat more chicken to keep up zinc levels, they can advise a greater consumption of selected foods to increase other nutrients that tend to be in short supply in a person's diet. Egg yolks, brown rice and nuts are a good source of thiamin. Foods as diverse as cheeses, mushrooms and parsley provide riboflavin, a vitamin important for metabolism in cells. In light of the growing evidence of the benefits of undernutrition, the elderly might be better served if they were advised to eat selected foods rather than just to ingest more calories.

They are not told this principally because so little is known about nutrition. The RDAs, not only those for calories but also for nutrient intake, were set up in 1941 when much of the country's food was going to feed troops overseas. They were conceived for the people at home to ensure that they did not rely on the easier to obtain but nutritionally emptier foods like white bread and rice that lined grocery-market shelves. Though based on voluminous research, the standards are approximations at best and are by no means suited to each person. Since they came into being, they have been revised nine times and are currently undergoing their tenth revision.

Until two decades ago, nutrition research was a humdrum field occupied by statisticians and people content to twiddle their thumbs while waiting to see the effects of a certain diet. But in the 1970s, research sparked into life. Heart disease had become the country's number one killer; stroke was not far behind. Both had been tentatively linked to animal fat and cholesterol. And the ties between diet and some forms of cancer were beginning to be acknowledged. But even with this impetus, nutrition research, like most science, is a field best suited to those with great patience. Results of experiments do not appear overnight or even in the same decade in which they are initiated. The field is still in its youth. Our emotional and social ties to food run strong. Health gurus and pill doctors have grabbed the opportunity to jump between the question marks and come forth with what sounds like irrefutable advice. Solid nutritionists are put on the defensive. Not only is their research snail-paced, even the most definitive findings cannot match the most facile claims of the feel-good-with-a-pill advocates.

One of the biggest worries of nutritionists these days, according to Dr. Linda Meyers, a nutritionist at the National Academy of Sciences, are the effects of what she terms "preventive nutrients"—the megadoses of vitamins and minerals, over ten times the RDA—that people are popping with increasing regularity. Relatively little is known about what will happen as a result. Learning the results has become one of the Academy's major research fronts. "We tend to be conservative about nutrients because we just don't know what they do," Meyers says. "We are worried about a number of them. Even vitamin B_6, which everyone thought was as safe as could be, turns out to have some bad side effects." Pyridoxine, which this water-soluble vitamin is also known as, is a favorite of bodybuilders and of women hoping to alleviate premenstrual pain and/or encourage fertility. Taken in extended megadoses—over 2000 milligrams per day—it can cause numbness and slowed reflexes. Recovery can take over a year.

One example of the conservative inclination of the Academy's Food and Nutrition Board is its RDA for vitamin C. Sixty milligrams a day is all that is recommended for an adult. According to this guideline, it is difficult not to overdose on the vitamin, especially in the summertime with the increased availability of fruits and vegetables, which some people blissfully consume while continuing to pop pills. After all, one orange contains 50 mg. of vitamin C, a serving of potato, 20 mg., and a serving of peas, 30 mg. That makes 100 mg. without even trying. If, one summer day, you gobble down a dozen or so strawberries, you will have added 60 mg. A half a cantaloupe adds another 30 or so. Hundreds of reports have appeared proclaiming the benefits of this vitamin. Some say it picks up the immune system, others that it prevents cancer and lowers cholesterol, and yet others, notably Dr. Linus Pauling, the Nobel Prize winner, that it retards aging. Only recent research has come up with anything bad to say about vitamin C; doses of 1500 milligrams per day can result in anemia and super megadoses of 10 grams a day can cause the formation of kidney stones. Anyone who consumes this amount of a vitamin is asking for something bad to happen. It is like eating a dozen eggs a day because you have heard that eggs are full of protein.

Without *any* vitamin C, however, you get scurvy. Your gums bleed, your teeth fall out and your joints weaken. By taking just a little bit of the vitamin, you will never face this problem. That is the only information that the Food and Nutrition Board or any other established medical/scientific organization deems solid, hence the low RDA.

Fat-soluble vitamins like A, D, E, and K are more hazardous than water-soluble ones. They lodge in the fat and accumulate there. Vitamin A is the most popular because it's supposed to ward off cancer. The indications are that it does. But overdosing on this vitamin can lead to serious consequences. The most typical are nausea and vomiting followed by irritability, dehydration, swelling and possible hemorrhaging. Too much vitamin E can result in depression.

The dietary guidelines developed by the U.S. Department of Agriculture in 1980, which are different from the RDAs, urge that Americans consume a wide variety of foods. While meat, potatoes and a green vegetable may be fine, as long as the meat is lean, this traditional diet may miss some of the more exotic nutrients most abundant in foods not so frequently eaten. Almonds, for instance, are slivered, crushed, and sprinkled for taste and decoration, not for their high content of calcium, potassium and magnesium. And we would all do well to consume sunflower seeds, rich in zinc, copper and selenium.

What the Department of Agriculture is trying to do is persuade us to return to a diet that resembles that of the turn of the century, a diet far higher in carbohydrates than the one we consume today. Back then, 56 percent of the American diet was carbohydrates, 32 percent fat, and 12 percent protein. Now, it's 46 percent carbohydrates, 42 percent fat and 12 percent protein. And a huge amount of carbohydrates—18 percent—consists of processed foods, nutritional parlance for junk food. Milk consumption plummeted by almost 10 percent between 1962 and 1982, while soft drink consumption jumped by more than 15 percent, and beer five percent, according to the Agriculture Department. The message from the USDA is that we should abandon the diet that we came to be so proud of in the 1950s, when much of the population could finally afford marbled steak and eggs Benedict, and begin eating the food that most of the world's poor consumes—grains, fruits, vegetables and beans. This, incidentally, is the diet that the late Nathan Pritikin advocated for years.

The USDA came forth with its advice in 1980. Has America changed its eating habits as a result? While signs of a shift toward a healthier diet are all around us, especially in urban environments, the food that the majority of people eat is pretty much what it has been for the past twenty years. One reason is that food habits are hard to break, but perhaps the prime reason is that people think that a change to a healthier diet costs a lot more than they are paying now. But health-food stores, with their exorbitant prices, do not have a monopoly on a healthy diet. And you do not have to pay "lite" mayonnaise's high price in order to cut down on calories and cholesterol. Probably the best thing you can do is use less regular mayonnaise and get meat off your plate two or three times a week. Don't change your diet, adjust it.

That is what the food industry is trying to do with its low-calorie products. But all the TV commercials that plug "lite" beer are not turning beer drinkers around. In fact, industry executives say that despite the advertising and hoopla, low-calorie foods will probably never command more than 10 percent of the market.

Some restaurants are beginning to replace the less-popular items on their menus with vegetarian dishes. But look at the restaurants. They are generally the high-priced ones that cater to the wealthy, the aware and the trendy. Joe's Diner does not serve a vegetarian casserole. And even if it did, not many customers would order it, according to the results of a 1982 survey on nutrition conducted in a blue-collar neighborhood of New Rochelle, just north of New York City. The 300-plus respondents were ethnically mixed, with an age and income range typical of America. The findings, which could easily apply to a large segment of the American population, were alarming. While most of the people surveyed were well aware of the value of good nutrition, very few tried to improve their diet. Most people knew that being overweight could lead to heart disease, and over 50 percent thought that *they* were overweight. Yet dieting came up as the least popular way of losing weight. Further, just over half those people who informed the researchers that they were concerned about their diet also said that they ate cream cheese and sour cream, two fatty foods notorious for their high cholesterol count. Another of the survey's unfortunate findings was that people who are most concerned about nutrition do not tend to eat more nutritional food than those who have no concern about what they eat.

Food feeds more than our bodies. It fuels our emotions; it soothes our depressions and frustrations and it helps us to mix socially. Going to a dinner party and not eating anything is like going to a beach in a business suit. As one forty-five-year-old member of a New York public relations firm said to me at a reception, "Sure, I nibble at all these goodies. I know that they are bad for me. I know the drinks are doing all sorts of things to my insides. But I also know that I enjoy all this fluff and it keeps me happier in my job. Besides, I feel fine. When I don't, I'll stop." Maybe this person will be able to stop himself but the fact that he "feels fine" should not in itself reassure him. Countless people who have suffered heart attacks felt fine ten minutes before an attack.

The American Heart Association and its colleagues would do well to hit us where it hurts—run a campaign on the dangers of fried eggs for breakfast, steak for supper and a six-pack every weekend by showing us what happens when someone has a heart attack, by giving us a close-up of a stroke victim rather than by just talking about the dangers.

Exercise—The Way to a Longer Life?

There may be an easier way to live longer than to half-starve ourselves. Exercise may be the answer. Researchers have been hard put to acknowledge the connection between exercise and increased life expectancy until recently, though common sense has long indicated a solid link in the same way that common sense told us that smoking led to lung cancer and pulmonary problems. At last, common sense prevailed when two elaborate studies were published in mid-1984 that proved that exercise reduces both heart disease and hypertension. One study examined the life-style and weekly energy expenditure of 17,000 Harvard alumni aged thirty-five to seventy-four. Those who burned 2000 calories per week no matter how they exercised—climbing stairs, walking city streets, or through sports—had a 50 percent lesser risk of having a heart attack than their less active former college mates.

The researchers, led by Ralph S. Paffenbarger of both the Stanford School of Medicine and the Harvard School of Public Health, estimated that if all 17,000 alumni had expended 2000 calories per week through exercise, the number of heart attacks would have been reduced by 26 percent. As it was, 572 men out of the 17,000, or three percent, suffered heart attacks; 215 were fatal. The researchers also discovered that the risk of heart attack was neither increased nor decreased by participation in athletics during college years. The key is what you do athletically after you graduate. The college football jock and the chess champion run the same risk of heart disease (when all the other factors influencing heart disease are excluded) if neither of them exercises after college. However, the study also found that those who had played on athletic teams during their college years, or who had exercised regularly in other ways, were more likely to continue exercising after graduating. Other more general findings that came out of the study included: the greater the energy output during exercise, the less chance of a heart attack. People who run regularly, in other words, have a greater chance of avoiding a heart attack than those who exercise by walking the dog twice a day.

The second study correlated physical activity with hypertension by surveying 6000 people in Dallas. The participants, aged twenty to sixty-five, were followed for up to twelve years. The crucial finding was that those who got no exercise were about 50 percent more likely to develop hypertension than those who exercised, a discovery that might provide a plot line for the producers of *Dallas*. Can you imagine the tension that would be engendered by having J.R. diagnosed in the last episodes of a season as suffering from gross hypertension which puts him in imminent danger of a heart attack? He begins a rigorous and regular exercise program. But a scoundrel from a competing oil company that has designs on Ewing Oil hears about J.R.'s health problem. He sees a golden opportunity for a buy-out. If he can make things hot for J.R., the increased stress just might do the trick. He arranges for a scandal to break wide open—an illegitimate child, a blackmailing mistress, a tax-evasion charge—you name it. J.R. is out running somewhere on the ranch. He does not know of the latest disaster until informed on his earphone intercom that he has taken to wearing since he began jogging across the range. He clutches his breast, of course, then staggers and falls. Cut to hospital room and scene of around J.R. Shaking heads and J.R.'s ashen face suggest that the situation is not hopeful. Will he live, and if so, will he be able to preside over Ewing Oil? You have to wait all summer to find out.

Though the Harvard and Dallas studies are among the most recent, others have come up with similar results. A twenty-two-year study of San Francisco longshoremen and heart-attack rates showed that those cargo handlers and dockworkers who burned off more than 8500 calories per week during their work suffered half as many fatal heart attacks as their colleagues who expended fewer calories. As it was, 400, or 10 percent of the 4000 workers studied, died of heart attacks during the twenty-two-year period.

Similar studies have compared letter carriers to postal workers (people who sort mail) in Washington, D.C.; bus drivers to bus conductors, the ones who walk up and down the aisles collecting fares, in London; and farmers to people in more sedentary occupations in North Dakota. Each study has found that the people who get rid of the most calories over a given period are at a significantly lower risk of dying from a heart attack.

Exercise used to be a bad word. Those who had had heart attacks were told that they could never play tennis, swim or exert themselves again. They were even advised to steer clear of sex. Pregnant women were not supposed to run. In 1976, I was told I had a minor lung ailment, and my internist advised me to lay off exercise until further notice. Exercise is a strain on the body, he informed me, and a strain on my lungs might exacerbate the situation. He might not be so quick to condemn exercise now. Millions of words, hundreds of articles in both the popular and scientific press, and scores of books have been written on the benefits of exertion. The results are obvious, at least in urban areas. Joggers and bicyclists crowd city parks across the country. Swimming is the second most popular form of exercise in the country; walking is the first. Health clubs exist in every suburban mall. Social gatherings are sprinkled with chatter about the latest marathon or, as one elderly man said to me: "I remember everyone talking about the sporting events they had just seen. Now everyone is talking about the events they just did."

Even so, 41 percent of the country's adult population gets no regular exercise, according to an elaborate 1979 survey (one of the most recent) on fitness in America conducted by Louis Harris and Associates at the behest of Perrier, the French sparkling-water enterprise. Though 59 percent of those polled said that they regularly exercised, far above the 29 percent in a 1961 survey, it is sobering to realize that some forms of exercise that people say they regularly pursue are not really exercise at all. Over 30 percent think that bowling or playing golf is a good way to keep fit. By all counts, playing baseball, bowling and playing golf are lousy ways to exercise. They do not require a greater amount of oxygen to be transported through the body, as jogging does; they do not require that the heart pump more blood; and they do not appreciably lower cholesterol. The only real good that these sports do is to stretch muscles.

The Harris researchers broke exercise down into the categories of time spent per week and calories burned. The most active exercisers were those who spent at least 306 minutes (just over five hours) per week and who burned at least 1500 calories while exercising. Only 15 percent of the country's regular exercisers qualified for this most-active-exerciser category. Most of these were young men under thirty-five years. To put this calorie expenditure into some perspective, a 150-pound person jogging 10 mph burns around 900 calories per hour. Casual bicycling for the same weight person uses up 660 calories per hour; squash, 600 per hour; swimming laps, 600; brisk walking, 450; chopping wood, 400; normal walking, 300, gardening, 220; keeping house, 180; and sitting, 100.

The two other categories included moderate exercisers—those who exercised for at least 204 minutes per week (just under three and one half hours) and the least active—people who exercised for only 150 minutes per week (just under two hours). The survey found that as much as 28 percent of the country's regular exercisers fall into the less-active category. Not very impressive.

Almost half the people questioned said that they did not have enough time. Fifteen percent came up with bad weather as their excuse. Worse still, 18 percent were bold enough to say that they were too lazy or not interested. But the greatest misfortune, or the greatest embarrassment, is that people who exercised were more likely to smoke than people who get no exercise. While it's understandable that bowlers smoke because they do not have to exert themselves to pursue their sport, it is disheartening to discover that 45 percent of those who swim for their exercise also smoke, as do 42 percent of those who play basketball.

There is a considerable amount of misunderstanding about

the benefits of exercise and proper diet, a misunderstanding that can be traced by observing how death rates from specific diseases have changed over the years. While heart disease is the country's leading cause of death today, it was the fourth-leading cause in 1900. And diabetes, which is a major cause of death today, is not even listed among the top ten killers in 1900. Yet almost 30 percent of the population thinks that exercise should not be pursued because it leads to overeating, according to the Harris survey. Almost half those questioned think that people who jog or lift weights become fanatics and another half say that they do not exercise regularly because the sudden exertion would be unhealthy.

You swim for your principal exercise, joining the 26 million Americans who do the same thing, or you run, like 18 million Americans. You are on the tenth lap of a mile-long workout or you are just completing the second mile of a five-mile run. It is boring; it is hard; you have a lot of work on your desk in the office. You have not yet found your pace and you are not sure that you are going to today. Your lungs are struggling to take in enough air. Your muscles feel like rubber. This is no fun, you say; this is a waste of time. Shall I quit?

But you keep going, at least most people do. Why? For two reasons. The first has to do with plain, simple pride. You know the body protests too easily. You know that the pain you feel now in your lungs and muscles will not compare to the pain of guilt and wounded pride that you will feel if you stop. Jim Shapiro, an ultra-marathon runner who wrote the book, *Meditations from the Breakdown Lane: Running across America,* an account of his experience doing just that, told me how he began running: "I was about twenty-four and I saw I was getting a potbelly. That really shocked me. I began running about five miles a day. Then I began noticing older runners, people in their forties, fifties and sixties who were doing ultra-marathon running. I got this sense that there was an unlimited ocean of strength that you could keep refining and hammering away at, like a Japanese swordmaker folds and refolds the molten metal that he is tempering. After that, I worked myself up to fifty miles a day. Where was the limit? It seemed as if there were none."

There is a limit, of course, but the pride one feels from such exertion does not recognize it. This feeling may have a physical as well as psychological origin. The pain and stress of exertion causes the brain to secrete substances called endorphins, which are not only natural painkillers but opiates as well. They give you a high. Some researchers think that runners suffer to a certain extent from addiction to endorphins. They have to get their fix every day and if they do not, they become irritable and depressed. It is not surprising then that the Harris survey found that people who got a lot of exercise felt much better about themselves than those who got only a little. People who exercise reported that they felt less tired, more relaxed, more disciplined, had more self-confidence, were more productive at work and had better sex lives than those who exercise less.

Beyond making you feel good about yourself, running, swimming, bicycling, walking and similar sorts of exercise demand the repetitive use of large muscles—principally those of the legs, shoulders and arms. The continued exertion calls for oxygen. People who cannot supply oxygen quickly get tired quickly and their muscles ache with lactic acid, a substance that dampens the metabolism of muscle cells. The capacity of the lungs to take in more oxygen and the heart and arteries to circulate it around the body is what the benefits of exercise are all about. But we realize more than ever that oxygen is a double-edged sword. The more the body can absorb, the better shape we are in. But oxygen is a poison, as we saw in the last chapter, that creates free radicals that ravage our cells. The more oxygen you get into your bloodstream, the greater the potential for free-radical damage. There must be a balance somewhere; that is for future gerontological research to determine.

When your lungs' ability to take in oxygen and your cardiovascular system's capacity to distribute it equals your muscles' demand for it, you have reached what exercise therapists call "steady state." And if you can maintain "steady state" for twenty minutes three times a week so that your heart beats at least 70 to 85 percent of capacity, you will have achieved the exalted state of physical fitness. Exercise gurus call this "training effect." How can you calculate 70 and 85 percent of your maximum heartbeat? Simple. Subtract your age from the number 220. Now multiply the answer, first by .70 and then by .85. A fifty-year-old man subtracting his age from 220 will get 170. This number, multiplied by .70 and by .85 will give him a range between 119 and 145, the rate at which his heart should beat for at least twenty minutes per exercise session. If this is the case, he is fit.

His maximum oxygen intake has increased. And his heart beats more slowly and with greater volume under strain than it would if he were not in shape. More oxygen enters the tissues, blood-sugar levels are better maintained, neuromuscular coordination improved, low density lipids (the bad kind of cholesterol) reduced and high density lipids (the good kind of cholesterol) increased.

The death of Jim Fixx in July 1984 of a heart attack shocked those who had been persuaded by his best-selling book to take up this form of exercise. He was their patron saint. He had told them how good running would be for them. And then at fifty-two he died while jogging down a Vermont country road. Murmurs were heard that maybe Fixx's advice was idealistic, that the benefits of exercise were not all that the exercise movement cracked them up to be. The blasphemy of those cynics was right. Exercise does not ensure perpetual good health, and it certainly does not preclude the need for physical checkups. That was where Fixx went wrong. He did not have a regular physician. His father had had his first heart attack when he was thirty-five and had died of a second at forty-three. Yet Fixx had not had a physical examination for a number of years. He may have been scared by what a doctor would find or he may have thought that running would overcome any heart condition. Fixx's belief in the merits of running may have blinded him to his genes and to his own mortality. A few weeks before he died, he apparently complained to his sister of exhaustion and a tightness in his throat after exercising, two key signals that the heart may be under strain.

Even so, it is probable that Fixx extended his life by perhaps a decade through his running.

Solid evidence of the benefits of exercise exists in the form of eighty-six-year-old Paul E. Spangler, a retired surgeon who lives in San Luis Obispo, California. Dr. Spangler is in remarkable shape. He began running when he was sixty-seven because he was afraid of heart disease, though he had no indication of it. He started at two or three miles a day and worked himself up to ten. After he retired, running, and to a certain extent swimming, became his life through Master's competitions (track, field and swimming events for those forty and over). By 1977, Spangler, then seventy-seven, held fourteen world records for track and distance running in the seventy-five-to-seventy-nine-year-old category. Now, he holds over forty world records. A few weeks after he turned eighty-five in March 1984, he set world records for his age class (85 to 89) in a five-mile and twenty-kilometer race. "The trouble is," he says, "that there are no records in my age category, so I set a record any time I compete." One consequence is that his motivation has lessened. "I don't feel like driving myself like I did before," he told me resignedly. "I guess I am slowing down a bit." Still, he runs six miles and swims half a mile six days out of the week.

In 1977, Dr. James L. Webb of California Polytechnic State University's Human Performance Laboratory put Spangler through a series of tests and found, not surprisingly, that he was in much better shape than his more sedentary peers. His degree of physical fitness was, in fact, more typical of people two-thirds his age. Spangler's cholesterol count was only 201 milligrams per milliliter of blood, whereas that of most men his age ranges between 260 and 285. His resting blood pressure was a youthful 120/70. The usual for that age is 145/82. His resting heart rate was 55 beats per minute; normal would have been 65. And his maximum oxygen intake was just over three liters per minute, far above the normal range of between 1.71 and 2.23.

Paul Spangler is a lucky man. There is probably not one chance in a million that he will die of a heart attack, much less even suffer one. Most elderly people are not so fortunate. Heart disease is the leading cause of death among those over sixty-five, accounting for almost 45 percent of the deaths. Of the 17,000 men surveyed in the Harvard alumni study, over two thirds of the 572 heart attacks suffered during the duration of the research period occurred in men over fifty-five. A similar risk was discovered in the San Francisco longshoremen who were older than fifty-five. Perhaps this danger is one reason why the Harris researchers mentioned earlier found that the elderly take a unique view of the benefits of exercise. Over 70 percent of the people over fifty thought that exercises that strengthen the heart and improve circulation are the most important. The same percentage also believed that swimming three times a week for an hour each time will keep one physically fit. But when it comes to actually doing exercise, older people put in a poor showing. More than one quarter of the population over fifty gets no exercise. Only three percent of the people over sixty-five consider themselves highly active exercisers. That so few elderly people exercise might well be due to the attitudes that much of the population have toward them. Almost one fifth of the population thinks that the middle-aged and the elderly do not need any exercise other than walking. As one brash young jogger in a bright red Gortex suit said to me, "These hunched over old people that get out there in their warm-up suits really kill me. They're like cocker spaniels trying to be greyhounds."

An increasing number of the elderly would like to be and are perfectly capable of running all over this youth-centric individual. Over 1500 runners in the 1984 New York City Marathon were past fifty. Nineteen were over seventy and one was eighty-five. In an article in *The New York Times Magazine,* writer Alex Ward cites evidence that "the age barrier in sports is all the way down." There is fifty-three-year-old Hal Higdon who has run in marathons for the past twenty-five years. There is Marion Irvine, a fifty-four-year-old Dominican nun who began running only in 1978. In 1983, she qualified for the Olympic trials, but says she runs mainly because "I love the feeling of my body in motion." There are hundreds of other people in their forties, fifties and sixties who are not only running but swimming, rowing and cross-country skiing.

While it is fine to learn about the benefits of exercise in staving off heart attacks and how running has slowed Paul Spangler's aging, William M. Bortz II, a researcher at the Palo Alto Medical Clinic in Palo Alto, California, wanted to know more about the mechanisms at work. Since he was located close to NASA's astronaut-training center at Edwards Air Force Base, he was able to get hold of data on the effects of weightlessness and confinement on the human body. The Soviets had found that calcium drains from the bones of their astronauts at the astounding rate of four grams per month during long space flights. After Bortz learned this, he concluded that many elderly people, though not weightless, are similarly confined and thus prone to losing substantial amounts of calcium.

Bortz, a fifty-four-year-old marathon runner, had torn an Achilles tendon during a race. When he saw his right leg after six weeks in a plaster cast, any doubt he may have had about his confinement theory vanished. "It [his leg] had all the appearance of belonging to a person forty years older. It was withered, stiff and painful," he wrote in a 1982 article in the *Journal of the American Medical Association.* Bortz's theory suggests that many of the changes commonly thought of as being part of the aging process are not due so much to aging as to increasing physical disuse. His idea thus unites astronauts, the bedridden and the aged in the common bond of deterioration because of inactivity.

By examining the work of other researchers, Bortz put together some significant information about the benefits of exercise: that if a seventy-year-old person begins to exercise moderately, he can recapture the capability to transport oxygen that he enjoyed (unwittingly, no doubt) fifteen years earlier. And if the same person were to whip himself into topnotch shape, he would regain forty years of oxygen transport capacity, which is just about what Paul Spangler has done. Even a bedridden person can regain some of his capacity to transport oxygen by doing exercises in bed.

Bortz also found that elderly people who exercise tend to be much leaner than those who do not; they have higher amounts of neurotransmitters, the lubricants of the brain's chemical reactions, and their sex hormones remain at higher levels. Exercise can also help to limber up stiff joints. Victims of arthritis and bursitis may be discouraged about exercising, in which case, a vicious circle begins; the less a joint is used, the rustier it feels and the more reluctant is its owner to try it out. Prolonged disuse will cause muscles, tendons and ligaments to lose their stretch. Joints will become frozen. So familiar is the sight of the elderly moving stiffly, their grimaces betraying their aches and pains, that we regard the state as natural and normal. It is not. But the elderly have to work to get and keep themselves in shape. And if they do not continue exercising, they will be right back where they started within eight weeks' time.

The key to Bortz's message is the old, overused adage, "Use it or lose it," which has cropped up a number of times in this book. That so many people fall into the trap of letting their bodies stiffen up, wither and replace muscle with fat is a sad commentary on our society, for we have traditionally over-played mental and social capabilities and downgraded physical fitness. We have also ignored our evolutionary heritage in which survival depended every bit on being as physically fit as it did on being mentally agile.

Tips on Nutrition and Exercise

Nutrition

The only proven way for animals to increase their life span is through calorie restriction. Theoretically, this should work for people, but it should not be attempted unless you are under the strict supervision of a physician or a registered dietitian. Because the consequences of severe calorie restriction on growth and development are little known, children should be ex-cluded from any program. Do not readily accept advice from a nutritionist or a dietitian who is not registered. Anyone can attach labels to his or her name. A *registered* dietitian, however, is registered by the American Dietetic Association. For this, a dietitian must have a bachelor's degree in food or nutrition from a four-year college, must have undergone clinical training and must pass ongoing competency examinations administered by the association. There are 37,000 registered dietitians in this country. These people have the right to carry the initials "R. D." (registered dietitian) after their name. Most such dietitians charge from $30 to $50 a visit. To locate registered dietitians in your area, consult your physician, call your local heart or diabetes association or write to the American Dietetic Associa-tion, 430 North Michigan Avenue, Chicago, IL 60611 (312-280-5000).

A less expensive way to restrict your diet is by eating wisely. These days, newspapers and magazines are full of information on the findings of health and diet studies. Depending upon the publication, there is a certain amount of hype and gee-whiz to each report; and diet and nutrition information can get terri-bly confusing as a result. It's hard to know what is absolutely true, partially true, or merely what appears to be true because the writer has chosen background research material that fits

his or her bias. Another reason for the confusion is that nutrition is a field in which a lot of new information is constantly
appearing. One month we are told to eat oily fish like bluefish,
mackerel and salmon because the oil breaks up accumulations
of fatty deposits in our cells. The next month we are told to
keep away from oily fish because it builds up our cholesterol
levels.

If you keep alert to articles on diet and nutrition in responsible publications, you will find, however, that certain basic research findings, like the link between cholesterol and animal
fats in the diet and heart disease, are repeated over and over
again, whereas the fringe findings, such as the discovery of an
aphrodisiac that grows in a species of tree in West Africa, get
a big splash and then disappear. Follow the information that
you see repeated. The repetition means that the information
has been implicitly approved by the informal array of doctors,
scientists and readers who know something about the subject.

Also, the U.S. Department of Agriculture publishes a great
deal of information on the nutritive value of foods and ways
to prepare them. Write to USDA, Human Nutrition Information Service, Hyattsville, MD 20782, for a list of publications. A book covering the entire subject comprehensibly and
authoritatively is *Jane Brody's Nutrition Book,* by Jane Brody (W.
W. Norton & Co., 1981).

Exercise

If you think you should exercise—and you should—but do not
want to begin on your own, join a health club, a "Y" or a local
gymnasium program. If you want to compete, the best way to
do so for running, swimming, track or race-walking is to get
involved in the Master's competition program, ostensibly for
those over forty. There is, however, a sub-master's program
for those over thirty. The Master's program is a loosely orga-
nized network of running, track and swimming clubs that hold
meets across the country almost every weekend. Unfortunately, there is no one organization you can contact to find out
how to join the program. The best way is to visit a local running or swimming club. You will probably be given the name
of an individual, not necessarily an administrator of the club,
who acts as regional coordinator. As elusive as the network is,
Master's competition is enormously popular among older peo-

ple who are tired of jogging or swimming on their own and want to compete against others. This is not to say that a sixty-five-year-old will find himself or herself competing against a forty-year-old. All competitions are grouped in five-year intervals, though specific events may be held at the same time. A six-mile race, for example, may attract people from forty to ninety years old, but those in the race will be competing only with those in their age group.

How Much Exercise?

Physicians advise people over fifty who have not exercised in many years to begin by walking briskly, followed by a period of walking alternated with jogging. You should do this until your body becomes accustomed to the new demands, stresses and strains. It might be two weeks or a month before you can really begin jogging. The amount of exercise a person needs and can endure varies tremendously from person to person. Very generally, older people can get plenty of exercise by running three miles three times a week.

You should exercise so that your heart beats from 70 to 85 percent of capacity for at least twenty minutes during an exercise period. To find out what your maximum heart beat is, you can go to a doctor and ask for a stress test. But there is a simpler and cheaper way: take the number 220 and subtract your age from it; then multiply the difference by both .70 and .85. This will give you the range between 70 and 85 percent of your maximum heart rate. Here is an example. A forty-two-year-old person subtracts his age from 220 and gets 178. This number, multiplied by .70 and .85, respectively, will give him a range between 125 and 151. His heart beat should fall within this range for at least twenty minutes every time he exercises. Heart rate can be determined by taking your pulse.

The best way to know when your heart is beating fast enough to benefit your cardiovascular system is to warm up for five minutes before taking your pulse. Though it probably will not have reached the 70 percent mark, it will be close and will help you get a bearing on your heart as you begin to exercise. Five minutes later you might want to check your pulse again. If it has climbed above the 70 percent mark, keep up that pace for at least twenty minutes. It is not hard to take your pulse while exercising, particularly running. But you must have a watch with a sweep hand. Stop running for a moment so you can find your pulse; count the beats for ten seconds and multiply by six.

Warning Signs

When you begin exercising after a long time away from it, you will undoubtedly experience some unpleasant, even alarming, sensations, though your doctor has checked you out and given you some advice on how far to push yourself. You should pay attention to these feelings. The following chart,* based on the advice of Dr. Lenore Zohman, director of Cardiopulmonary Rehabilitation at Montefiore Hospital and Medical Center in New York City, will help you put them in perspective:

Symptom	*Cause and Action to Take*
Irregular heart beat, palpitations, fluttering or slowing of pulse while exercising. Symptoms may occur during exercise or as many as 24 hours later.	*Consult your doctor as soon as possible, though the condition may be due to a harmless disorder of cardiac rhythm.*
Pain or pressure in center of chest or in arms or throat. Symptoms may occur after exercise.	*Again, consult your doctor as soon as possible. Symptoms may be due to heart strain.*
Dizziness, light-headedness, lack of coordination, confusion, cold sweat, fainting. Occurs when exercising or immediately after.	*May be due to not enough blood getting to brain. Put your head between your legs or lie down with feet higher than head.*
Nausea or vomiting during or immediately after exercise.	*Not enough oxygen is getting to the intestines. Slow down. Exercise less strenuously.*
Out of breath ten minutes after exercising.	*Heart and lungs being worked too hard. Exercise less strenuously.*
Shin splints (intense pain in shins or lower legs).	*You should get shoes with thicker soles or run on a softer surface.*
Insomnia after exercising.	*You are exercising too hard.*

*Much of the material in this chart appeared in the booklet *Beyond Diet . . . Exercise Your Way to Fitness and Heart Health,* by Dr. Zohman, printed as a public service by Mazola Corn Oil.

Calf-muscle pain.	*Strained muscle. This may be due to faulty circulation.*
Side stitch (cramp).	*Caused by a spasm in the diaphragm muscle that separates the chest from the intestines. Sit down and lean forward until the pain recedes.*

Informal Exercise

You can get your cardiovascular system in shape without taking up such a structured exercise regime as running or swimming. Aerobic exercise, the kind that will benefit your heart and arteries, comes in many forms as long as you do it regularly and do enough of it so your heart beats gets within the 70 to 85 percent range of maximum for at least twenty-minute stretches. You can walk to work, for example. If you walk at a good clip, five miles per hour, you will burn off around 450 calories per hour. Test if you are walking far enough or fast enough by taking your pulse just after you begin and again when you reach your destination. If it falls within the 70 to 85 percent of maximum heart rate, you will know that you are helping your cardiovascular system. Climb stairs instead of taking an elevator. This is an especially convenient aerobic exercise if you work or live in a high-rise building. Do housework that keeps you busy for long stretches of time—scrubbing the floor, washing windows, chopping wood—rather than stop and start work.

Books on the Subject

deVries, Herbert, and Hales, Dianne, *Fitness after 50: An Exercise Prescription for Life-Long Health*, Scribner's, 1982.
Fonda, Jane, *Women Coming of Age*, Simon and Schuster, 1984.
Jerome, John, *Staying with It: On Becoming an Athlete*, The Viking Press, 1984.

Chapter 6

Searching for Longevity

*B*ertie Dotson sits on the edge of her house porch in Robertson County, Kentucky. Her house is tiny, only two or three rooms. The porch tilts crazily to the left. Bertie is on the lower end, skinny little legs in battered black shoes firmly on the ground, skinny little arms planted on knees covered by a tattered dress, and gnarled hands cupping her chin. As she always does on nice summer days, she stares out at the dirt road through cataract-clouded eyes. Only a few cars pass. The people in them invariably wave but Bertie never acknowledges their greeting. A passing car is only a blur to her; she cannot tell where the vehicle ends and the cloud of dust it raises begins.

From the distance of the road to the porch, she looks like a waif thinking grand thoughts about life within her dollhouse.

Actually Bertie is thinking about her one hundred and third birthday party a few weeks off. "It's gonna be down beside the fishin' lake," she blurts out in a high-pitched voice, her mouth empty of teeth. Fogged as her eyes are, they dance with delight for a moment before her face lapses into a shy, almost scared expression. "They say it's gonna be as big as the one they gave me for my one hundredth. I guess they think they better give me another good one before the bad man comes an' gets me."

She looks down at her worn shoes, her yellow-white hair falling over her face in wisps. "Yep," she perks up suddenly, "I cain't even milk my cow anymore without gettin' tired. He's

142

gonna come soon, but I hope the good Lord'll keep him away until after my party."*

In the late 1970s a group of anthropologists at the University of Kentucky in Lexington got very excited over people like Bertie. The possible existence of long-lived societies is a continual fascination, their elusiveness a continual frustration. The anthropologists wondered if Robertson County would prove to be this country's center of long-lived people. A decade earlier, the Western world had been treated to stories of people in three societies—in parts of Soviet Georgia, in the Ecuadorian Andes and in northern Pakistan—who were said to reach fantastic ages, occasionally one hundred fifty years. It did not take much follow-up investigation to learn that such age claims were highly exaggerated. Soviet Georgia remains of special interest, however, because of its number of centenarians, though gerontologists are at loggerheads over the extent of longevity there.

One of the first American researchers to investigate the original Soviet claims was the anthropologist Sula Benet. Polish-born, Benet had spent childhood summers in parts of Soviet Georgia with her family, who went there to "take the waters." Though her description of the people and their life-style is detailed and accurate, she was entirely gullible. Other researchers, including Dr. Alexander Leaf, a medical professor at Harvard Medical School and a staff member of Massachusetts General Hospital, were initially only slightly less gullible. But protests from the dissident Soviet geneticist, Zhores A. Medvedev, now living in England, made people reconsider. In 1974, he published an article in *The Gerontologist* that pointed out the following: There was absolutely no proof of longevity since the Soviet government did not begin keeping birth records until 1932 and most baptismal records, another source of verification of longevity claims, had been destroyed after the Bolshevik Revolution; the results of physical tests on those who claimed to be centenarians proved to be comparable to those of people half their age; and more male centenarians turned up than female, a suspicious finding since it contradicts the recognized dictum that females live longer than males.

---

*Late in 1984, Bertie became almost completely blind. Members of her family persuaded her to move to a nearby nursing home. She lives there now.

Some Soviet gerontologists agree with Medvedev's observations, but this does not deny the existence of longevity in Soviet Georgia. Though claims of anyone living more than one hundred twenty years are assumed to be false, a 1979 census of Abkhazia, a tiny Soviet republic between the Black Sea and the Caucasus mountains, turned up 241 centenarians out of a population of 520,000, five times the percentage of the United States. Here, according to the 1980 census, there are only 30,000 people over one hundred years old. Some American gerontologists and statisticians debate the centenarian figures of both censuses.

Why might long life be more common in Soviet Georgia? Though complex, the reasons are not subtle. If nothing else, they point to the physical damage we do to ourselves by the way we live and eat and the psychological damage we do by the way we regard the elderly. The main beneficial factors there are diet, physical activity, respect for the elderly and genetics. First, diet. Perhaps of greatest importance is that the Abkhasians eat much less than we do. The average adult consumes from 1500 to 2000 calories per day. Adult Americans generally ingest from 500 to 1000 more calories per day than this, according to the National Center for Health Statistics, and some nutritionists think the Center's numbers are conservative. Almost three quarters of the Abkhasians' diet consists of milk, milk products and vegetables. They also eat small amounts of meat, mostly mutton, that they boil, roast or fry. The people are adamant about the freshness of their foods, particularly their vegetables and fruit, which they pick only just before a meal. Garden salads for breakfast are popular. The most common vegetables are all the ones we eat, with the addition of estragon (tarragon), turnip, kohlrabi, radish and Jerusalem artichoke. They also eat a lot of nuts, especially walnuts, and herbs and spices like coriander, savory, basil and mint, which they mix into pungent sauces. They are also fond of sour sauces made from plums, barberries, dewberries, pomegranates, green grapes and tomatoes. Americans who visit Abkhazia come back drooling with stories of the delicious fare, especially the stews that have simmered in these sauces.

With a diet like this, the Abkhasians, though not eating a great deal (gluttony at the table is frowned upon and being overweight is openly scorned), consume high quantities of vitamins and minerals, one possible reason for their low rate of atherosclerosis despite the abundant intake of dairy products. Low cholesterol counts are typical of all age groups; 150 to 180 milligrams per deciliter of blood was the average in the early 1970s when Sula Benet studied the people there. In this country, the average cholesterol count is 220.

Here are the ingredients of a typical day's meals, according to G. G. Kopeshavidze, a Soviet nutritionist who presented a paper on the Abkhasian diet at the First Soviet-American Symposium on Longevity Research in the Caucasus, this one in 1978 in Tbilisi, the capital of Soviet Georgia:

Breakfast: Corn meal porridge with cheese, boiled kidney beans or lima beans, fresh vegetables, boiled eggs, boiled or fried meat, boiled or sour milk.
Lunch: Porridge with sour milk, pita-like bread with cheese.
Dinner: Porridge with cheese, boiled beans, fresh vegetables, sour milk and honey.

In addition, at each meal most Abkhasians drink matzoni, which is something like yogurt, and men drink two or three glasses of wine.

Day-to-day existence in the little villages that are scattered over the western slopes of the Caucasus Mountains is based on herding and raising fruits and vegetables, requiring a physically active life in rough terrain. The elderly never entirely withdraw; they just gradually reduce the number of hours they work. Nonagenerian women splitting wood and centenarians on top of ladders picking fruit are common sights.

But gerontologists feel that the most important reason for longevity among these people is the respect in which they are held. Soviet Georgia is one of the few places in the world, Japan being another, where the older you are, the better your social position. (Respect for the elderly in Japan, however, is rapidly diminishing as Western values become more predominant.) Those over ninety are not categorized as "the elderly" or "the aged"; and they are not condescendingly referred to as having reached their "sunset" or "golden" years. They are called *dolgozhiteli,* which means "the long-living," a label that conveys a high status for them. Many of the frequent and lavish toasts during family celebrations and gatherings typically end with "May he live to be one hundred twenty years old." The long-living preside over extended families, are sought out for advice by family members and are called upon to make decisions. Sons, writes Benet, rarely go off on their own when they are grown. Rather, they stay within the influence of the extended family and under the tutelage of its oldest member. Even so, the authority of this person is often symbolic. While he will sit at the head of the table, a younger member may administer the family's holdings. The long-living hold the family's moral, ethical and traditional reins.

Before the 1917 revolution, the area had long been one of noble families with vast holdings and poor peasants with little. Respect for the elderly was one of the few traditions that the classes shared. Soviet administrators found themselves in a dilemma. Though a class society was the antithesis of Soviet political philosophy, the prospect of building a classless society in Soviet Georgia, known for its relative autonomy, did not seem worth the effort.

A solution was found in the elderly and, through it, their status was upgraded. Traditionally, villages were governed by a council of elders. Beginning in the 1950s, the Soviet government granted the council increased powers. In return, the council communicated Soviet ideals to the villagers. Soviet administrators knew that this way their aims would be listened to far more attentively than if they had been introduced by a Soviet bureaucrat. Also, by increasing the powers of the elderly, the Soviets avoided having to squash factions vying for the government's favors.

Much less is known about longevity in the other two regions where it has been studied—in Vilcabamba, a valley in the Ecuadorian Andes, and among the Hunza, a group of people living under the Karakoram Mountains of Pakistan. The industrialized world became excited about longevity in the Andes after a 1971 Ecuadorian census turned up nine centenarians among Vilcabamba's population of 819, a rate unheard of anywhere else. This news was interpreted to mean that tiny Vilcabamba must hold the key to everlasting life. In fact, the valley has long enjoyed a reputation as an undeveloped health spa. The Incas bathed in nearby hot springs and Alexander Leaf, the principal initial investigator of Vilcabamban longevity, mentions that a Yankee ship captain visiting the area in 1851 was struck by meeting several elderly people, one of whom claimed he was one hundred eleven years old.

Shortly after the 1971 census was publicized, Leaf paid a visit to Vilcabamba and met the centenarians. Besides being impressed by the poverty and squalor that the people lived in ("When we asked various villagers how long it had been since they had last bathed," Leaf wrote in an article in *Scientific American,* "the responses showed that many had not done so for two years"), he was encouraged to learn that the average elderly Vilcabamban consumed about 1200 calories a day that consisted of from 200 to 250 grams of carbohydrates, 35 to 38 grams of protein and only 12 to 19 grams of fat. The results of this diet, not unexpectedly, were an extremely low rate of heart disease and atherosclerosis. But Leaf was still baffled by the number of centenarians. He went away thinking that it must be due to genetics, for those who claimed that they were over one hundred appeared to be European rather than Indian.

A few years later he returned to analyze the blood of these people and found, to his disappointment and frustration, that their ancestors were of *both* European and Indian descent. Again he went away baffled. But he was also suspicious. One of the best known of the centenarians was a man named Miguel Carpio, who told Leaf during his first visit to the valley that he was one hundred twenty-one years old. When Leaf returned four years later, Carpio made the mistake of telling him that he was one hundred thirty-two years old. His credibility was dealt a further blow when Leaf searched for his baptismal record and found that the pages holding Carpio's birth and baptismal record were gone, either destroyed by fire or torn out.

Two anthropologists, Richard B. Mazess and Sylvia H. Forman, solved the mystery. They spent months compiling genealogies of all the inhabitants of Vilcabamba. The result: Those who claimed to be centenarians had not only lied about their ages, they had been able to do so by assuming the records of their relatives with the same names and offering them up as proof. Not one of the self-proclaimed centenarians was one hundred. The oldest was ninety-six.

It seemed strange, initially, to researchers that these people should go to all this trouble to add years to their lives, especially when, unlike the Abkhasians, elderly Vilcabambans were given no special treatment. But Leaf remembered that a local governor had referred to the elderly once as Vilcabamba's "oil wells." That phrase stuck. He was also amazed to find, during one of his return visits, a freshly paved highway leading to Vilcabamba from the coast, presumably for the benefit of tourists who might visit the village and valley to seek the key to immortality. In fact, a Japanese concern was planning to build a health spa to continue the Incan tradition of five hundred years earlier.

Even if the Vilcabambans did lie about their age, their rate of cardiovascular disease is far lower than ours, confirming once again the benefits of a low-calorie, low-fat, high-carbohydrate diet.

What is striking about research among the Hunza, a group of people living in relative isolation for centuries, is that until recently there had never been a shred of evidence of longevity among them. Even so, scientists and other visitors from the West created a legend of long lives for these mountain-dwelling people. The legend did not begin with James Hilton's *Lost Horizon*, the story of a valley in the Himalayas where the climate is perfect. According to American writer Dan Georgakas in *The Methuselah Factors*, an account of longevity claims, the myth may have begun with descriptions of the Hunza by Sir Robert McCarrison, a British Army surgeon who was stationed among them. Though sickness, disease and malnutrition were rampant, he preferred to believe that the Hunza were immune to the aches and pains typical of aging. Some of this thinking is understandable, for the Hunza are very agile people, able to farm narrow mountain terraces even in old age.

McCarrison's glowing reports paved the way for decades of idealists who came back with incredible tales of Hunza health and, by implication, longevity. Even Alexander Leaf got caught up in the euphoria; but after going all the way to Pakistan, he returned with the observation that, since the Hunza had no written language, it was impossible to verify the ages of those few people who claimed they were over one hundred. The only significant finding that came out of Leaf's exploration was a note on nutrition. While the Hunza diet might not be ideal, it is low in calories and high in carbohydrates. The average male consumes around 1900 calories per day.

Dr. M. John Murray, a University of Minnesota cardiologist who spent the summers of 1983 and 1984 among the Hunza, claims to have located eleven who are over one hundred years old. The eldest is one hundred twenty-two. Dr. Murray says that every one of these centenarians can verify his or her age. But actual age is not so important to him as the fact that these people remain active. "In this country, centenarians are most often in wheelchairs," he told me. "There, they are out in the fields." Dr. Murray attributes much of the difference to diet.

In searching for strongholds of longevity in this country, scientists have turned to religious groups such as the Mormons, the Amish, the Mennonites and the Seventh-Day Adventists, religions whose strict codes of behavior and diet prevent followers from poisoning themselves with the food and vices that many people find enjoyable. Cancer rates in all four groups are less than in the population at large. Mormon males suffer half the cancer incidence of other males, according to information cited by Kenneth R. Pelletier in his book, *Longevity, Fulfilling Our Biological Potential.* As a result, observant male Mormons have a life expectancy seven years longer than that of the general male population. Most of these added years are thought to be due to the Mormon prohibition against smoking. Mormons also consume very little alcohol, coffee, tea and soft drinks.

Seventh-Day Adventists, who do not smoke or drink and who are quasi vegetarians, restricting their animal-product consumption to eggs, milk, butter and cheese, suffer a much lower rate of cancer of the colon than the population at large. The Amish are interesting for a slightly different reason. Though their diet is stereotypically American, with animal fat galore and high calories, it does not include junk food. Yet the male death rate among the Amish from cancer, heart disease, stroke, pulmonary diseases and accidents is markedly lower than average. But there is a higher incidence of lymph cancer and leukemia, perhaps because of the high amounts of pesticides and chemical fertilizers that the Amish use. That they suffer less from cardiovascular disease and stroke is attributed to the great amount of exercise that Amish men get as traditional farmers who till their fields with horse and plow.

Bertie Dotson's people are farmers, too. During the nineteenth century, her ancestors and those of the 2300 people who live near her, all of Scots-Irish heritage, migrated down the Ohio River and across West Virginia from Pennsylvania, where many of the Amish live, to Robertson County, a tiny corner of hills and hollows tucked away in northwestern Kentucky. The faces of the farm boys here do not look much different from those of street urchins in Dublin. The people were not always a mixture of Scots-Irish. Their ancestors came to this country, some as Scottish and some as Irish immigrants, to work the coal mines of Pennsylvania and to farm on the side. Over the years they intermarried. When the Pennsylvania coal mines were exhausted, they moved south, some of them ending up in Robertson County where the absence of mining forced them into farming.

Robertson County, one of the smallest counties in the state, has only one town, Mount Olivet, a name suggestive of the importance that Christianity plays here. Earl Linville, the town's mayor for twenty years, says of the county, "We're just a little bit behind everywhere else in the country." No major highway passes through the county; it has no airport, no railroad, no industry, no movie theater, no hospital, no doctors and no ambulance. If a sick person has to be taken to a hospital fast, the coroner in Mount Olivet comes with his hearse to rush the patient to a hospital in an adjoining county.

The only reason anyone might have heard of Robertson County before the University of Kentucky anthropologists began their research there is that Blue Licks State Park, the site of the Revolutionary War's last battle, is located there. Even then the local colonists were a bit behind the rest of the country. The battle occurred two weeks after the British surrendered at Yorktown. Daniel Boone's son, Israel, was killed in it.

Of less tourist interest is that the average life expectancy of the county's people is seventy-seven years, three years above the national average. Further, around 20 percent of its population is over sixty years old, contrasting with the national average of 11 percent. The difference between the elderly of Robertson County and those of Miami Beach, where the numbers also run extraordinarily high, is that most of the old people in the county were born there. Miami Beach's elderly are transplanted northerners and midwesterners. Of those over sixty in Robertson County, almost one quarter are eighty or older. But these statistics do not mean that Bertie Dotson has any friends her age. In mid-1984, only two or three centenarians lived in the county. Bertie was by far the healthiest.

Scientists discovered Robertson County mostly because of Dr. Vera Rubin, the head of a tiny anthropological research organization, the Research Institute for the Study of Man, tucked into an elegant townhouse on Manhattan's upper East Side. Until her death early in 1985, Dr. Rubin, who was Russian-born and had an intimate knowledge of Soviet Georgia, was intrigued with the possibility of finding a similar stronghold of longevity in this country. She and her staff at the Research Institute spent an entire summer sifting through census reports looking for population clusters where a large percentage of the inhabitants were over sixty-five.

The 1970 Census turned up seven counties in Kentucky and some parts of Ohio that looked promising. Robertson County in Kentucky was, very conveniently, only an hour's drive north of the University of Kentucky at Lexington. In 1976, the National Institute on Aging granted pilot funds to an anthropological team at the university for a preliminary investigation of the county. It was the beginning of a six-year period of lavish funding that ended in mid-1982.

What attracted Dr. Rubin and the University of Kentucky anthropologists to the county was its superficial similarities to Abkhazia. It was a pale imitation, however, because the county's centenarians numbered two or three rather than in the hundreds. Nevertheless it was all we had. The terrain was hilly; 85 percent of the adult males were tobacco farmers, a type of agriculture that allows the continuous participation of the elderly; the diet appeared to be nutritional, judging from the number of gardens scattered around and by the fact that so many people put up their garden produce for winter consumption; and it appeared that the elderly were by and large in charge of their families and had not been shunted into nursing homes. There also was the added kicker that the spring water in the hills was full of minerals. In 1862 a health spa with a two-hundred-room hotel had been built on the Licking River. Mineral water from its spring was bottled and sold until the early part of this century, when the spring failed.

The county encompasses some of the strangest landforms in the eastern United States. The last glaciation 18,000 years ago left a massive terminal moraine. Erosion carved this pile of gravel into a maze of gullies and steep-sided ridges which are now covered by layers of rich soil. Roads trace the snaking ridges upward to Mount Olivet. On each side, the land falls off steeply to the hardwood-lined creeks and hollows below.

Most of the houses along the roads outside Mount Olivet are painted a white that has quickly dulled under the ceaseless winds. Like Bertie Dotson's, most have a front porch that tilts to one side. Barns out back sag, and the occasional outhouse looks like it is just about to fall over.

The little houses grow closer together as you get near town, finally passing a sign announcing Mount Olivet's population of six hundred, an exaggerated figure. The town runs along two streets at right angles to each other. The only traffic light is at their intersection, though it is hardly needed since the streets are empty of moving vehicles much of the day. There is nothing physically outstanding about Mount Olivet with the exception of the county courthouse, a massive, squat nineteenth-century building constructed of bricks of such delicate color that they look as though they are about to melt.

Mount Olivet's elderly do not conform to stereotype. They obviously have more on their minds than just getting through the next day. They are spry; they tend to hold themselves erect and they have a little bounce to their step. No shuffling here. You see few morose or unfriendly faces, even when a stranger like me passes them on the sidewalk. A nod or a "hello" is the least of their acknowledgment. More typically, they are curious; they questioned me about what I was doing in Mount Olivet and gave me their condolences when I told them that I live in New York City. To them, Mount Olivet is the best place on earth; they had heard all the stories of crime, poverty and discrimination elsewhere, but there have been only three murders in Robertson County. Though almost 30 percent of the county's population lives below the poverty line, rural poverty in a mild or moderate climate is not as severe as statisticians might lead one to believe. While people may not have enough income to purchase a week's supply of food, they have the space for and the tradition of growing their own. A house without a kitchen garden in Robertson County is like a farm without a barn.

Lucy Linville, a distant relative of the mayor, was the first person I chatted with during my short stay in Mount Olivet. She was ninety years old, had all her teeth, decent eyesight and hearing, and a purple wig with curls on top. "I got this," she explained to me, "so when I go out, I don't have to spend a lot of time in front of a mirror fixing up my hair. I can just plop this on my head and be out the door." I was charmed by the woman after I saw her leap out of a chair like a child. I commented on her suppleness. "Want to see me touch my toes?" she asked. And she did. Then she twisted her wrists, wiggled her fingers and kicked her legs.

Lucy grew up on a farm just outside of town. During most of her childhood, she helped her father with his tobacco plants. She had to walk over five miles to school and the same distance back each day until she was sixteen. When she got married, she moved to another farm and had two children, a boy and a girl. Her daughter died at eighteen months. Her son was killed in a car accident when he was forty, leaving her four grandsons, none of whom lives near her. After her husband died a few years ago, she lived alone on the farm but moved into town when an apartment complex for the elderly was put up.

Now she spends a lot of time alone, mostly reading. "I read romance novels. What do you think I am going to do, sit at home and twiddle my fingers all day long?" She also reads religious pamphlets, not so much for their messages as to check the accuracy of their Biblical quotations against what the Bible says. "You know, a lot of those quotes are just plain wrong," she points out.

The elderly men also show spirit. There are three places in town where they meet. One is Mitchell's Restaurant, an old-fashioned place with high ceilings, walls that were once white and a floor that once shone. There are always some older men there at the Formica tables talking about tobacco farming. They never leave off farming, even when they are too old to work the fields. Most still own some land. They rent it to younger farmers just starting out, and a partnership typically develops between owner and renter. The owner purchases the tobacco seed and decides when to plant and harvest, thus exerting considerable control over his land. He often assists in the harvest as well, in the job of stripping the big leaves from the stalks.

Each Wednesday the Licking Valley Community Action Program serves a hot lunch to Robertson County residents who are at or below the poverty level. The elderly flock to the community center though many of them are not in dire financial straits. Food takes a secondary role to socializing. The women make no pretense about it. Their bright print dresses sparkle against the hall's pale-green walls. They have freshly set their hair, and their rouge and lipstick turn their faces into beacons. Like schoolgirls at a dance, they cluster around one of the long tables, jumping up from their chairs with new bits of gossip and chatter.

The men, far fewer in number than the women, hold themselves more somberly. They sit quietly at a separate table from the women's, their lunch before them. But they do more than eat. They chitchat about "the girls" at the next table; they kid Chester, a big, hairy-chested man with only one tooth visible in his mouth, about his new thirty-nine-year-old wife, over thirty years younger than he. Occasionally, a "girl" approaches the men. Chester invariably grabs her and gives her a squeeze. "It's nice to make these ladies jump," he says to the other men, "but you gotta be careful or they'll be all over you."

Another man, named Sadie, so sad-faced his solemnity has a funny edge about it, shakes his head. "No, 'tain't true," he says. "I wish it were but you got to prod these girls with a stick before they look at you."

"Oh, Sadie, you jus' give 'em a smile. That sad face of yours will make 'em blush," another man encourages. Sadie blushes.

And they talk about being old, about a man they all know who was just taken to the hospital with "failing kidneys." But the conversation soon regains its humor. A man named Lemmy often leads the change from reflection to laughter. He does not have an ounce of fat on him. The skin on his arms and cheeks is smooth. In his bib overalls, he looks like an aged child.

Lemmy has a set of fine strong teeth. He looks up at a man without even *one* tooth in his mouth. Eating is a struggle for the man. He is having difficulty keeping lima beans in his mouth. Lemmy perks up, his long neck rising from out of overalls, and stares. He begins nodding excitedly. "That's it," he shouts. "That's it, you got 'em, boy. Hold onto them beans. Don' let 'em slip. There you go. You got 'em fair and square."

The man grins an empty-mouthed, proud grin. "Yep, they didn't beat me this time. Say, you got some teeth there. Where'd you get 'em made?"

"They was made when I was a little baby," Lemmy replies.

"Guess that means I still got some baby in me. An' I still like to suck lollipops, too."

The banter rambles on, but the noise that the women are making predominates. Eventually the men fall silent, finish their meal and wander out, one of them muttering, "I jus' cain't stand all that cackling. That's what it is. No, that's wrong. It's screaming, an' I still cain't stand it."

The noise of the women during the lunches is the ostensible reason that the elderly men of Robertson County established The Loafers' Club. It is a storefront on Main Street with a soda machine, a bunch of wooden folding chairs and several rows of dilapidated seats taken from a movie theater. Anyone walking by on the sidewalk can look through the big windows and see who is inside. Any male in the county who can afford the five-dollar-a-month membership fee can join. But it is mostly a place where the old men hang out, each one in his accustomed chair. The Loafers' Club is not just a clubhouse where the men beat a retreat from cackling women. It is also a place where children seek favors and advice from the older generation. Every afternoon the battered screen door continuously crashes closed as children file in to report some bit of news about tobacco, ask a grandfather for a quarter, tell an uncle that he is wanted at home, or ask someone else where a tool or a piece of machinery is kept. Here, in these ratty and scarred chairs, sits the council of elders of Robertson County, a living window display that mocks the seclusion that old people are so often forced into or force themselves into.

The task that the anthropologists set out to do—to discover the secret of aging of the people of Robertson County, though they would never refer to it this way—was mammoth in scope. "We knew that this was going to take time but we had no idea of the details to be attended to," says Dr. David J. Wolf, the project's co-leader. Dr. Wolf, a physical anthropologist who specializes in genetics, had first to examine the people's background. Genealogies had to be constructed. His staff had to probe hereditary factors. They had to analyze the food that the people ate and how they prepared it; they had to see what they raised in their gardens and how much of it they consumed; they had to determine the properties of the water they drank, the stresses they were under; their relationships with members of their families, with their peers and with the younger generation. The people of Robertson County were thrilled: never had so much attention been lavished upon them.

After six years, the project fell flat on its face. Little had been learned and close to one million dollars had been spent. Almost nothing had been published. The anthropologists were barely on speaking terms. In June 1982, the National Institute on Aging refused further funding. The anthropologists were dumbfounded. The people of Robertson County are still bewildered but put the end of the research down to government bungling rather than to a lack of organization on the part of the researchers.

David Wolf is now a forensic anthropologist with the Kentucky Department of Justice. If someone drowns or is fatally burned in a fire or a car accident, Wolf is called in to examine the remains to determine if there was foul play. One half of Wolf's office in the State Office Building in Frankfort, Kentucky, contains little piles of bones and skulls of possible murder victims whose cases Wolf is working on. Some go back to the turn of the century. The other half is filled with file cabinets containing material gathered during the "Longevity Project," as the anthropologists refer to it. "It's all there," Wolf told me, pointing to the cabinets. "It just has to be analyzed and written up. I'm planning on getting to it soon." He talks as if the project is still ongoing. He says that he sometimes cannot believe that the National Institute on Aging refused further funding.

The only concrete finding that came out of the years of research was some basic nutritional information which coincides with that found in other communities where a high percentage of elderly people have lived since birth. Generally, those over sixty in Robertson County consume about 1600 calories per day with a high intake of iron and vitamins A and C. Calcium and zinc are the only nutrients they tend to be deficient in. Another possibly significant bit of information is that almost 70 percent of the population grows its own vegetables and most of these people freeze them for winter consumption. But the fried food and animal-rich diet typical of much of the country has come to the county. Over 80 percent of the annual deaths are caused by cardiovascular disease, a big jump from the early years of this century when the county's big killers were tuberculosis, influenza and pneumonia.

That the National Institute canceled funding for the project appears not to be entirely because of the lack of concrete information coming out of the research. By 1982, the bloom was off studies on longevity. The Vilcabambans had made some researchers look foolish; explorers and dreamers had romanticized the Hunza; and longevity among the Abkhasians seemed suspect.

But what about all the elderly people in The Loafers' Club and at the Wednesday lunches? There is a reason that there are so many of them, probably the same reason why there are so many in Abkhazia. In both places, the elderly serve a purpose. They are liked, respected and sought out. Fear of eventual isolation is a recurring nightmare for those beginning to think about their own later years and a constant source of guilt for those who have placed their elderly relatives in nursing homes and institutions. One elderly woman who sits in silence each day in a wheelchair in the corridors of a nursing home complains, "There is nothing to do here. Just because I am in a wheelchair, everyone assumes I am feebleminded. Whenever I try to talk to a nurse, she just smiles at me. Whenever I talk to another resident, I get stared at like I'm crazy." For such people, the golden years become hollow years and senior citizens become social misfits.

This does not typically happen in Abkhazia and few signs of it are evident in Robertson County. The old people in The Loafers' Club are a source of learning and of merriment for the children of the town. When the old men begin talking about tobacco prices, the harvests and the droughts, young eyes open wide. And when no audience is present, the old men turn to each other, take up a bit of gossip and turn it around until they are all in a huddle of murmurs and quiet laughter.

Chapter 7

The Blessing and Burden of Stress

*P*rivileged few of us are free of the pain, anxiety and depression that stress can bring. It is perhaps a prerequisite of human intelligence that we maneuver ourselves or are forced into excruciatingly demanding and uncertain situations, and when that happens hormones and neurotransmitters start racing. Unremitting stress over the years can result in sometimes fatal disease. In short, stress can have a considerable impact on how many years we live. Some researchers now believe that stress is one of the prime causes of aging. Laboratory research on animals suggests that the older we grow, the more the stress hormones flow, leaving us victims of their ability to destroy us as well as to activate us.

The Blessing

Without some stress we would be marshmallows, squishy and soft and with no hard edges with which to face the world. We would have less incentive to learn; we would see little merit in competing; and we would have little desire to excel. And short-term stress serves a very beneficial purpose. The hormones and other substances that pump through us when we narrowly avoid a traffic accident ready mind and body to act fast. What happens today when someone senses an intruder and what happened 300,000 years ago when one of our ancestors sensed the proximity of a saber-toothed tiger are the same. A chemical domino effect begins in our heads and goes all the way to our toes. The hypothalamus secretes a hormone called corticotropin-releasing factor (CRF) which travels to the pituitary gland nearby, where it triggers the release of adrenocorticotropic hormone (ACTH). The bloodstream whisks ACTH to our adrenal glands, sitting atop the kidneys. The adrenals secrete the hormones cortisol and epinephrine, also known as adrenaline. Both do remarkable things to the body to ready it for the pending emergency. They help grind to a halt the body's nonessential activities such as digestion, growth, reproductive functions and, most important for the subject at hand, immunity. They suppress the sensation of pain. They increase heart output and blood pressure, dilate blood vessels in the muscles and increase blood sugar to give the cells an extra shot of energy. They cause the pupils to dilate and they clear the mind.

The overall effect is that the body is poised and ready for action; and the mind, cleared of cobwebs, is sharp and prepared to concentrate on what lies ahead. Carnival operators long ago realized that they could make a living from these hormonal reactions. Who has not thrilled at the sensation of seemingly being launched into orbit on the tilt-a-whirl or crashing to the ground from the height of a roller coaster? Recent studies suggest that those in powerful positions get the same kind of exhilaration from the control they exert. They become addicted to the chemical rushes from the stresses of their exalted situations.

The Burden

Besides closing off the body's nonessential activities, the cortisol secreted by the adrenals circulates back up both to the pituitary, in a feedback loop to alert that gland that it has secreted enough ACTH, and to the hypothalamus, where it inhibits further CRF release. This switching-off device works very well for the occasional period of stress; the hormonal flow ceases and the body returns to its business of digesting food, growing, repairing itself and fighting off disease. Increasingly, however, chronic stress is replacing the occasional emergency. Modern society has turned us into constant worriers and strivers, always whispering to ourselves, as Mayor Koch of New York is wont to ask aloud, "How'm I doing?"

The blessings of consciousness have also enabled us to do something that no other species is able to do—to worry without end, often for absurd reasons and about things that we have no control over. The hormonal results are that the pituitary is probably in action far more frequently than it was in our ancestors, flooding the adrenals with ACTH, which in turn secretes adrenaline, putting the body on constant alert. The results can be unfortunate. People under prolonged stress tend to be sick more often than others. How many honeymoons have been spoiled when the bride or the groom comes down with a cold the day after the wedding, the culmination of many months of planning and stress; how many vacations are spoiled by anxiety-producing heightened workloads in anticipation of a period of relaxation. Young parents often run a gamut of sickness after the arrival of a new baby and the drastic change in their accustomed life-style that the newcomer brings. And ulcers. Stress and peptic ulcers go together like tension and headaches, though no medical proof of a connection exists in either case. Yet everyone has heard of the harried manager, the young mother burdened with small children and no help, the accused awaiting trial, and the soldier awaiting possible death in battle who develop ulcers. Whether people with ulcers are under more stress than others or whether they are less able to cope with stress is unknown. Even the physical cause of ulcers has not been precisely determined, though it appears to be associated with an increase in gastric acid secretion, in peristalsis, and in blood flow. Laboratory studies indicate that guilt, hostility, resentment, frustration and anxiety produce such increases.

Medical research, though conservative by nature, has at last begun to pay attention to the influence that the mind has over the body. Even my internist, a die-hard traditionalist who rolls his eyes at the mention of psychology, has taken to asking me how I am feeling—"Are you happy?"—"How's your work going?"—"Do you feel frustrated?"—before a periodic physical examination. Holistic medicine—the integration of mind and body—has long lingered on the fringes of medical practice, a fuzzy area filled with idealists. But the ecology movement of the 1960s started people thinking in terms of indirect influences. In the case of ecology, this meant the long-term effects that pollutants, unrestricted development and overuse had on the environment. Such thinking also made plausible the notion that the same kind of indirect assault could take place on the body because of the workings of the mind. Since then, holistic medicine, with increasingly rapid acceptance, has become a respected part of medical thought. Articles on the mind-body relationship are cropping up in such established publications as *The New England Journal of Medicine, The Journal of the American Medical Association, Science* and *Lancet.* Two organizations were recently formed—the American Institute of Stress and the Institute for the Advancement of Health—to separate solid research findings and implications from wishful thinking and to disseminate the former.

Credit for convincing the reputable research community to look further into the effects of stress must go to Hans Selye, who, in 1925, as a young Hungarian medical student at the University of Prague, was intrigued by the number of cases he saw of people suffering without explanation from rashes, aching joints and gastrointestinal disturbances. Doctors in those days had no idea what was wrong with such patients and advised young Selye to await the development of more concrete symptoms before making a diagnosis.

Ten years later, Selye was researching sex hormones as an assistant in the biochemistry department of McGill University in Montreal. In the course of experimentation, he noticed that whenever he injected rats with various foreign substances, the animals reacted in the same way: their adrenal glands enlarged; their lymph nodes, spleen and thymus—all structures related to the immune system—shrank; and ulcers developed in the stomach and in the small intestine. Selye assumed that the reaction had something to do with the kinds of extracts—solutions derived from ovaries and placental tissue. So he injected other substances into the animals to compare the results and he exposed them to heat, cold and forced exercise. No matter the source of stress, the same thing happened to the animals. Selye, who died in 1982, assigned the name "general adaptation syndrome" to the phenomenon. Today, it is simply called stress, which, though a simpler term, is far too general to account for the incredibly complex chemical interactions that take place when our bodies are confronted with an alarming and perhaps prolonged stimulus. Nevertheless, Seyle's general adaptation syndrome stands as the foundation for what happens to us when the toll of daily life becomes too much for our minds and bodies to bear. Even so, relatively little is understood about what stress does to us. One of the latest theories is that our bodies react differently to different kinds of stress. Some stress may be good for us while other types are harmful.

It is no longer a pop psychology theory that we can stress ourselves sick; it is medical fact, though the mechanisms remain elusive. NASA found that the immune systems of Skylab astronauts were depressed on the day of splashdown, and two of the astronauts on the ill-fated Apollo 13 mission developed severe infections. Not many of us will get the chance to fly in space but everyone encounters more mundane experiences that have an equal or worse effect. While the death of a spouse is one of life's most wrenching misfortunes, we all must endure other stress-laden events, such as taking out a mortgage or loan, conflicts with in-laws or with a boss, changing careers, or seeing a child leave home. The effects of such occurrences have been studied by scientists since 1967, when psychiatrists Thomas Holmes and Richard Rahe first developed their Social Readjustment Rating Scale. The scale consists of forty-three events that often happen to people, each one carrying an associated score. Losing a spouse has a score of 100; being fired from your job scores 47 in contributing to stress; and minor scrapes with the law, such as getting a speeding ticket, rate an 11.

In one oft-cited study, over 2500 men on three navy cruisers were asked to fill out a version of the scale during the six-month period prior to active duty. Based on their scores, the men were categorized as being either at high risk or at low risk of getting sick. After the ships put to sea, researchers were able to correlate stress level with sickness by keeping track of the number of sick-bay calls made by each man. Those in the high-risk group got sick 50 percent more often than those in the low-risk group. During an outbreak of diarrhea on one of the cruisers, there were twice as many cases among the high-risk group. The greatest amount of sickness occurred whenever the ships were ordered to a new location, times that entailed increased stress because of additional workloads and apprehensiveness about safety.

Study after study using the Holmes-Rahe rating scale has concluded that the more changes one encounters during a lifetime, the more frequent will be illness. Bleak as this sounds, Holmes also states that people can reduce their risk of illness by familiarizing themselves with the forty-three life events. This

Event	Value	Event	Value
1. Death of spouse	100	23. Son or daughter leaving home	29
2. Divorce	73		
3. Marital separation	65	24. Trouble with in-laws	29
4. Jail term	63	25. Outstanding personal achievement	28
5. Death of close family member	63		
		26. Spouse begins or stops work	26
6. Personal injury or illness	53		
		27. Begin or end school	26
7. Marriage	50	28. Change in living conditions	25
8. Fired at work	47		
9. Marital reconciliation	45	29. Revision of personal habits	24
10. Retirement	45	30. Trouble with boss	23
11. Change in health of family member	44	31. Change in work hours or conditions	20
12. Pregnancy	40	32. Change in residence	20
13. Sex difficulties	39	33. Change in schools	20
14. Gain of new family member	39	34. Change in recreation	19
15. Business readjustment	39	35. Change in church activities	19
16. Change in financial state	38	36. Change in social activities	18
17. Death of close friend	37	37. Mortgage or loan for a lesser purpose	17
18. Change to different line of work	36	38. Change in sleeping habits	16
19. Change in number of arguments with spouse	35	39. Change in number of family get-togethers	15
20. Mortgage or loan for a major purpose	31	40. Change in eating habits	15
21. Foreclosure of mortgage or loan	30	41. Vacation	13
		42. Christmas	12
22. Change in responsibilities at work	29	43. Minor violations of the law	11

way you can put stressful experiences in perspective and steel yourself for them by making an effort to relax, by eating well and by generally taking care of yourself during a painful experience. Here is the scale, each event with a number. The higher the number, the greater the stress. To see what kind of stress you are under, find the occurrences that have happened to you over the past year, multiply their number by the times they have happened, and add the results. If you score over 300, you may be, depending upon your personality, suffering a period of major stress. If your score is under 150, your stress level is minimal.

What about lesser griefs that we all suffer every day—the traffic jams, the man next to you who will not put out his cigar, the ranting drunk on the street corner, the clamoring children? One 1970 study came up with predictable results—the greater the number of even small stresses, the greater the number of symptoms of sickness, albeit these symptoms were so minor as not to merit medical attention. Thomas Holmes, who was also the lead researcher in this study, asked eighty people to fill out a form every day for two weeks recording symptoms of illness such as backache, headache, colds, nausea and vomiting, skin rashes and diarrhea.

He also asked them to keep track of their emotional states—tense, elated, irritable, angry, joyful, etc.—and to fill out a rating scale similar to the one developed earlier by him and Rahe. It turned out that seemingly insignificant events such as dieting or overeating, sleeping less or more, a change in social activities or in working hours were the most common sources of stress. And the physical symptoms of sickness that these changes precipitated—at least one supposes that this was the reason—were skin rashes, runny noses, sore throats, nausea and muscle aches and pains, complaints that are voiced every day in the office. Though a skin rash, by far the most common symptom, is not very dramatic, the researchers point out that the skin is the body's first line of defense and, by implication, the first tissue to be attacked by the environment when the body's immunity is down.

Stress and Immunity

One finding of this and similar studies is that as soon as a period of minor, short-term stress is over, the immune function resumes its normal guardianship over the body. The present frontier of stress research is concentrated on two areas: on the intriguing evidence that not everyone succumbs to the damage that even short-term stress can bring and that long-term stress is far more harmful than short-term stress.

People who suffer from foul breath have become very good guinea pigs for some new stress research. The association between stress and bad breath has been recognized for centuries. In the fourth century B.C., Xenophon described it in Greek soldiers. And during World War I, bad breath took on its more colorful and colloquial name—trench mouth—not because the breath of those who had it smelled like an open sewer but because soldiers fighting in the trenches were often afflicted.

The most frequent cause of bad breath is periodontal disease, characterized by gum bleeding, ulceration and general rotting of the tissues. Why this happens has a lot to do with stress. Ronald B. Cogen, a professor of dentistry at the University of Alabama School of Dentistry, conducted a three-year study of 100 people with necrotizing ulcerative gingivitis, as trench mouth is called in medical terminology, and 100 controls—people matched for age, sex and degree of dental plaque—who did not have the disease. His most consistent finding was that those with the disease had elevated levels of cortisol, one of the adrenal hormones, an indication that the person was under stress. Cogen also discovered that the lymphocytes in patients with the disease responded to bacteria with only 60 percent of the effectiveness of the controls. In other words, their immune response to this antigen had only 60 percent of the strength of normal people.

Stress and psychology appeared to dictate why cortisol secretion was high and immune response low. The people with trench mouth reported more stressful events in their lives than the controls and took these events more seriously than many other people would. They also tended to be anxious and depressed by nature. Though the study was terminated at the end of three years, one would assume that if the victims took themselves to a dentist and had the necessary cleaning and repair work done *and* if the source of stress was eliminated at the same time, their immune response would increase. If bacteria then persisted in attacking their gums, the rejuvenated immune system would have the strength to kill them off.

Most studies on stress have certainly suggested that immunity and stress seesaw up and down depending upon the be-

ginning and end of the stressful period. The decreased immunity in astronauts is one example. The day after splashdown, immune functions began to return to normal. Marathon
runners are prone to get sick after a race because of depressed
immunity, but lymphocyte responsiveness pops right back up.
But what about long-term stress? The results are just beginning to come in. One study of what happens after the death
of a spouse found that immunity was depressed for periods of
two months up to a year. The study, conducted by Steven J.
Schleifer and associates at Mount Sinai School of Medicine in
New York, looked at the immune responses of fifteen men
whose wives were dying of breast cancer.

The immune responses of three of the men were still dropping a year after the death of their wives. Schleifer told me
that two of these men had young children to take care of. And
for the third, the course of his wife's disease was what Schleifer terms "extraordinary . . . horrible toward the end." These
special situations were the only reasons the researchers could
pick out for the continued depression of these men's immune
systems.

Schleifer was attracted to the relationship between the death
of a spouse and the immune response in the surviving mate
because of the high death rate of widows and widowers relatively soon after their mates had died. He noted that 700,000
persons over the age of fifty lose their spouses each year. Thirty-
five thousand of the widows and widowers die within a year.
Seven thousand, or 20 percent, of these can be directly linked
to the death of a husband or a wife.

The Mount Sinai researchers had assumed that the prime
reason for depressed immunity during stress is decreased lymphocyte production. But lymphocyte numbers in the men
studied stayed about the same before and after the death of a
spouse. The reason for the depression confirmed Cogen's
findings about periodontal disease; lymphocytes in the widowers were far less *active* than they would be normally.

Given the magnitude and the duration of the stress and the
consequent long period of depressed immunity when disease
could strike with little resistance, it is no wonder that so many
people who have lost a spouse tend to die, seemingly for reasons directly tied to their loss. Psychologists believe that more
men than women die under these circumstances because men

are socialized to contain their grief. Women tend to let their emotions show and they are able to gain psychological and emotional strength from family, friends and others who have faced similar tragedy.

No one really knows even now what the cumulative damage is of years and years of stress, great and small. "One has to be very careful," says Schleifer, "of looking at these kinds of studies and then saying that someone is going to get sick. I think the most we can say is that studies like ours show that an experience like bereavement can change the immune system. What that change really means, we do not yet know. It does not necessarily mean that we are going to get certain illnesses. Also, to what extent are medical disorders psychological? We know that stress leads to psychological changes. But if your psychological state is good, you can have a cold and go about your normal business. If you are depressed, a mere cold will seem horrible." Presumably, then, those who are depressed and have colds will be more apt to say they are sick.

Some researchers cite victims of Cushing's disease as examples of what can happen under a constant barrage of stress. The rare disease, most frequently caused by a pituitary tumor, makes that gland oversecrete ACTH, which then causes the hypersecretion of epinephrine and cortisol. The body closes down its nonessential activities, just as it does during stress. The results are not pleasant. The immune response decreases; growth in children ceases; osteoporosis is common. The secretion of stress-induced hormones causes the release of cholesterol from storage sites in the body; atherosclerosis is common, as is hypertension. Other symptoms of the disease include diabetes, muscle deterioration, the growth of fatty pads, skin inflammation and thymus tumors.

Work—A Major Cause of Stress

Work is the area in which the effects of stress have been most studied. Every occupation has certain stress-provoking traits. And everyone brings to his or her work specific characteristics that include personality, ability, psychological needs and family background. As Hans Selye suggested long ago, every physical, psychological and social factor can be a source of stress.

But some degree of stress is a necessary motivation. You can be told to produce so many analyses per week or you can be told to produce an analysis only when you feel like it. At a certain point along this continuum, probably in the middle, the demands, stimulation and rewards are just right and coincide with the abilities and the needs of most people. Those who have such jobs are the lucky few. How work environments produce stress that leads to illness provides telling evidence of the power of the turmoil that churns within us.

One morning in 1972, thirty-five keypunch operators working in the data center of a university in a midwestern town of 50,000 became ill with nausea, vomiting, dizziness and fainting. Ten of the workers had to be taken to the medical center of the university for treatment; all the employees were evacuated and the data center closed. Extensive testing of the air in the building and the blood and urine of all the affected workers failed to locate any traces of a noxious gas. A traditional biomedical explanation could not account for why these thirty-five workers became sick.

Social scientists took up the search. They noted that those who were most unhappy with their job reported the most severe symptoms during the outbreak. The sick said that they did not like the fact that a supervisor observed them at work from the psychologically superior perch offered by a glass booth. They also complained that they were not allowed to dress the way they wanted to. Yet another common complaint was the constant noise at a nearby construction site. Not only were workers unnerved by dynamite blasts but by the roar of a diesel engine that had been moved under one of the windows of the data center.

Though the link between the workers' illness and stress was never firmly established, there is little doubt in scientific circles that work conditions caused it. Similar incidents have been reported in other industrial settings, including an electronics plant, a shoe factory and a textile plant. Workers in the electronics plant were under stress because different supervisors gave them so many conflicting orders that they could not carry out their duties. Many of the workers in the shoe factory were experiencing deep financial difficulties. Investigators found that those in the direst straits suffered the greatest amount of sickness.

The stress that air traffic controllers must endure is horrendous. According to the air traffic controllers' union, their life expectancy is only fifty-three years. In a study in which 4000 controllers were compared to 8000 air force technicians, high blood pressure was four times more common among the controllers. The incidence of peptic ulcers was twice as high, especially among younger controllers. The busier the airport, the higher the rate of disease.

Then there is the stress of just getting to work. Everyone knows that commuting can be stressful, a subject well studied by Swedish researchers. One study found that the more crowded a train, the higher the level of epinephrine secretion by its riders.

Even if vocational stress does not make us physically ill, it can change our outlook. A tough day at the office can ruin us for the theater or a dinner that evening. A blue Monday makes us want to crawl into bed as soon as we get home. Researchers have looked at what mechanization did to the attitudes of sawmill workers whose job consisted of cutting lumber in the same way over and over again. Each cut lasted no more than ten seconds, during which time the worker was totally dependent on his saw and had to give what he was doing his undivided attention or risk serious injury. These workers were compared to two other groups at the mill whose jobs were not subject to machine control and who had more autonomy.

Those who were assigned to the power saws had a higher rate of absenteeism. They also participated less often in organizations outside of work and in their union activities. The power-saw operators also had the highest levels of epinephrine and norepinephrine. (Norepinephrine is secreted by the nerve endings throughout the body during times of stress.) The two substances were measured in high amounts in the workers before they even began work in the morning. By midmorning, levels slightly decreased but then steadily increased throughout the day and peaked just before the end of work.

Other studies on job-related stress have focused on personality. Much has been written about the Type A personality, that generally austere and pressured individual who is apt to have a heart attack. Type A people can make life hell for themselves and for those around them. They tend to be ambitious, inflexible, competitive, impulsive and constantly in a rush. They feel guilty when they take a vacation. They crave power and recognition. They tend not to have too many friends because they are very self-centered. They are often unduly aggressive and hostile. You know you have come upon a Type A if he or she constantly plays with a pencil, fidgets, taps a foot on the floor. Their speech is full of odd breathing sounds, short bursts of laughter and mutterings. They often try to finish your sentence for you.

The Type A, brought to our attention in the late 1950s by the cardiologists Meyer Friedman and Ray Rosenman, incorporates many of the coveted attributes of success in American culture, the kind that bring honors and promotions in the workplace. A century and a half ago, Type A's were rare. There were fewer arenas that provoked them to act out their jittery aggressiveness. Type A's are in greatest danger when they are thrown into the heat of competition. Once these people withdraw from the pressure, through retirement, for example, they are able to simmer down and enjoy life.

While we hear much about high-powered business executives, doctors and lawyers possessing Type-A traits, what about blue-collar workers? They can be in even more danger of heart problems than executives. The less control they have in their jobs, the greater the risk, according to research by Robert A. Karasek, an industrial engineering professor at Columbia University, who led a study of over 5000 Swedish and American workers. Assembly-line workers, says Karasek, are from 70 to 200 times more likely to suffer heart attacks than management personnel. And people who have the least control over their jobs have about a five times greater chance of having heart disease than do people with the highest amount of control. Those in the worst position, as far as stress is concerned, are people with low control and high psychological demands in their jobs. These dangerous occupations include cooks, cashiers, fire fighters, telephone operators, waiters, freight handlers and garment stitchers. In many of these jobs, machines set the pace, allowing the worker little freedom to develop skills or use imagination. Being a cook must be one of the most harried occupations in the world, the physical environment stifling, the pace exhausting and the gratitude almost nonexistent. Cashiers are never praised for taking money. Their days are marked by a never-ending line of impatient faces. And telephone operators must live in one of the most occupationally anonymous worlds imaginable.

The physical mechanisms leading from stress to heart disease have not been entirely deciphered. One of the characteristics of stress, in keeping with the primitive fight-or-flee response set off by the hypothalamus, is increased heart rate that, if combined with possible high blood pressure and perhaps atherosclerosis, is grounds for a heart attack. Another theory is that stress causes the release of norepinephrine in nerve endings in the heart as well as in nerve endings throughout the body. The hormone's excessive release can result in a very specific kind of damage during a heart attack, easily recognizable by a coroner.

Despite the traditional separation of mind and body in medical circles, the bind between heart and mind for the lay person is so inextricable that it makes up part of our language and belief system. Phrases like "brokenhearted," "to one's heart's content," "heart of gold" and "lose heart" tell of the strong ties. Now, a British research team claims that it can predict who will have a heart attack within a year by assessing a person's psychological state. After gathering information on the mental attitudes of 235 men between forty and sixty-five, the researchers correctly predicted 81 percent of the time who would have a heart attack. The victims tended to be those who were worried, felt sad, anxious and had little libido. In other words, they were under stress.

The subtlety of the relationship between heart and mind is also revealed by the findings of the Framingham Heart Study, in progress since 1950. One part of the huge study found that among 269 couples, aged forty-five to sixty-four, men married to women with more than a high school education were 2.6 times more likely to have heart disease than men married to women with a grammar school education. Also, men married to women who held white-collar jobs were over three times more likely to get heart disease. Another finding was that the husbands of women who worked outside the home but in unpleasant situations, such as not having a supportive boss or not having any opportunities for promotion, suffered a higher amount of heart disease than those whose wives were satisfied with their work environment. The anger and frustration that the wives brought home with them from work colored the home environment to such an extent that the husbands were deeply affected. They may have developed heart disease because they saw their wives suffering and felt powerless to change the situation, a form of stress. Suzanne G. Hayes, the principal investigator of this part of the study, also theorizes that husbands just may not understand what is bothering their wives but are nevertheless frustrated by the constant gripes and complaints.

The Cancer Connection

People have theorized for centuries that stress promotes cancer. Galen, the second-century Greek physician and writer, noted that melancholy women were more prone to cancer than other women were. And eighteenth-century British physicians, writes Dr. Paul J. Rosch, president of the American Institute of Stress, saw a relationship between grief and cancer. In an article in *Comprehensive Therapy*, Rosch also cites anecdotal observations and informal studies showing that those who are most likely to get cancer have certain personality traits or have gone through severe emotional strain, such as losing someone close to them. A feeling of helplessness about one's circumstances or about life in general can lead to cancer. Observation after observation points out that those who bottle up their emotions and who are unable to show anger are cancer targets. There is also some evidence that lonely people without close ties to a parent and people who are distrustful are cancer-prone.

Stress is the common marker in all these cases. Though the reason some people get cancer and others escape it are not known, the causes of the disease are all around us in the form of carcinogens—substances in the environment, whether manmade or naturally occurring pollutants, and in the food we eat. Scientists believe that 80 percent of cancer is caused by these carcinogens. Most people do not get cancer because their immune systems are able to effectively fight off carcinogens. Since one of the hallmarks of stress is decreased immunity, the link between depressed mental state and cancer may thus be the immune system. But so far proof has been elusive.

Much more is known about how stress influences people who *have* cancer than is known about how it influences people toward getting it. If you have cancer and get mad at it, even at your doctors, you will fare much better than those who react calmly. In fact, cancer patients who, as one research report stated, put on a "facade of pleasantness" and "painful acquiescence" succumb faster than those who put up a fight by ranting and raving about their dilemma.

This makes sense in light of the research showing that those who can show their emotions are less likely to suffer stress related diseases. Even those Type A's who are able to relax from time to time, laugh and dance and put their goals in perspective, tend not only to succeed but to do so without having a heart attack.

Stress and Aging—An Inevitable Relationship

Age brings a shift in the type of stress that we are likely to come under, a change that can be but does not have to be frightening. Stress can stem from worries about money, health and the too-easily-feared boredom of retirement. Social security payments and a pension may force a reduction in expenses. Medical costs begin to rise. Eyesight and hearing may start to fail. Friends die off. Children move out of the home. Feelings of no longer being important to anything or anyone may begin to crop up.

Are elderly people under more stress than younger ones? This may be impossible to answer. As Steven Schleifer says, "People certainly seem to undergo more major life events as they get older. But there are many day-to-day events that they do not have to deal with." The great majority of elderly people that I have talked with invariably state that although they feel they have more judgment and wisdom than they had in their younger years, the physical, social and financial compromises that they must make are a constant source of irritation and anxiety. As one seventy-five-year-old man said to me, "Now that I have reached this age, I feel frustrated just thinking about what an effort it is to get around."

Elderly rats, like victims of Cushing's disease, offer a clue to the dire results of long periods of anxiety and depression. Rats and people respond to stress through a release of similar hormones. What happens to halt these reactions is similar, also. In aged rats the feedback loop that circles cortisol up to the pituitary and the hypothalamus to stop the release of ACTH does not work so well.

Robert M. Sapolsky, a researcher at the Salk Institute, is one of those who has been attempting to examine the interaction in rats between aging and stress. What first struck Sapolsky, a small man with a Paul Bunyan beard, dangling locks and excited eyes, is that the stress response, i.e., hormone secretion, in old rats that he examined always seemed half-turned-on, even if the rats were not under stress. He also noticed that stressed older rats took a much longer time to return to normal after a period of stress.

Analyses of hormone levels in these rats showed that they had high amounts of ACTH, the hormone secreted by the pituitary, thus indicating that cortisol was not able to make the pituitary turn off its production of ACTH. "You don't get the right switch-off signal. The brain has not figured out that it's time to stop secreting," Sapolsky told me in his laboratory. The next problem in Sapolsky's search for the secret of stress response in elderly rats was to figure out what part of the brain was not working right. Every cell has specific hormone receptors either on its surface or in its cytoplasm. Once bound, the hormones will then be transported to the cell's DNA so that the cell can carry out the hormone's instructions.

Sapolsky's first suspicion, of course, was that something was the matter with the receptors of the pituitary gland cells. But he found no damage there, a disappointment of sorts, because it meant that he would have to analyze almost every part of the complex chemistry of the brain to find the reason that cortisol was not able to turn off the production of ACTH. He found his answer in the hippocampus, a mysterious and little-known section of the brain. Located near the hypothalamus and pituitary, the hippocampus influences memory, learning ability and depression. Another of its functions, it turns out, is to signal the pituitary, either directly or indirectly, to turn off ACTH secretion. Discovering that the hippocampus assumed this role added a new link to the chain of command that activates or inactivates stress response. But what went wrong with this link in elderly rats?

Brain cells come in two sorts—the neurons, which are the nerve cells, and the glia, the support cells. Sapolsky wondered if the source of the problem was damage to just the receptors of the hippocampal neurons or whether entire neurons in this part of the brain were malfunctioning. The answer is that both were true. And here is where the possible damage of chronic stress comes in. Rats—not necessarily old ones—under heavy stress for short periods will lose 40 percent of the receptors of their hippocampal neural cells. After the stress is over, the receptors will grow back. But if the stress is continuous for three or four months, the damage is far more severe; entire hippocampal neurons die. And when that happens, there is no way for the hippocampus to alert the pituitary to stop ACTH production. The result is that stress hormones run wild and free through the body, falsely telling it that there is a never-ending emergency. In order to meet the supposed emergency, cells throughout the body give up the energy they have stored. Eventually, they starve, which is why aged rats suffer the following symptoms: muscle atrophy, diabetes, osteoporosis, decreased lymphocytes and, of course, immunosuppression. And, it follows, old rats are much less able to fight off cancer than are younger ones. When tumor-producing cells were injected into old rats that were subsequently placed under stress, massive tumor growths developed, as opposed to much smaller growths in younger rats given the same kind of treatment.

Since hormonal levels in elderly people are, in Sapolsky's words, "surprisingly similar to those of an old rat," it should come as no surprise that old people and rats suffer many of the same ailments. But Sapolsky will not commit himself to saying that the human dilemma is the same as the rat's. "You see a trend in that direction in older humans," he says. "Three out of five studies say it looks like the hormonal stress response in older people is comparable to that of an older rat. One out of five definitely says yes; one out of five definitely says no."

Sapolsky's findings would indicate that there is no escape from the hormonal flow of the stress response in the elderly, though this conclusion is based solely on work with laboratory animals. What is not known is whether efforts to avoid or to temper stress during your younger years will affect hormonal release during your later years. Even if they do, relating low stress to longevity may not be the most appropriate way of thinking about the matter. It may be better to think of stress as a possible instigator of fatal disease in the same way that poor sanitation paves the way for typhoid, tuberculosis and dysentery.

Yet so complicated are the chemical balances as a result of stress that some researchers believe that certain kinds of stress may even be beneficial. Robert Ader, a psychiatrist at the University of Rochester Medical School, thinks that the release of some adrenal hormones may help the body resist infection. And then there is the quirk that cancer victims who get mad at the disease live longer than those who accept it.

Lessening Stress's Bad Side

More and more information is coming to light about two aspects of stress: that certain people, aside from the stereotypical Type A individual, might be prone to disease as a result of stress; and that it may be possible to avoid disease by learning to temper stress.

In a study of immunosuppression, stress and personality, John Jemmott, a Princeton University psychologist, and his colleagues found that the immune response of dental students under stress acted in different ways depending upon personality. The immune response they chose to study was immunoglobin A, an antibody in saliva that fights off viral and bacterial infections. To see if personality was related to antibody secretion levels, they divided the students into two groups: those who were very ambitious, and those who were more concerned with maintaining friendships than with gaining power. Though antibody secretion decreased in both groups during exams, the group more concerned about friendships consistently maintained higher levels. And after the exam period was over, the antibody levels in this group bounced back, whereas antibody levels in the group of power-seekers continued to decrease. The reason may be, says Jemmott, that members of this group were worried about their performance or that they suddenly found themselves without a challenge.

So one of the ways to resist disease may be to broaden your perspective to include the rapport and feelings of well-being that are part of friendship. The road to power can be very lonely if one does not share some feelings and show some caring for others. Loneliness is one reason why widowers have a harder time adjusting than widows. And while the spirit of competition is fine, too much of it taken too seriously tends to foster aggressivity, hostility and ultimately guilt, all traits leading to possible heart disease.

If stress is harmful, why are so many people who are under its considerable influence able to cope so well? To find out something about the secrets of coping, psychologist Suzanne Kobasa conducted an eight-year study of executives of the American Telephone and Telegraph Company during the impending divestiture of the company, a time when stress ran rampant. The main ingredient for coping, she found, is what she calls "hardiness." And her definition of hardiness means commitment to important values, a sense of control over what you are doing, and the ability to look at change as a challenge rather than as a frustration. The hardy AT&T executives, Kobasa reported in an article in *American Health* magazine, were not necessarily those whom you might expect. They were not the highest up the corporate ladder or the best paid or the best educated. Rather they were those executives who were committed to themselves, their careers and their families. They felt they were in control of their lives rather than merely going through the paces of living. And they looked forward to the challenges offered by the breakup of the company. These people were also anxious to resolve conflicts rather than to let them simmer. And they accepted advice from colleagues and family members. Advice from the family was not always constructive, though. If a person is under professional stress and a family member offers everlasting love as a means of support, it will not help resolve the conflict. But if they offer solutions or at least a perspective on the problem, that is the kind of support that the stressed can use.

While you cannot change your personality overnight to learn to cope, Kobasa's findings can help to achieve a better way to handle stress. If you do not like the challenges, for example, ask yourself why and look for the hidden opportunities in them. Another way to cope more easily is to practice enforced relaxation. Meditation, as oversung as it is, does reduce blood pressure and high serum cholesterol levels, though the cause may not be meditation per se but the relaxation and the desperately needed peace that accompanies it. Just retiring for fifteen to twenty minutes a day in a quiet spot will help. Some studies say that this reduces the secretion of stress hormones.

The old standby, exercise, is still another way of coping with stress. By releasing endorphins, the substances in the brain that control pain and produce a kind of relaxed euphoria, exercise calms the mind as it strengthens the body.

The amount of stress that we live under is not going to diminish unless we try to reduce its presence. This can be done. Factory environments can be made more pleasant. Bureaucracies can be humanized. Education can include programs on coping with stress. The tendency seems to be, though, to make our lives more complicated in the interests of efficiency. The ubiquitous computer was supposed to make things easier for us. It does to some extent. But some management efficiency experts have turned the technology into Big Brother, who constantly assesses each employee's productivity and sends reports back to the boss. The chances are that stress is going to grow. To a certain extent it will be up to us to try to wrestle it to the ground and put it under our control. If we do not, it is bound to increase both the toll it takes by making us sick and the influence it exerts over how long we live.

Stress, Disease and Coping

Though no evidence exists that less stress can extend our lives, laboratory evidence in animals and anecdotal evidence in humans suggests that too much of it or not being able to cope with it can shorten life expectancy principally by reducing the efficiency of the immune response, thus opening the way for disease. The risk of heart disease is the most firmly established result of stress. Type A individuals are at great risk because of their competitiveness, aggressiveness, hostility and ever-striving nature. They find it extremely difficult, sometimes impossible, to relax.

As well as increasing the risk of heart attack, stress can also result in the following:

• higher serum cholesterol levels
• atherosclerosis

- ulcers
- cancer (the relationship is theoretical but there are centuries of anecdotal evidence)
- multiple sclerosis (another tentative relationship)
- infertility
- impotence
- bad breath
- colds, headaches, muscle and joint aches, backaches, gastrointestinal problems, skin eruptions and rashes.

Coping

- The most common source of long-term stress is a job that does not offer any degree of independence and innovation but has great psychological demands. Granted that it is easier said than done, you should try to get out of such a position and into one in which you will be more in control of what you do.
- Try not to be hostile. The hostility that sometimes comes with competition usually results in loneliness and guilt, both common sources of stress. Competition is fine but you do not have to isolate yourself to pursue a goal.
- Regular exercise not only benefits the muscles and the cardiovascular system but also stimulates the production of endorphins, substances secreted by the brain that act as a natural opiate. Also, exercise offers a means of getting away from all the pressures. The pressure during exercise is all yours, between your will and your body. Satisfaction at having pushed your body toward a goal may defuse some of the conflicts back at the office.
- Meditation is another good way of giving yourself a break from the turmoil of work or family. Physically remove yourself from the source of your stress for twenty minutes or so every day. Sit on a pillow with your legs crossed, close your eyes and try not to think of anything. While it may be difficult at first to force your mind not to drift back to problems, persevere. You will find that after twenty minutes of this, you will feel refreshed and more alert.
- Stress workshops and centers, best found through gymnasiums or exercise clubs, offer various exercise and meditation programs that are structured and supervised. But do not be taken in by meditation hype. There is strong evidence that

the only thing meditation will do as far as reducing the effects of stress is concerned is to get you away from it for a while. Mantras, then, may be all fluff.

Small Tips

- If you feel under stress, don't just churn and seethe inside and get more frustrated. Figure out the underlying reason. If the problem is your boss's manner toward you, analyze the situation from both his or her point of view and from yours. Maybe your boss is under pressure from above. Maybe you will discover that you are not performing as well as you could.
- Make lists as a way of reducing stress. Make a list of what causes you stress and tack it up on the wall so you have in front of you what makes you uptight. Make a list of the ways in which you could have better handled a stressful situation. If your life seems cluttered with details, make a list of the really essential things you have to get done and of the unessential things you would like to do. Stick to doing the essential things.
- Discipline yourself. Give yourself a set amount of time in which to do something and then do it. If that does not work, keep doing whatever it is you have to do until you are finished. Interrupting yourself or letting yourself be interrupted contributes to a lack of efficiency, a good source of stress.
- Don't bottle things up. If someone is being unfair to you, let him or her know it. You will feel better and the chances are the person will have more respect for you.

Chapter 8

Desire Never Has to Die

Waning sexuality is one of the greatest fears of aging. While the prospect of diminished attractiveness is not a topic of conversation that people are anxious to bring up, they do so indirectly in a daily whirl of chatter about cosmetics, fashions, suntans, exercise and food, much of which is a way of asking, "How can I make myself sexier?" or "Am I becoming less sexy?"

Conversations about the even greater fear—losing one's desire for sex, losing the libido that plunges adolescents into fantasies of sexual derring-do—are rarely heard. Vanishing sexual drive is too close to the loss of an essential ingredient of life itself.

The fear has little basis in reality. It is a generational apprehension conceived by those approaching middle age and fueled by the disparity between Victorian repression and hormonal influences. Pushed by androgens and estrogens, youth pays great mind to sex but is consistently reminded through a variety of societal mores that sexuality is for them alone. The middle-aged can dabble with it. The elderly can remember it but should refrain from indulging in it. Unburdened by hormonal taskmasters, older generations are expected to reinforce to young people that life after fifty can be lived very well without sex, thank you. More importantly, older people are expected to unwittingly perpetuate the myth that sex is an evil vestige of our animal past and an unfortunate necessity for procreation. Grandparents should have raised themselves above such base desires and if any sexual drive lingers, it is a quaint aberration which should not be encouraged. How many adults have scolded nursing-home administrators for allowing their parents to have a "boyfriend" or a "girlfriend" and to hold hands? It happens all too often.

Impotence and the Power of Suggestion

Biological changes within ourselves are another equally important reason why the fear of losing interest in sex is common with the approach of middle age. For the first time, a man may notice that his penis does not lift its head to the heights that it once did. A woman may notice that her vagina does not invitingly moisten within seconds of being stimulated as it did when she was in her late twenties and thirties. We are forced to live with such a premium placed on sexual prowess, on the merits of animal sexual attraction beneath the perfume, inside the jeans and within a gown's folds that any change is a threat. But we do not have to be threatened. As with much of aging, understanding what is happening is the key to alleviating anxiety.

Very few people lose their libido. When it does happen, males are usually the victims. Anxiety is one of the leading reasons, often about money and career—the male climacteric. A fifty-year-old man is most vulnerable. His expenses have never been higher. He has achieved a status in his career that makes others look up to him. But the struggle to keep up the pace that drove him to those heights can be physically and psychologically overwhelming. He can fall at any time and the chances are he knows that he is dispensable. Yet he has worked twenty-five to thirty years for this moment. If he stumbles, he may never again get on track. He will be adrift, a sea lion wallowing in the shallows without the strength to haul himself ashore and establish a territory. Sex is far from his mind, but he feels he must perform.

He may even be bored with sex—at least as far as with his wife is concerned. Certainly the prospect of sex at this age is different from what it was twenty years ago; the expectation of sleeping for the 2500th time with the same woman, after all, does not hold the excitement that even the 500th time did. His wife undoubtedly feels the same about her husband. One night he gets into bed with his wife and the inevitable happens. They both find that his penis is as bored as he is. It refuses to make a pretense. Suddenly, the boredom takes on a sinister edge. He is vulnerable in his job, financially pressured, expected to successfully continue to compete but feeling the hot breath of colleagues fifteen years his junior—and now impotent. A limp penis can never be willed to rise. The stronghold of manliness has been assaulted and defeated. The choice is obvious: depression and collapse, or a search for a new self. And so begin many affairs with younger women. As Gail Sheehy wrote in *Passages*, ". . . the greatest temptation in the change-of-life affair is the fireworks of romantic love. What could be more splendidly therapeutic in dispelling middlescent gloom? While the blaze is high, it bathes us again in aureoles of beauty and strength, eclipses this dreary review of past and present, fixes time in the breathless present, or better still, delivers us back to the cheerful selfishness of adolescent infatuation."

While such bliss may be invigorating, it frequently dies an early death, cut short not only by discovery and guilt but also by the differences in sexual needs and capabilities. While a young woman of twenty-five may be happy to spend an entire weekend lovemaking, a fifty-year-old man's penis may not oblige though its master may yearn for more.

Physiologically imposed impotence, on the other hand, is rare. Sexual desire runs strong in the human body from the first churnings of adolescence to the last hand-holding of old age. Disease does get in the way occasionally. Almost any physical ailment can cause a decrease in potency and desire. Victims of emphysema and angina frequently complain of impotence. Alcohol can dampen potency. One of the most common reasons for impaired sexual functioning is hypertension, not that hypertension in itself is responsible, but the drugs given to lower blood pressure often are. Heart attack is another common cause of impotence. Again, the actual reason is indirect but is largely based on the fear that exertion during sex will precipitate another attack. This common fear is greatly overrated. Though an orgasm in a healthy young man increases the heart rate to the 140–180-beats-per-minute range, a study of forty-eight middle-aged men with heart disease found that the average heart rate during orgasm was the equivalent of just over 117 beats per minute. This is not significantly lower than the average heart rate during everyday work activity which has been measured at 120 beats per minute. (Stressful periods can make the pulse jump.) The risk of suffering a heart attack during sex increases, however, in an extramarital affair. A Japanese study of 5559 sudden deaths found that 34 had occurred during sexual intercourse. Eighteen were caused by heart attack and all of the victims were having an extramarital affair when they died.

The Prostate—Every Man's Problem

Prostate problems are the greatest cause of physiological impotence in men. The prostate is a gland that encircles the urethra just below the bladder. It contains and secretes the milky part of the semen and is necessary to transport and nourish sperm on its voyage through the penis and into the vagina during ejaculation. In early adulthood, it is about the size of a grape but after forty it begins growing in most men, gradually constricting the urethra and the free flow of urine. The result is the condition known as prostatitis. Symptoms can be frustrating. Frequent urination is common but the flow is often weak. Straining to empty the bladder can cause hernias or hemorrhoids. When the bladder never completely empties, bladder infections can result. Occasionally, the prostate grows so large that it intrudes into the bladder, reducing its size so much that urine remains in the kidneys and causes even more severe infections.

Why the prostate begins growing is unknown but is thought to be related to changes in the secretion of hormones. Castrated men never have prostate problems. And under certain circumstances, flare-ups are only sporadic in some men. Studies have shown that inflammations in these men often occur following the resumption of sexual activity after a period of abstention, a change that would tend to alter levels of hormone secretion.

Inflammation occurs at one time or another in 30 percent of all men between the ages of forty and fifty. The frequency slowly increases until over one half the male population eighty years and older suffers from it. In most cases, the problem is benign, but prostate cancer is fairly common in older men. It accounts for 15 percent of all cancers in white males and 21 percent in black males, though it goes undiagnosed in many more men. It causes 20,000 deaths per year. Though this form of cancer almost never occurs in men under forty, it can creep up after this age without any warning symptoms. A rectal examination by a physician can detect the cancer in the early stages when it can often be cured without surgery. Such an examination should be included in every physical checkup after forty.

If the pain is constant and severe and the risk of infection in the bladder and kidneys is high, surgery is required even if the prostate enlargement has been diagnosed as benign. Two types of surgery deal with benign growth. The usual fear on the part of the patient is that either one will result in impotency. This is nonsense. The simplest technique involves the insertion of a device into the bladder through the urethra that cuts away part of the growth that bulges into the bladder. The procedure involves a week-long hospital stay.

The second type of surgery involves making an incision in the lower abdomen. Once exposed, the swollen prostate can be partially removed. These two procedures cannot possibly affect potency from a physical standpoint. But both result in what medical jargon has termed retrograde ejaculation, which does not mean an ejaculation of lower quality, but one in which the semen travels into the bladder rather than through the penis. It is then expelled along with the urine. This is not a hardship unless you want to father children. The only change in sensation is that the semen cannot be felt leaving the penis, nor is the woman aware of it, as she once may have been.

A third type of surgery is reserved for a severely malignant prostate. This is accomplished either through an incision in the lower abdomen or, in more severe cases, through the perineum—the area between the scrotum and the anus. Impotency almost always results from the latter operation because of damage to the nerves that control erection. Though prostate cancer is far more common in elderly than in younger men, it moves so slowly in the elderly that it is often left alone. The case is quite different for a man in his fifties. There, the disease can move more rapidly, metastasizing to other areas. Surgery would probably be recommended for the removal of the entire prostate and the nearby tissues.

Less drastic techniques are being developed to deal with this form of cancer if it has been detected before advancing too far. One involves destroying cancerous prostate tissue by freezing it. Another is the use of radiation pinpointed on the affected area. Still another is an attempt to halt the cancer by administering female hormones.

Diabetes is another cause of physiological impotence, affecting about half those who have the disease. In men, impotence may be one of the first signs of Type II diabetes, the kind that strikes later in life. The early indications are a loss of firmness of erection and an inability to maintain an erection for an extended period. One reason is the accumulation of chemical substances in nerves throughout the body, the penis included. Another reason is the damage to blood vessels that is typical of diabetes. Erectile tissue is very prone because it is laced with small vessels.

Diabetic women also suffer from the failure of erectile tissue, particularly the clitoris, to react to stimulation. Some women are unable to have an orgasm because of the lack of sensation. Fortunately, some of these problems in both men and women can be partially eliminated with proper dosages of insulin or oral medications.

Impotence in women used to be labeled frigidity, a male-conceived explanation suggesting coldness and lack of interest. Sexual dysfunction, a far more clinical turn of words, is now the preferred term. Aging has very little to do with sexual dysfunction. Women who suffer from it range from those having no interest in sex to those who are unable to have an orgasm. Most reasons, with the exception of diabetes, are psychogenic. Even women who have had a hysterectomy and removal of their ovaries are perfectly capable of having a normal sex life. By the time such an operation is needed, sexual behavior patterns have been established for many years and take precedence over the lessening of hormonal output.

Adult Sex—A Calmer Affair

Given the number of over-sixty-year-olds, organic impotence and dysfunction are relatively rare while psychogenic sexual problems are theoretically correctable. This is not to say that changes in sexual interest and drive do not occur. They are inevitable. People usually become aware of change after they turn fifty. In one study, over 70 percent of men and 78 percent of women from fifty-one to fifty-five years old said that they were aware of decreasing sexual interest. William Masters and Virginia Johnson pioneered the observation of such changes; much of what follows comes from their work, compiled and published in 1966 in *Human Sexual Response* and refined, added to, and much elaborated in *Human Sexual Inadequacy,* published in 1970. How does a woman's sexual response change with the years? As expected, sex becomes a calmer and less demanding affair which needs fewer occasions on which to express itself. Yet some women become more responsive after menopause and may even burst forth with an outpouring of desire which is really a way of expressing freedom—freedom from the fear of pregnancy, from children, from being a day-to-day parent—free to make love at any opportunity. Physiologically, such feelings of abandon may be due to the drop in estrogen (the principal female sex hormone) that permits testosterone (the principal sex hormone of males but which women have in lesser amounts) to come forward.

The flush typical of sexual excitement disappears with increasing age. Nipples very gradually lose their ability to become erect. And breast-size increases, common in younger women who are sexually excited, no longer occur in most older women. Yet the clitoris reacts to stimulation regardless of age by increasing its diameter as it becomes congested. The vagina and labia of older women, however, show marked changes. After menopause, the vagina becomes, as Masters and Johnson say, "steroid-starved." Its walls lose their purplish and well-nourished mien. Instead, the vagina walls become papery-thin and fragile. In addition, the postmenopausal vagina contracts in length and shrinks in width by 40 to 50 percent. It also loses its amazing elasticity and may require one to three minutes to become lubricated after the onset of sexual stimulation, rather than the ten to thirty seconds needed by younger women.

Though a woman's ability to have an orgasm never dies, it does dwindle with age. The number of orgasmic contractions decreases and they can be so painful that some women avoid reaching that point of excitement. The pain during intercourse from dryness, fragility of the vaginal walls, loss of elasticity and shrinking depth is known as dyspareunia, common in some women following menopause and thought to be caused primarily by a decrease in estrogen secretion. Some of these problems as well as the much-discussed menopausal hot flashes can be alleviated by vaginal creams or oral estrogen-replace-ment therapy, though both carry the danger of causing en-dometrial cancer. One study found that women who use estrogen therapy are up to fourteen times more likely to get cancer. It has been known for some time that women on birth-control pills rarely get endometrial cancer. Could it be that es-trogen in the pill taken during one's younger years confers protection postmenopause? The answer is yes, according to a study conducted by Nancy Lee at the Center for Disease Con-trol in Atlanta. Postmenopausal women on estrogen therapy who had been on the pill had a 50 percent less chance of get-ting cancer than those using estrogen who had never been on the pill. Estrogen therapy still carries risks but these can be considerably reduced by adding the female sex hormone pro-gesterone to the regimen.

A far safer and more natural way to avoid dyspareunia is to keep up sexual activity. Numerous studies have concluded that those women who maintain an active sex life before, during and after menopause stand a much greater chance of preserv-ing youthful and well-preserved vaginas. One of the most re-cent studies, conducted by the Rutgers University psychiatric-gynecological team of Sandra Lieblum and Gloria Bachmann, suggests that ongoing sexual activity's role in keeping the va-gina fit has less to do with estrogen loss than with the level of circulating androgens—male hormones. Those women with higher androgen levels, their production stimulated by fre-quent sexual activity, including masturbation, had far fewer physical problems with their genitals than those women who refrained from sex.

Three of the women Masters and Johnson observed prove the point. Two were between sixty-one and seventy years old and the third was seventy-three. They all secreted vaginal lu-bricants seconds after the initiation of sexual stimulation. The only reason the baffled researchers could offer is that out of the group of elderly women they studied, these three alone maintained active sex lives, having "sexual connections," as Masters and Johnson term it, once or twice a week without fail.

The physical sexual changes that occur in males are more obvious only to the degree that the male sex organs are more obvious. A fifty-plus-year-old man takes fifteen or twenty sec-onds to become fully erect in contrast to the instant erection of a twenty-year-old. And the erection that an elderly man produces will not be rock hard or rise to a 45-degree or higher angle. Rather, it will be firm, capable and horizontal. Unlike a surging adolescent, an older man cannot keep an erection indefinitely even if the stimulation is constant. And the need to ejaculate is not so strong, a characteristic that may improve one's sex life because of the more relaxed course that lovemaking can take. But the lack of need can also panic the insecure or the uninformed by being interpreted as one more sign of the impending impotence that tradition says the elderly must live with. Nonsense. It's an opportunity to be able to enjoy long bouts in bed uninterrupted by youth's pressure to ejaculate.

Once the orgasm comes, and bear in mind that middle-aged and elderly men are often just as happy if they do not ejaculate every time, it is not as intense as it once was since the contractions are fewer. As an indication of the weaker ejaculation, consider the comparative distances that older and younger men can propel their semen. A young man's will fly up to two feet through the air, a fifty-year-old-plus man's only half that distance if he is lucky. And if he has had an erection for a long time, his semen may not go anywhere. It may just seep from the urethra during orgasm. Immediately afterward, his penis will go limp and may literally slip out of the vagina, as if it were exhausted. Hours may go by before it can rise again.

Why the Changes Happen

Why does the gap between desire and ability occur, gradually turning into a chasm of frustration which can only occasionally be crossed on a fragile bridge of encouraging caresses and unhurried lovemaking? Researchers do not know exactly why the sexual behavior of men and women changes with age except that it is obviously due to the process of aging itself. Part of the pattern in both sexes is due to changes in androgen levels, of which testosterone is the leading figure. It is known, of course, that in women estrogen levels begin decreasing around age fifty. The role of androgens in women is not so clear. As has been mentioned, those women with higher androgen levels appear to suffer less vaginal atrophy; and in some women, a combined androgen-estrogen therapy might do more good in restoring both vaginal lubrication and libido than estrogen therapy alone, though the combination is so experimental it is never used clinically.

In males, the role of testosterone is clearer, though still baffling to the research community. What testosterone does on a day-to-day basis has long been known. Produced in the testicles, though some comes from the adrenal glands (all the testosterone that *females* produce originates in the adrenal glands), the hormone is responsible for the development and functioning of the male reproductive system and for such physical traits as beard growth, deep voice and muscular development. It is also tied to such psychological traits as aggressiveness, territoriality and some cognitive skills. Beyond these, Julian Davidson, a Stanford University physiologist who looks at testosterone in humans as well as in laboratory animals, has found that the hormone has a direct effect on sexual activity. In one of his studies, hypogonadal men (men with impaired testicular functioning) given testosterone every four weeks had over twice as many erections as they had before treatment. They also masturbated much more, quadrupled their attempts at sexual intercourse and had many more orgasms. Their erections also were achieved more readily both when the men fantasized and when they were shown films. Endocrinologists tell us that getting an erection while viewing a pornographic film is relatively "easy." It does not take much testosterone to produce a reaction. But to concoct a sexual fantasy and get an erection as a result requires internal, as opposed to external, stimulation to originate the fantasy. Davidson's work suggests that testosterone replacement therapy not only helps an unresponsive penis to become erect but may even stimulate the man's libido.

These tests dovetail with the research by S. Mitchell Harman of the Gerontology Research Center, mentioned in Chapter 4, that shows those men who had the highest testosterone levels were the most sexually active while those men with the least sexual activity had the lowest levels of testosterone. One interpretation is that continued sexual activity stimulates testosterone production. Another interpretation is that people who are in good health tend to maintain their level of hormonal secretions. The men that Harman studied were all in good physical and mental health and were financially secure. The very tentative implications are, then, that if you are healthy in the most inclusive sense of the word, you will produce more testosterone and be more sexually alive, though it is unknown if testosterone comes before sex or sex before testosterone. Julian Davidson succinctly puts the issue in lay language: "It might be," he says, "that sex is just one aspect of being in good health. After all, if you are healthy, you're apt to be sexy."

Other indications exist that testosterone, sexual activity and social status go hand in hand. The classic study that opened up this field of research was done in the early 1970s on rhesus monkeys at the Yerkes Regional Primate Research Center in Atlanta by Robert M. Rose, a physiologist then at Boston University School of Medicine. Endocrinologists had previously noted that dominant male rhesus monkeys had higher testosterone levels than subordinate ones, but it was unknown whether the levels rose as a result of the animals being intrinsically dominant or whether those animals that had high initial levels were able to assume positions of leadership more easily. To determine which came first, the hormone or the status, Rose put each of four adult males in a separate enclosure for two-week periods with a group of sexually receptive females. In this artificial atmosphere, one that would never occur under normal circumstances, testosterone levels of males jumped, tripling in some cases, leading Rose to believe that an environment in which males enjoyed unopposed sexual access to females and were undisputed leaders—an environment void of the everyday hassles and stress that most male monkeys encounter—prompted the testosterone increase. To prove this point, he took the lucky males from their blissful environment and put each one, again separately, in with a group of strange males. They were immediately attacked and harassed. Testosterone levels plunged an average of 80 percent. But when these subdued males were put back in with the all-female group, their testosterone jumped back up to the previously high levels. "The most important finding of the study," says Rose, now chairman of psychiatry and behavioral sciences at the University of Texas Medical School, "is that it showed the strong relationship between testosterone levels and environment."

The interplay between hormonal levels and feelings of well-being are now becoming clearer, though precise measuring techniques are still in their infancy. "It would appear," says Estelle Ramey, a physiologist at Georgetown University's School of Medicine, "that the endocrine system operates best when a person feels that he or she is in control." In rats, testosterone levels fall following an electric shock to the foot. Testosterone in humans decreases following surgery. One study showed that testosterone plummeted during the initial and most stressful weeks of army officers' training at Fort Benning, Georgia. Much of the stress during the first twelve weeks of the twenty-three-week course was due to the constant evaluation that each candidate underwent, his performance often being reviewed and ranked by his peers. The social pressure experienced must have been similar to that suffered when the rhesus monkeys were thrown in with a group of strange males. As with the monkeys, the testosterone level in the candidate officers bounced back when the stressful period of the course was over and they entered the more prestigious second half of the training.

These effects of stress make sense from an evolutionary point of view. Aggression and territoriality, the principal behaviorial traits that testosterone produces in animals and, to some extent, in men, are leadership traits. But animals under stress, whether because of injury or an uncertain social status, do not make good leaders. The social cohesion of a group as a whole, then, would be enhanced if an unfit leader was replaced or no longer in a position to pass his genes on, leaving the role open to a more competent individual.

The amount of androgens secreted can also be tied to our evolutionary past—through their influence on cognitive skills. A recent study by Daniel B. Hier and William F. Crowley, Jr., suggests that men whose genitals fail to mature in adolescence and thus fail to secrete appropriate amounts of androgens have a much less developed ability to understand the relationship between objects and space than those with normal levels, as measured by the length of time it took each to place shaped figures in the correct holes or to calculate space relationships between different figures. However, the verbal ability of these low-androgen men was no different from that of the controls.

Commenting on the study, S. Mitchell Harman at the Gerontology Research Center suggests that a sophisticated spatial ability, which implies both a heightened visual-stimuli threshold and an ability to concentrate were crucial for primitive man if one accepts the thesis that males evolved as hunters. We might be different beings today if our ancestors had not been able to spot potential prey in the monotony of the African plains and track it for days at a time.

While the role of testosterone in maintaining male sexual capability is incontestable, there is no getting around the fact that sexual activity decreases with age while testosterone levels may stay the same. Obviously, there is more to male sexual arousal than testosterone. One possibility is that cells become less sensitive to testosterone as the years go by. When the testes and the adrenal glands are directed to manufacture and secrete more testosterone and other androgens, each hormone heads for relevant cells—muscle cells that tense the body, cells that dilate veins and erectile tissue, cells that secrete lubricants, etc. Studies with rats indicate that the cells' hormonal receptors decrease in number with aging. This has not yet been tested in humans. Some researchers theorize, though, that one reason testosterone-replacement therapy may not always be successful is that the cells' receptors are so diminished that no additional amount of testosterone will achieve the desired response.

Yet another theory is that neurotransmitters, those chemicals secreted in the brain to carry messages from one neuron to another, might be responsible for at least some decreased sexual vigor. The secretion of neurotransmitters, which include dopamine, acetylcholine and serotonin, diminishes with aging. Men with Alzheimer's disease (see Chapter 9) become impotent due to the dwindling of acetylcholine, which activates the parasympathetic nervous system, which in turn helps males maintain an erection. The vaginas of women with Alzheimer's disease are dryer than normal. Medication that inhibits the secretion of acetylcholine (used in the treatment of peptic ulcers and colitis) tend to decrease sexual arousal. And people with Parkinson's disease also do not become sexually aroused, partially because of age but also because the disease is accompanied by a decrease in dopamine secretions. One side effect of the common therapy for the disease—doses of L dopa, which is converted into dopamine in the body—may increase the libido of some people.

The Persistence of Desire

While sexual desire may wane, it rarely dies. A study of the sex lives of 4246 Americans aged fifty and older that was sponsored by Consumer's Union and written by Edward M. Brecher (published in 1984 under the title *Love, Sex and Aging* by Little, Brown and Company) found that, although respondents to a questionnaire were very much aware of a lessening sexual drive, their sex lives were still relatively active. The results of the survey are probably not representative of the fifty-plus population in this country. First, most of the people who responded were readers of *Consumer Reports,* in which notice of the study had been announced. Second, those who took the time to answer the questions were undoubtedly interested in sex and were sexually active. Someone who does not wish to reveal the details of his or her sex life, even anonymously, or who is angry that he or she can no longer have sex, is not likely to answer questions on the subject. Nevertheless, 93 percent of the women and 98 percent of the men in their fifties and 81 percent of the women and 91 percent of the men in their sixties said that they had active sex lives. And 75 percent of the women and 94 percent of the men in their fifties said that they had a strong to moderate interest in sex. Most of those surveyed felt that sex was very important; 83 percent of the women and 96 percent of the men in their fifties felt that sex was moderately to very important for them. Sixty-three percent of the women and 76 percent of the men in their seventies felt the same way.

This survey is one of several that reinforces the observation of many sexual-behavior researchers that sexual interest among some women *in*creases over time. Eighteen percent of the women but only 11 percent of the men in their fifties said that their interest in sex was stronger than it had been when they were in their forties. And the greater interest in sex of these women was equally true of women in their seventies. Sex researchers have often noted that the biggest sexual complaint of elderly women is not dying desire, drier vaginas, or more difficulty reaching orgasm; it is, rather, the dearth of partners. Statistically, this makes sense; women live an average of seven years longer than men and are generally three years younger than their husbands. Unless they find new partners, they must thus live ten years of lonely sex or no sex.

Limp penises and shrunken vaginas, however, do not stop the elderly from having sex. The Consumer Union study discovered that the aging and the elderly have devised an array of methods to satisfy their sexual interests in the face of less-than-firm penises and less-than-moist vaginas. "Stuffing" is one whereby lovers will literally stuff a flaccid penis into the vagina. One seventy-four-year-old man wrote about the foot rests he had rigged up at the foot of his and his wife's bed so his wife could place herself in the best stuffing position.

Ninety-four percent of the women surveyed said they like to stimulate their own clitoris during intercourse. Mutual masturbation is a common practice. Eighty-two percent of the women said they enjoyed receiving cunnilingus and 95 percent of the men reported that they enjoyed performing it.

While younger people are concerned about premature ejaculation and frequency of orgasm, the imaginations of older people have roamed far and wide to find satisfaction with what they have left. Given the physical problems of the elderly, many younger people would have headed for the sex-therapist's couch. But the elderly tend to work out problems and techniques for themselves.

One eighty-four-year-old woman relates, "Believe it or not, masturbation is tiring for an older person. Therefore, vibrators are a blessing." A sixty-eight-year-old man reports that he makes love to his wife with both penis and vibrator. A lot of older people (63 percent in the survey) enjoy masturbation. Even many of those who think masturbation is wrong do it, a continuation of a "sinful" activity they enjoyed during their adolescence which, they must have noted, did them no harm.

Sexual fantasizing is a common way for the elderly to become excited. Many of the fantasies are really memories of special times years earlier. Reading pornographic material or watching pornographic films is another means of arousal used by old and young alike. One elderly couple reports that they sit in bed with pornographic books, the wife reading aloud, and stimulate each other. Some people say that they use pornography as a way of initiating fantasies. What is clear is that a lot of elderly people refuse to put away their sexuality. The fires may be dying but the embers are still glowing.

New Horizons for Sexuality

Sex is a far gentler form of relaxation for the elderly than it is for youth. The incredible surges of sexual tension of adolescence have long since disappeared. Even the pressures to perform have lessened. Robert Butler, chairman of Mount Sinai Medical Center's Department of Geriatrics, and his wife, Myrna Lewis, talk about the second language of sex in their book, *Sex after Sixty.* The first language of sex, they state, is for younger people. It serves biological and procreational needs and is wonderfully invigorating. The second language of sex, which is by no means restricted to the elderly, has the power to communicate love, pleasure and shared intimacy. It can be a morning in bed together; a caress that so many couples under the pressure of child-rearing and careers forget to give each other; it can be a time for complete romance with no need to submit to the biological encumbrances and pressures that accompany youthful sex; and it can be an affirmation that despite the encroachment of physical and perhaps financial ills that aging often brings, sexual communication, no matter how altered from that of younger days, is the warmest kind of intimacy.

Butler and Lewis also point out that continued sexuality is a sign of defiance against the societal stereotype that the elderly should put away sex. The sensuality, warmth, compassion and sensitivity that are often part of sexuality among the elderly are traits that are sorely missed by younger people unhappy with their own start-and-stop sex lives. The elderly might do well to start a sex-therapy institute open only to youth. Sessions might be entitled "Sex and Sensitivity," "Lovemaking Before and After Orgasm" and "Sex and Caressing." Sex, viewed through the intimacy of age, can be far more comprehensive than the rumpled sheets of a double bed or an accounting of the number of times a couple makes love each week.

Alfred C. Kinsey, the great sex-behavior researcher, was the first to note that sexual activity in youth is the key to good sex in old age. One of his investigations involved a survey of how males sexually relieve themselves. Masturbation, of course, was high on the list. Though adolescence in boys begins around fourteen, some enter the period at the age of ten or eleven.

Kinsey found that those who turned the corner earlier began their sex lives earlier, mostly through masturbation. But boys who entered adolescence later, after fourteen, usually waited a year or more before beginning to masturbate. What astounded Kinsey and his colleagues was that the boys who began masturbating early tended to keep up their sexual activity to a far greater extent and for many more years than those who began later. Men from forty-six to fifty years old who had begun their sex lives at a very early age, perhaps even in pre-adolescence, were 20 percent more active than those in the same age group who had gone through puberty later and who had consequently begun sexual explorations later. Similarly and more recently, Clyde E. Martin, one of Kinsey's associates, who later worked at the Gerontology Research Center, found that high sexual activity during the first years of marriage generally results in more frequent than average sexual encounters during later years.

Why the difference? Kinsey felt that some of the reasons were basic: those boys who entered adolescence at a very early age felt many fewer restraints from those who developed later. These little boys could masturbate in glorious ecstasy without being instilled with the fear that if they "abused themselves" they would become dwarfs and turn into idiots. (The belief that masturbation causes insanity, incidentally, probably goes back to the Greek writers Diocles and Empedocles, who believed that semen was part of the brain and spinal marrow. According to these early sexologists, the more you masturbated, the more your brain shrank.) Older boys, though, were forewarned that sinful desires were about to take hold and they better keep their hands above the table. Kinsey also theorized that these early masturbators had established a pattern of sexual release which they had followed for years and they were not about to let old age force them to change their ways. Sex, it turns out, is as much a force of habit as it is of emotion and hormones. Findings on the effects of early masturbation on female sexual behavior are far less precise; in the late 1940s and early '50s, when Kinsey did his research, acknowledgment of female masturbation was hesitant and the consequent pleasures and problems more uncertain.

Kinsey believed that there must be other reasons besides beginning sex at an early age to account for why certain people remain sexually active while others lose desire. Some people give it up because they drink too much, and alcohol not only reduces potency but lowers testosterone levels. Overeating and obesity have also been found to diminish testosterone. Another reason is that some elderly couples just get sick of each other and stay together only because to do so is easier than separating.

Reasons for remaining sexually active include the theory, already mentioned, that a richer sex life causes higher than average androgen levels in both older men and women. The elevation may, in turn, increase desire. Another observation is that sexual activity—even the thought of sex for men—stimulates testosterone production. Research in this area is limited to anecdotal evidence. A 1970 issue of *Nature* carried an anonymous but credible letter by a young scientist who, much to the amusement of physiologists and endocrinologists, recounted one effect of periodic field trips he made to an isolated island where he stayed for several weeks at a time. The young man noticed that during his first days on the island his beard growth diminished but became heavier just before he left to return to the mainland, where he anticipated ending his self-imposed celibacy. By measuring the weight of the shavings, the man determined that his beard was heaviest just before he resumed his sex life.

In all the unknowns of why some aging people keep up their sex lives, researchers agree upon two points. The first is that sexual functioning and ability decline through the years, a given that cannot be remedied. The second is, yet again, that old adage, used frequently by William Masters in his presentations, "Use it or lose it." Kinsey showed that it was true. Masters and Johnson have shown it. Millions of elderly people who continue to enjoy sex show it, even though their children may snicker and their peers may turn away in embarrassment. Yet those people who refuse to give up their sex lives know a secret that continues to warm their beds at night and their hearts during the day.

Sex Comes to Terms with Aging

A waning of interest in sex over the years and a lessened ability to express oneself sexually are inevitable. But the aging and the elderly are just as capable of giving and receiving sexual satisfaction as a person in his or her twenties or thirties. Desire never dies, contrary to myth and common fear.

No one should ever outgrow sex. It is a basic and valid form of communication. But increasing physical ills do take their toll. Prostate problems are common among men, although in most cases they do not lead to impotence. A lack of lubrication, common among women, can be remedied with the proper medication. The greatest number of problems are psychogenic—a turning away from sex because the mind often exaggerates the effects of a relatively minor physical ailment.

The greatest challenge of the aging is to come to grips with the changes that they are undergoing. Initially, the changes may be frightening. In men they may include: a less-firm erection, a longer time required to get an erection, a less-pronounced need to have an orgasm, a less-intense orgasm, a smaller amount of semen ejaculated and a rapid loss of erection after ejaculation. Both men and women may be alarmed by these changes; a man may think he is heading for impotence, a woman that she has failed as a lover is the man does not have a firm erection or an orgasm. Common changes in women, aside from menopause, the most dramatic change of all, include: more time required for vaginal lubrication to occur, less lubrication, thinner vaginal walls, less elasticity of the vagina and a narrower entrance.

Post-fifty is when a gentler sexual relationship is appropriate. Everything requires more time. Erections are attained in a minute rather than a second. Vaginal lubrication takes longer. For the man, one of the great blessings of older sex is that the pressure to ejaculate disappears. Pleasurable though the need may be for the youth, it is inconvenient baggage that brings to a quick halt many an evening's lovemaking. In a sense, then, aging brings on an opportunity for making love over long stretches of time.

Older women do not have to worry about pregnancy and the

dampening effect on a sensual atmosphere that the use of some birth-control devices entails. Children are likely to be grown and out of the house. No more jumping out of bed at 3 A.M. to comfort a child through a nightmare. There is now ample time for the intimacies of relaxed lovemaking and the special, warm communication that unhurried sex creates. Sexual explorations ranging from different positions to the use of pornographic material to vibrators can be pursued without inhibition.

The ultimate key to a satisfying sex life during middle and old age is to have had an active sex life during one's younger years. All the scientific evidence points to the fact that people who began their sex lives early continue having sex and desiring sexual relationships far into old age.

Chapter 9

Alzheimer's Disease: The Elusive Cause

My mother was diagnosed as having Alzheimer's disease in the spring of 1978, before it was recognized as a national tragedy. When my sister and I told my mother's friends what she had, their faces went blank. Even after we explained to them the little we had learned about the disease, we got only stares of uncomprehending horror. It's hard to grasp a disease that rots the mind.

My father had died several months before the tentative diagnosis was made, tentative because a brain autopsy or biopsy is the only way to make a firm diagnosis, and the latter involves risks in the elderly. I was living in Louisiana at the time, deep in research for a book I was writing. After my father's funeral, I stayed with my mother in the big old family farmhouse for a few weeks before returning to work.

She seemed subdued but accepting of the enormous adjustment that she would have to make. She was sixty-six years old and had been married to and living with the same person for almost forty years. It had not been an easy marriage. My father was a dominating man who demanded and received attention. Devotion to him had become a way of life for her, even though it had forced her to give up some of her main interests of younger years. Now that the overpowering figure in her life was gone, I hoped that she might return to the art and music that she had often wistfully mentioned. Encouragingly, she had said a number of times during these weeks, "You know, I almost feel free now."

After I left to return to Louisiana, my sister called to say that our mother had been in the car accident I mentioned in the Preface.

Though my mother had not been injured in the accident, her physician recommended that she see a neurologist. The neurologist asked her what month it was. She made a few incorrect guesses. He asked her who was President. JFK, my mother answered. It was 1978 and, of course, Jimmy Carter was President. He asked her to count backward from twenty. She couldn't.

Afterward, my mother said she did not like that man and called him insensitive and cold.

The neurologist ordered brain scans. They showed that my mother's brain was considerably shrunken. That, together with her apparently reduced ability to recall commonplace knowledge, made a diagnosis of senile dementia of the Alzheimer's type more appropriate than dementia caused by atherosclerosis. As far as anyone knew, she had never had a stroke, another possible cause of dementia; and the brain scans showed no tumors. The diagnosis, however, was tentative.

After the neurologist told my mother what he thought she had, she railed against him and voiced her opinion that he might be "a little strange in the head." I never heard her mention the disease again until two years ago, five years after the diagnosis, when she told me that she knew "something was wrong up here," pointing to her head.

I did not believe any of it, initially. Oh yes, I could understand it intellectually. But it seemed nonsensical that one month my mother should appear mentally competent and the next be diagnosed as having such a horrible disease. And it was impossible to think that over the coming years she would slowly be reduced to a drooling, vegetable state.

But it occurred to my sister and me that maybe she had not been so normal in recent years. Then it dawned on me—she had developed an incredibly subtle cover-up. I will never know if it was consciously done or not. Always dependent on and submissive to my father, she had taken to turning to him for more than just advice on what she should wear and what meal to prepare. Over the past year or so, we recalled, she had counted on him to take over her daily thinking. If she were asked, for example, where she had spent a recent vacation, she might answer, "Oh, we had a most marvelous time. We discovered a wonderful place. Let me see, it was"—and then with a note of irritated urgency, as if so much were going on in her life that she could not be expected to remember every detail—"Oh, Bill, *where* did we go?" My father, perhaps an unwitting accomplice, willingly supplied the required information, which my mother then smoothly picked up on. In social gatherings, they made quite a team. Their friends always commented on how compatible they seemed.

Gradually my father took over day-to-day doings. I remember being surprised that he had assumed the management of the household. He did all the food shopping. He cooked almost every meal. Once I even found him washing the kitchen floor. My mother said that he liked to keep busy in his retirement.

I did not see her until a few months after the diagnosis. The first morning of a brief stay with her, I was awakened by a bitter smell and ran downstairs to see what was burning. I found my mother in the kitchen vacantly staring at the stove on which the coffeepot was percolating. She had emptied into the basket an entire jar of instant coffee, which had turned into a tarlike substance, with the liquid in the pot having the consistency of molasses. When I told my mother that instant coffee was not supposed to be put into a percolator, a sad, confused look came over her face. She shrugged and simply said she had forgotten how to make coffee. She had also forgotten, I discovered, how to turn a key in a lock, to wind clocks, to turn on the burglar alarm, to water the plants and to record the checks she had written out. Notices from the bank were on her desk, warning her that she had overdrawn her account. I showed her where to write the amounts of the checks in her checkbook. She nodded her head in apparent understanding. Then I discovered that she no longer could add or subtract.

Keeping track of the amount in a checking account was one thing; making coffee was another. I got mad. How could someone who had made coffee for so many years suddenly forget? I took her through the steps of brewing coffee, reminding her where the can of ground coffee was kept in the refrigerator, how full the basket should be and how much water to put in the percolator. The next morning, my mother did not make coffee. I asked her what happened. She said she thought we had run out of coffee because she could not find any.

Such incidents jolted me. They made me feel guilty, too. They were the first lessons in the cruel course that Alzheimer's takes, particularly harsh at this point because my mother could still function perfectly well on a superficial level and seemed physically healthy. She just forgot everything. At times, I found myself drawing a mental picture of her brain being eaten away. What was going to happen to my mother, it occurred to me, was precisely the opposite of what happens to an infant. At two months a baby begins to smile. When the disease had succeeded in destroying a certain part of her brain, my mother would forget how to smile. A baby begins to walk at around one year. My mother would forget to walk. At two years, a toddler learns to hold in urine and feces. Alzheimer's victims become incontinent; at a certain point, they have to be diapered. A child learns to talk at two. My mother would forget how to talk, even how to swallow properly. What would happen to my mother reminded me of what happened to HAL, the computer in the movie *2001*. As its circuits were pulled one by one, the computer's thought processes became simpler and simpler until all it could do was sing nursery rhymes.

Of all the things my mother forgot, though, she never forgot how to make a superb beef stew with rosemary seasoning. How she retained the knack for seasoning like that is as much a mystery to me as her increasing memory loss.

My mother was not an adventurous person. Her house was truly her home. She loved every square inch of it, from hand-hewn rafters to holes in the walls where winter's wind came whistling in. My sister and I fleetingly talked about moving her to a nursing home. We knew it would come down to that—we moving her, we making the decision. My mother froze when we brought up the possibility. She would not budge. Guiltily, we shoved the prospect aside. We doubled our guilt at the same time by acknowledging to each other that neither of us wanted her to live with us. We knew what would happen—that she would need our care around the clock. Our own families, we agreed, came before taking care of our own mother.

So we compromised. We hired people to live with her in her house. Trained nurses at $200 a day were far too expensive, so we found untrained people—young couples and single women in the midst of deciding what they wanted to do with their lives. Each lasted for six months to a year. My mother, normally a generous woman, treated them like servants, dismissing them with a regal nod or icy voice. They were strangers invading her home, her last grip on a reality that was becoming more and more unreal to her with each passing day. What is more, she complained, these people served her supper at five-thirty and did not even consider the social grace of a cocktail before dinner.

She did show her generosity in one way to these caretakers. She gave them money, so lavishly that they became addicted to it. She bought them clothes; she bought them books; she bought them whatever they wanted. Whenever they went to buy food for the house, she stuffed bills into their hands. We will never know if they pocketed the change, but soon the bank was calling to tell us our mother was constantly overdrawn. And she donated money to every cause that came her way. The charities swarmed to her like sharks in a feeding frenzy. As soon as she sent them a check, they came back for another.

Two years ago, my sister and I moved my mother into a nursing home, twenty minutes away from my sister's house. Two years before the move, we had placed her name on a waiting list. The administration told us that we were lucky. The usual waiting period is four to five years. My mother visited the home before we put her on the waiting list. She said she would never be caught dead there. She complained about all the "feeble-minded" people she had seen. After a room finally opened up for her, she just nodded her head. During the intervening two years, I think she realized that living in the old farmhouse was too much. She was silently acknowledging that life was getting so foreign to her that it did not much matter where she lived.

Her friends were outraged. They thought that we wanted to get rid of her. Some of them told us that nothing was wrong with her, even after one social gathering during which she began to take off her clothes saying that it was time for bed. They insisted that she was still "just upset" over her husband's death. Most of the time, they commented far too extravagantly on how well my mother looked and how she had adapted so well to the loneliness. Some extended tentative invitations to my mother for lunch or dinner, but they rarely followed up on them. In fact, they began to ignore her despite their adamant proclamations that she was fine. For her to move away from them into a home was a threat, I supposed, a sign that their little clique was falling apart and that they might be the next to go.

She lived in the nursing home for four years. While she used to say that she was not happy there and her complaints about the staff and the food were almost constant, they lessened over time until her only gripes were that the nurses strapped her into her bed and wheelchair. My sister used to take her out for lunch once a week but that had to stop. My mother became so lost in a restaurant that she kept asking where they were and why weren't they back at the home. She felt safe there; in a way, it had become her new home.

But life there was far from peaceful for her or her family. The disease played a cruel trick on her. While her memory loss seemed to stabilize for a time, her motor coordination all but vanished. She lost the knowledge of how to move her feet. I watched her trying to put one foot in front of the other but nothing happened. She became bedridden and bound to a wheelchair.

Her mind, though, remained relatively alert, at least for a time. She recognized family and friends and talked about her grandchildren endlessly. She knew where she was living. From time to time, she exclaimed bitterly that she was wasting her remaining days and that she should "take the bull by the horns," as she said, and do something constructive with her life. Early last spring, something happened to her mind. It suddenly seemed to go dead. She stared into space for hours at a time. When someone asked her a question, she just looked at the person blankly. She never answered. One evening, she called for a nurse from her bed and said that she did not feel well. About a second after she said this, she died. A brain autopsy showed that she indeed had had Alzheimer's. As sad as her death was, she avoided the worst of Alzheimer's disease.

The Growing Tragedy

Some two million people in this country alone are like my mother or will become like her. Most of them are over sixty-five, though the youngest person known to suffer from Alzheimer's, a Japanese woman, was only twenty-eight. Until recently, those under fifty were thought to get a different form of the disease from the elderly. But that distinction has been abandoned. It's the same disease, no matter the age. The only important difference is that the disease moves much faster in younger people, killing them in an average of four years. The average time for those over sixty-five is eight years. People have had it, though, for over twenty years before dying.

Alzheimer's is now the fourth leading cause of death in the elderly, a figure which is often disputed because the disease very rarely kills outright. Most of its victims die of infections, particularly aspirational pneumonia, a form of pneumonia resulting from food entering the lungs and causing infection. As the disease gnaws away at the brain, the neurons that permit normal swallowing are killed. Drooling and an inability to smile or talk are one result; swallowing food "the wrong way" is another.

While one hears more and more about the disease, the percentage of people getting it is not increasing. The number of people diagnosed with it, however, is rising as the population of elderly people increases. It strikes without discrimination wherever health care is advanced enough to allow a large population of elderly to survive. And as medical technology advances, Alzheimer's is bound to become increasingly common. In this country, about seven percent of those over sixty-five have it or are at risk of getting it, a figure that rises to 20 percent of those over eighty. The Census Bureau predicts that in 1990, thirty-two million Americans will be sixty-five or older, meaning that well over two million people will have Alzheimer's. Right now, the medical cost of caring for these people amounts to $20 billion annually. In fifteen years, it could be double that.

Some people would say that not much more is known about the disease now than in 1906 when it was first described by Alois Alzheimer, a German neurologist. He thought that it was caused by atherosclerosis, until recently believed to be the major cause of dementia, a catchall word often equated with senility which refers to a marked decrease in mental functioning. For many years, senility, Alzheimer's disease, senile dementia, feeblemindedness and the mental ravages of aging were all jumbled up. Now, definitions are clearer. Alzheimer's turns out to be far and away the leading cause of dementia. Over 60 percent of the nursing-home population of this country have it. Dementia can also be due to a variety of other causes, including depression (now called pseudo-dementia), stroke and brain tumor. But dementia is not, contrary to popular belief, a normal part of aging. In fact, most elderly people who are tested show little decline in cognitive function beyond minor forgetfulness. But they may be so brainwashed into thinking that age and mental fuzziness go together that they let their mental abilities and alertness decline.

No cure exists for Alzheimer's and various drugs have only questionable results. Yet Dr. Barry Reisberg, clinical director of the Geriatric Study and Treatment Program at the New York University Medical Center, and a pioneering investigator into the clinical side of Alzheimer's, disagrees heartily that little is known about it. "One of the major advances in the last few years," he says, "has been a clinical description. It used to be described in terms of other diseases. Now we know that it has a characteristic onset, presentation and course. Three years ago, we knew none of this."

Reisberg, who has written extensively on the disease, breaks it down into five stages. Forgetfulness does increase during the aging process, and at a certain point it can become so severe that a person will not retain information just read, find the right word during a conversation or function properly on the job. Such symptoms may mark the initial stages of Alzheimer's. Reisberg cautions, however, that these symptoms occur in many people as they get older. Though they may cause great anxiety, the symptoms do not get worse in 95 percent of the cases he has studied. And the mental functioning of even those who have been forced to give up their jobs does not worsen in 80 percent of the cases.

A fine line separates those who suffer a decline in normal mental functioning from those with the preliminary signs of Alzheimer's. Once crossed, this line marks the beginning of a downward plunge into mental mush. Initially, those with the disease deny that anything is wrong. They hide their forgetfulness with a remarkable degree of success by mustering up all their social skills so that others will come to their assistance and fill the memory gap.

The second stage of the disease is marked by a loss of personal history, of knowledge about political and world events, and the loss of the ability to do simple subtraction. Balancing a checkbook becomes impossible. The victim is easily over-whelmed by a complex task and tries to avoid what he or she might consider to be challenging.

In the third stage, a person forgets his telephone number and address, the names of grandchildren, the day of the week or the month. Choosing which clothing to wear becomes too great a task. A person in this stage may also develop a fear of bathing.

The fourth stage is marked by forgetting the name of one's husband or wife, and sometimes one's own name. The ability to recall recent events disappears. The victim will now require constant care. He or she cannot get dressed without help. Urinary and fecal incontinence develops. Shaving, washing, and brushing teeth cannot be done alone.

Reisberg characterizes the last stage as a time when "the brain can no longer tell the body what to do." At this stage the analogy with the death of HAL, the computer, is most evident. The victim can no longer walk. In a sad progression of events, he loses all ability to speak more than a few words. He communicates by grunting. He can no longer smile; the face becomes a mask. Motor functions die. The ability to swallow disappears and the patient is apt to drool. A stupor follows, mercifully ending with coma and death.

Living with and caring for a victim of Alzheimer's disease is a cruel ordeal. Jerome Stone, the president and founder of the National Alzheimer's Disease and Related Disorders Association (ADRDA) is the spouse of an Alzheimer's victim. He characterizes the disease as one that "robs the mind of the victim and breaks the hearts of the family," and he might well add that it can also virtually enslave the person or people who must take care of the victim. And if that person is a member of the family, the years of care can be very, very rough. Dr. Reisberg advises that such people join support groups, a listing of which is made available through a local ADRDA chapter. The ordeal is exacerbated by current health-care reimbursement policies. Medicare, designed for short-term treatment, will not pay the costs of caring for an Alzheimer's patient in a long-term care institution. Medicaid will not pay until the patient's assets are minuscule. In New York State, where the limits are high compared to other states, Medicaid will not pay unless a patient's assets are below $2850 and monthly income less than $392.

Professional at-home nursing care can cost from $200 to $300 a day depending upon where you live. A nursing home will cost at least $20,000 a year and private ones, which are usually more attractive physically and have a higher staff/resident ratio, often will not accept Medicaid payments. To comply with these cruelly archaic regulations, many victims of Alzheimer's disease and other neurological disorders are forced to "spend down," as the health-care industry terms the necessity of becoming poverty stricken before reimbursement becomes possible. Another way for an elderly person to spend-down is by distributing assets to family members so that in the event of long-term illness, Medicaid will pay for health costs. However, this requires advance planning. If assets are distributed when a person is in the early stages of disease, Medicaid may refuse to reimburse until the distributions have been used for medical payments. As the population grows older and detailed financial planning is required, a legal practice that focuses on the needs of the elderly is beginning to grow.

Through stage three of Alzheimer's—the time when patients can still dress themselves and eat with no help—the stress of living with a victim is more wrenching than draining. But during the fourth stage, care becomes a different matter. This is the time, says Dr. Reisberg, when most families decide to institutionalize victims. Violence and incontinence are the main reasons. Absorbent underwear and condom catheters—for men—can contain incontinence to some extent. Psychosis is the more severe problem. Victims will often forget not only the name of their spouse but will not even recognize him or her. When they go into their own kitchen, they see a stranger who will have the temerity to say that the two of them are married. Eventually, the afflicted may not even recognize the kitchen as being in his or her own home. Other rooms may become increasingly unfamiliar. This is a dangerous point, for the patient may then walk out the door of his house in search of a place that he knows. Once outside, everything is foreign. A person does not know who he is, where he is going, or where he came from. People in this condition should wear a bracelet stating that they suffer from acute memory loss. These are available through the Medic-Alert Foundation. Local ADRDA chapters and some pharmacies carry Medic-Alert order forms.

One of the characteristics of Alzheimer's patients is that, upon learning that they have the disease, they withdraw socially. They are ashamed, scared and confused. Although no amount of therapy will permit a victim to regain lost mental functioning, group therapy sessions can help preserve limited social functioning. In New York City, the International Center for the Disabled, a comprehensive rehabilitation organization, runs such a group for about twenty victims of dementia, most of whom are suffering from Alzheimer's disease. Other similar groups are springing up across the country. On the day I visited the New York group, Jed Levine, a therapist, was leading a discussion about the hot and humid weather that had suffocated the city for the past week. The members of the group were seated in a circle. Most were elderly, but a few were in their fifties. They all looked lost and unsure of themselves. Some were dozing off. Jed, a cheerful and encouraging young man, was asking them what was the best way to keep cool in the heat.

"Wet," one replied. And there was silence.

"That's a good way—stay wet," said Jed enthusiastically. "Any other suggestions?"

"Take it easy," someone offered.

"That's a good point," Jed responded. "What else?" No one volunteered. An elderly woman named Beatrice was staring off into space. Jed tried to get her attention. Much of his time is occupied by gently shaking these people back to the here and now. "Are you with us, Beatrice?" he asked. Beatrice nodded and looked confused. "What's on your mind?" Jed wanted to know.

"I was just thinking," she answered, "how good it is to be here and relax. It's good to be healthy enough to come here."

That bit of interaction, from how to handle the heat to trying to bring Beatrice back, plus a few interruptions as several people tried to wander off, consumed twenty minutes.

Physical exercise was next on the agenda. The group responded with greater enthusiasm, albeit in slow motion, by stretching, twirling their arms and waving their legs. The session ended with dancing. I was struck by how attentive the people were to each other. Those who could still walk grasped the hands of the wheelchair-confined victims and swayed them back and forth in their chairs.

Alzheimer's unites these people. They grapple for each other through the fog of fear and uncertainty that the disease has brought upon them. Unsure of what is wrong, who they are or where they are going, every day is a voyage into the unknown. Even before people with Alzheimer's are diagnosed, many of them sense something is wrong. The feeling becomes more and more pronounced as daily wanderings lead them farther into a foreign world. It's a feeling that disappears only when the disease has destroyed all the knowledge that a person accumulates over the years. After that, the remaining days are a vacuum.

The passage to emptiness also includes a return to childhood. The stop-off is evident in conversation, movements and the singing and the art that the members of the little group pursue. But unlike real childhood, this is a childhood that carries a burden of despair with it. It involves a gradual unlearning rather than a learning, along with a fearful awareness that what one knows today will be lost forever tomorrow.

Two elderly men stand side by side. Each holds a finger painting. They are scrutinizing the paintings trying to decide who did which one. Both men are neat and crisply dressed in short-sleeved shirts and open collars. Their physical stances—the way they look at each other, the way they point to the lines and colors on the drawings—tell of a different life. Ten years ago they could have been standing side by side in an investment banking firm, a law office, or an account executive's office, going over a financial statement, a brief or a contract. Now they are looking at squiggles and shapes and colors, trying to remember if they made them.

I am sitting with Daniel, the only person in the group who is capable of articulating his feelings about having the disease. He was diagnosed three years ago. Jed tells me that his mental condition has deteriorated rapidly over the last three months. He is fifty-three years old, the youngest member of the group. He used to be a priest. He looks fine, if your gaze does not linger—slender build, gray hair cut short, soft eyes and an easy smile. But if you look into his eyes for more than a second, there is a great chasm there. Now he is holding his hands in a praying position, the fingertips first grazing his chin and then caressing his lower lip.

"So you were telling me," I say, "about why you went to a doctor."

Daniel lowers his hands and gives me an embarrassed smile. Everything is done slowly. "Oh, was I?" he answers. "Yes, I just felt that something was wrong. I couldn't remember . . ." He stops talking and his eyes and face go blank, as though a light switch inside his head had been flicked off. Then irritation flits across his face. "What were we talking about? Can you just tell me?" He looks down at the floor and says sadly, "I forget so easily."

"About when you felt that something was wrong." I say.

"Oh, yes. I talked about it with a priest first. Then I saw a doctor. He told me I had the disease."

"What was your reaction?" I ask.

"I was mad. I wanted to say 'Don't do this to me. You can't do this to me.' Then I cried."

Daniel knows what is happening to him. He sees the world through clouded eyes, but he realizes that the fog is going to settle around him soon and never lift. He touches the ends of his fingers together again and says in his mild-mannered way, "I'm scared, I'm scared. I know what is happening but then I don't know. It's all so confusing."

He lives alone in Manhattan but he could not tell me just where. His days in his apartment are limited. I ask him what he is going to do in the future. As I ask, I notice that he becomes nervous and begins to tap his feet on the floor. He looks at me, puzzled, and hesitatingly asks me to repeat myself. When I do, he tells me that he is looking for a place in the Bronx that takes Alzheimer's victims.

I ask him how big his apartment is. He gets nervous again and I realize that it is because he knows that he is being called upon to recall facts and for him the recollection of facts is as difficult as catching a cloud. But he tries. "I have a bedroom and a living room and . . ." He clutches his temples and sobs out "Damn it; it's so hard to remember. I get so mad . . ." Then he resumes his praying position and stares vacantly at a bulletin board.

Later, during one of the therapy sessions when the twenty patients are seated in a circle again, a man with a heavy Eastern European accent blurts out, "Where am I?" He looks around him in panic, searching for something familiar. When he does not recognize anything, his panic deepens and he gets up from his chair and heads for the door. "The Nazis are coming. I hear them. They are going to put me on the train again. Isn't that right?" An attendant leads him back to his chair. Jed Levine calms him down by telling him what year it is, by assuring him that no Nazis will take him away, and by pointing out the other members of the group as his friends. After the man has resumed a vacant stare, Jed asks the group to talk about what has just happened. Daniel says to everyone, "I just feel lucky that I am not like that." I sense that it is said as a means of reassurance, that he knows that in the near future he could very well be like that.

Search For a Clue

What is this disease that cripples in such a horrifying way, that has caused such suffering at least since Roman times when its symptoms were first recorded, and that occurs in every society where life expectancy is long enough to let it reveal itself? The body of knowledge that has accumulated over the past five years has put the disease's cause within the grasp of scientists. Recombinant DNA technology may well be the final key that will unlock its most preciously held secrets.

The basic reason for the characteristic symptoms have been known since 1976. They are due to the gradual death of neurons deep in the brain, just above where it and the spinal column join in a region known as the basal nucleus. The neurons that dwell there are crucial for mental functioning because they produce and secrete the neurotransmitter acetylcholine which travels into the cerebral cortex, the brain's outer layer and the seat of learning and memory. Without acetylcholine, learning and memory, two prerequisites of normal daily life, disappear, leaving the victim lost and confused.

Like many of the brain's cells, the neurons that produce acetylcholine are great sprawling things with arms, technically called axons, that ascend to the cerebral cortex. When the brain senses that it must recall or learn a fact, acetylcholine is fired from the terminals of the axons across the synaptic cleft (the space between neurons) to the receiving arms, or dendrites, of the cerebral cortex neurons. These cells then are able to carry out the appropriate functions.

Eventually, the decay that has begun in the terminals and axons of the acetylcholine-producing neurons works its way into the cell's nucleus and kills it. But that happens only during the latter stages of the disease. The first physical sign that the cells are dying may be the appearance of senile plaques that consist of a fatty-looking substance called amyloid, which distends the neuron's axons and terminals. Until recently, amyloid was thought to be a waste product. Some researchers now think that it may play an important role in the disease.

Another characteristic sign is the presence of neurofibrillary tangles. These are pairs of filaments within neurons that wrap around each other like strands of rope and become so ensnarled that, under an electron microscope, they look like a loose ball of yarn. Researchers have no idea why they form or whether they bear any relationship to acetylcholine deficiency.

Plaques and tangles are not restricted to Alzheimer's disease; they are also common to a number of other dementia-causing illnesses, a fact that makes researchers wonder if all dementias are not related. Just the normal process of aging brings them on, though not with the frequency with which they appear in Alzheimer's victims. People with Parkinson's disease have tangles. Those with Down's syndrome have plaques and tangles. So do retired boxers or people who have had severe head injuries. Researchers used to think that the dementia commonly seen in elderly boxers—punch-drunkenness—was, in fact, Alzheimer's disease. The theory has now been discarded. But, ironically, a recent study of young Alzheimer's victims turned up the fact that 15 percent of them suffered head injuries during their youth that made them unconscious, whereas only four percent of the control group had suffered any head injury. The researcher who did the study, Albert Heyman at Duke University, is skeptical, however, that head injury is an important cause of the disease. "If you ask enough questions of these people," he says, "you are bound to find something common to all of them." Heyman may, however, be underplaying the study's significance. Another completely different study, done in a different part of the country, came up with identical results. The curiosity of researchers is now whetted and more studies along these lines will be forthcoming. Such inquiries are inspired in part by the question that has long intrigued researchers: what initiates the onset of Alzheimer's? Is it purely physiological or is there a psychological component as well? Does stress play a role?

Heyman also discovered that a far greater percentage of people with malfunction of the thyroid gland suffer from Alzheimer's. In one study, he found that 25 percent of a sample of women with the disease had had thyroid disease, whereas only seven percent of a control group had had thyroid problems. The connection is unknown. "The need to find a cause for this disease is so great that people will jump on anything," says Heyman.

Some researchers have blamed atherosclerosis. Though atherosclerosis may reduce blood flow to the brain, or, worse still, cause a stroke that results in a form of dementia, it does not cause Alzheimer's. Studies have also suggested that house painters are more apt to get the disease, but the evidence is inconclusive. Aluminum in the brain is another possibility. While an accumulation of aluminum is typical of Alzheimer's patients, people suffering from aluminum toxicity over long periods do not develop the disease. Still, some of the evidence is tantalizing. Daniel Perl at the University of Vermont has found that neurofibrillary tangles contain much higher concentrations of aluminum than normal neurons do. Other investigations that Perl participated in discovered aluminum in the brains of a high percentage of natives of the Pacific island of Guam who had died either of a form of dementia or of amyotrophic lateral sclerosis, a degenerative neuromuscular disease. Further research has shown that where a high amount of aluminum but low levels of calcium and magnesium are found in the soil and in drinking water, which is true of Guam as well as of Japan and New Guinea, there are greater incidences of the neuromuscular disease and of dementia. A similar breakdown of metabolic ability may result in Alzheimer's.

The disease may also be caused by a virus that could take over thirty years to express itself. It is known that several neurological diseases that produce dementia are caused by slow viruses. One is kuru, a mysterious disease found mainly in women and children of the Fore tribe, a group of 35,000 people living in the New Guinea highlands. When its cause was known, scientists studying Alzheimer's disease began looking for a link between slow viruses and Alzheimer's. In the Fore language, kuru means shivering and trembling. These are among the most benign of the symptoms. Stumbling and loss of coordination occur first. Then the trembling and shivering, along with jerking, begin. Some victims become cross-eyed. They slur their speech and lose their intellect and their motor functions. Within six to nine months, they are virtually paralyzed. Death from common infections quickly follows. Autopsies show deteriorated brains full of plaques which, though bearing little resemblance to those of Alzheimer's victims, have made researchers curious.

The reason why women and children are far more susceptible to kuru was discovered by D. Carleton Gajdusek, an anthropologist living among the Fore in the 1950s. Cannibalism had long been part of tribal mourning practice until missionaries put a stop to it. When someone in the tribe died, the eating of selected organs showed respect for the deceased. The brains usually fell to women and children.

The reason why brain-eating apparently precipitated the disease was obscure. A clue came from the study of scrapie, a neurological disease common to sheep and goats. Researchers discovered that this disease could be transmitted to other animals by injection, the transmitting agent being the slow virus. The obvious question: Was kuru a slow virus, too? The question could be answered only by seeing if an extract of brain tissue taken from a kuru victim and injected into an animal produced the disease. In 1965, Gajdusek infected a chimpanzee this way, proving that kuru was caused by a virus that took decades to incubate in humans.

Later, Gajdusek proved that Creutzfeldt-Jakob disease, another rare human dementia, is transmitted by a slow virus. The brains of victims of this disease sometimes have plaques. The logical research progression was to see if Alzheimer's could also be transmitted. Results have been disappointing. That Alzheimer's may be caused by a slow virus is not a dead issue, however, especially in light of the fact that the viruses that cause Creutzfeldt-Jakob disease, scrapie and kuru do not behave like ordinary viruses in that they can remain inactive for years. Common viruses such as those that cause chicken pox or mumps have very short lives. Also, when slow viruses become active, they do not cause any inflammation. They also show a host of more subtle differences. They cannot, for instance, be killed with ultraviolet light; they contain no proteins in common with their hosts; and they cannot cause a protein increase in the cerebrospinal fluid of their victims. In fact, Gajdusek, who received a Nobel Prize in 1976 for his work, says that it is with some "misgivings" on the part of researchers that slow viruses are labeled viruses at all.

Stanley B. Prusiner, at the University of California at San Francisco, has discovered that the substance of the plaques in scrapie—amyloid—appears to be similar to that of the plaques of Alzheimer's disease victims. The amyloid in scrapie is suspected of being the infectious agent for that disease. If Prusiner is correct that the amyloid of scrapie and Alzheimer's are similar, and that still must be proven, it will strongly suggest that a slow virus is at least partially responsible for Alzheimer's disease.

Whether amyloid, once thought to be a waste product of the disease, is actually its cause is hotly disputed among researchers. If it is so, the disease should be infectious. But Alzheimer's, unlike scrapie, has never been transmitted. "There is not one shred of evidence," says Dr. Peter Davies, a prominent researcher at Albert Einstein College of Medicine in New York, "of infectivity, even in the spouses of those who have it."

Finding the Faulty Gene

Davies who, with coworkers, discovered in 1976 that low levels of acetylcholine is the immediate cause of memory loss in Alzheimer's patients, leans toward genetics as the prime cause of the disease. But he does not preclude the involvement of a virus. He believes that somewhere in the human genome—the 23 pairs of chromosomes that we all have that are made up of about 150,000 proteins—there is one defective protein that is the culprit, and he means to find it. The abnormality could be caused by a virus that has become a part of the genetic material and is inherited from one generation to the next. If so, the virus would then play the role of catalyst, rather than be the cause of the disease.

Even if the disease is genetic, its inheritance is not straightforward. If the defect were dominant and one of your parents has it, you would have a fifty-fifty chance of getting it. This does happen, but only in families in which the disease tends to strike at an early age. Davies cites one family in Philadelphia that "is predictable as hell—generation after generation for six or seven generations, with age of onset between forty-three and forty-seven and death occurring between fifty-three and fifty-seven." But only seven percent of the population over sixty-five has the disease, too low a rate if it were caused merely through the straightforward inheritance of a dominant gene.

Even so, if a person gets Alzheimer's at an early age, say in his or her fifties, the theoretical chances of an offspring getting it around the same age approaches 50 percent. If the disease strikes much later, say in one's seventies or eighties, the chances of an offspring getting it are reduced to around 20 percent because that person may die of other causes. "Some people who are going to get the disease when they are ninety-three," says Davies by way of explanation, "have already died of a heart attack when they are seventy-nine."

The complicating factor is that the disease's time of onset is highly variable. A few people get it when they are in their forties; more in their sixties; and even more in their eighties. Davies and his colleagues have worked out a computer model showing that between the age of fifty and the theoretical age of one hundred fifty, the average age of onset is one hundred three years old, the time when 50 percent of those whose parents carried the gene would have the disease. Most people have died by this time, of course, so Alzheimer's would-be prevalence is not evident. If Davies's model is correct, the medical technology that is enabling people to live longer and longer will also mean an increasing number of Alzheimer's victims.

The disease could still have a genetic explanation even if it turns out not to be caused by a classically dominant gene. Some diseases are inherited in only a certain percentage of cases through a dominant gene; in other cases the disease is caused by sudden damage to that gene. The disease retinoblastoma (tumor of the retina) is contracted either way. Approximately 30 percent of the cases are inherited whereas 70 percent are due to damage to a particular gene for any number of reasons—a chromosome breaking when a cell divides, or radiation or pollutants.

Davies, a colorful Welshman, points out the difficulty of predicting who might get Alzheimer's by citing his own family. "My grandfather died at around seventy. I never really knew him. He was said to be a little senile, but I have no idea whether he had Alzheimer's. He smoked heavily and drank himself stupid. He could have had an alcoholic condition; he could have had strokes; he might have been a little wacko to begin with. And if my mother—his daughter—developed Alzheimer's now, I would not know if there was a family history because I do not know anything about her parents. In most cases you can't get that information. That's why the genetics of this disease are so goddamned complicated."

A necessary step in really understanding a hereditary disease, of course, is to find the faulty chromosome, or better yet the gene on the chromosome, or better still the proteins that make up the gene. Only 5000 of the approximately 150,000 proteins we possess have been identified after years of painstaking work and none appears to have any bearing on Alzheimer's disease. If it were not for the development of recombinant DNA technology, the likelihood of discovery would be one out of 145,000. But recombinant DNA technology allows a researcher to examine long pieces of genetic material from an Alzheimer's victim. By examining correlating pieces from other patients and from normal people, abnormalities can be discerned. If, for example, an abnormality is consistently found in one region of chromosome 21 in all samples from Alzheimer's patients, there is a good chance that the defective gene or protein will be on this chromosome.

Once Davies has a sufficient number of blood samples from members of the few families that suffer Alzheimer's from one generation to the next, he is, as he says, "going straight for chromosome 21." The reason: a possible connection between Down's syndrome and Alzheimer's disease is growing stronger as research into both diseases becomes more sophisticated. Down's syndrome is caused in most cases by an extra twenty-first chromosome. Alzheimer's researchers have noted that every victim of this retarding disease who survives into his or her thirties and forties develops symptoms that are identical to Alzheimer's.

In addition, Down's syndrome is far more common in families with a history of Alzheimer's disease. Dr. Leonard L. Heston of the University of Michigan found that a woman who develops Alzheimer's is three times more likely than average to have produced children with Down's syndrome. If further research establishes a connection, it will not mean that the same gene controls both diseases but it will point the finger at chromosome 21 as the culprit in Alzheimer's as well as in Down's syndrome.

Most of the research on chromosome 21 is concentrated on dissecting the chromosome DNA molecule by DNA molecule. Davies, who thinks this is a waste of time, proposes a quicker solution. He plans to begin his search with the proteins that are already known to be associated with the chromosome and, through recombinant DNA technology, "follow" how they create DNA. "Finding the defective protein with this new technology is relatively easy," he says, "but discovering how it causes Alzheimer's is another matter. We've never cracked one of these diseases before. It's not simple genetics. Finding out how the disease works is something that you get hooked on."

Is There a Therapy?

Efforts to treat Alzheimer's have not been successful. Research has taken two directions: attempts to increase the amount of acetylcholine in the brain; and to increase the efficiency of the acetylcholine that the brain still manufactures. The idea of boosting the supply of the neurotransmitter came from the success that this method had in alleviating the symptoms of Parkinson's disease, caused by a deficiency in the neurotransmitter dopamine. In the 1950s, researchers discovered that the body could turn the drug levodopa, commonly called L-dopa, into dopamine, thus replacing the actual neurotransmitter.

A means of increasing acetylcholine has not been found. Researchers initially thought that if Alzheimer's patients ate food rich in the substance lecithin, the precursor of choline, which in turn is the precursor to acetylcholine, the brain would manufacture more of the neurotransmitter. Egg yolks, meat and fish contain lecithin. You can buy it in pill form in health-food stores. But the brain of a normal person is able to manufacture all the acetylcholine it needs from a normal diet. Eating lecithin-rich foods will not produce more acetylcholine. And the brains of Alzheimer's victims cannot convert choline to acetylcholine because the neurons that make the neurotransmitter are dying. Kenneth L. Davis and his colleagues at Mount Sinai School of Medicine in New York have experimented with a drug to increase the acetylcholine production of the neurons that still function. However, the drug blocked the receptors in the neurons of the cerebral cortex that receive the messages carried by the neurotransmitter, with the result that there was no communication between the neurons.

The second therapeutic approach—to increase the efficiency of the acetylcholine still produced in the brain—has met with slightly more success. The drug in this effort is called physostigmine. In 1976, Davis gave the drug to a group of normal young people and found that their ability to learn increased by as much as 20 percent. "It was like science fiction. I was reminded of books I read when I was an adolescent; this seemed fantastic," Davis said. He gave the drug on an experimental basis to patients with Alzheimer's on the theory that their learning ability, too, would increase. One third showed no change at all and even the changes in the patients that improved were not all that dramatic. "They looked about one year better," Davis says, "but this means more to the investigator than it does to the patient."

Efforts are also being made to find a substance that mimics acetylcholine. The most hopeful is bethanechol chloride, which for the past year and a half has been pumped into the brains of four Alzheimer's patients via a long tube implanted in their abdomens. The research, under the direction of Dr. Robert E. Harbaugh of the Dartmouth Medical School, is still in very preliminary stages.

Researchers also hope that one day Alzheimer's patients may be able to receive a brain graft that will replace destroyed acetylcholine-producing neurons with fresh ones. Work in this area has been underway at the University of Lund in Sweden for over a decade. Its present emphasis is to try to overcome the decrease of neurotransmitters and some hormones in the aging brain by grafting brain tissue from younger rats to older ones. Two people with Parkinson's Disease have also received grafts of tissue from their own adrenal glands, a source of dopamine.

In the meantime, there is no cure for Alzheimer's disease.

Day to Day with Alzheimer's Disease

Around two million people in this country have Alzheimer's disease. Most of them are over sixty-five years old, including more than 50 percent of nursing-home residents. A person over sixty-five has about a seven-percent chance of getting it; for those over eighty, it is a 20-percent chance. The chances are much less for people in their forties and fifties. However, if you happen to come from a family in which the disease appears in each generation, you theoretically have about a 50-percent chance of getting it *if* a parent got it in his or her fifties. But if a parent was over seventy, your chances decrease to about 20 percent. It strikes without regard to race, color or sex and is known throughout the world where medical technology, nutrition and hygiene have made long life expectancy common.

All of us become more forgetful as we get older. The fear of losing one's mental capacities is so terrifying that merely forgetting to put the roast in the oven or whom you had lunch with yesterday can be traumatic. Physicians will tell you, however, that this kind of forgetfulness is common even in one's twenties and thirties. There is no need for concern unless your forgetfulness impairs day-to-day functioning or jeopardizes your job.

If that is the case, your physician will probably recommend that you see a neurologist. If there is a suspicion that something is amiss after the neurologist asks you some silly questions like what day of the week is it and who is President, he may want you to undergo some tests. One of these will probably be a computerized axial tomographic X ray of the brain (CAT scan). Or he may want to use the more recently developed nuclear magnetic resonance (NMR) technique. Both allow detailed pictures of the inside of the brain. Another test is an electroencephalograph, which measures the brain's electrical activity. Tests will also be given to measure blood flow and metabolism in different parts of the brain.

A diagnosis of Alzheimer's disease is usually made through a process of elimination based on the results of tests and of questioning by neurologists and psychiatrists. A brain scan serves to eliminate the possibility of damage from a stroke, a brain tumor or atherosclerosis. If a scan does not pick up any of these possibilities and if a person, while being questioned, shows forgetfulness of recent events and confusion that turns out not to be from depression or alcoholism, then a diagnosis of Alzheimer's disease will probably be made. The only information that a brain scan will pick up in an Alzheimer's victim is a degree of shrinking of the cerebral cortex, the brain's outer layer. But in an older person, shrinkage is normal, so this cannot really be used as an indication of the disease. Ordinarily, a definite diagnosis of Alzheimer's disease cannot be made until after death when a brain autopsy is performed.

Dr. Barry Reisberg, clinical director of the Geriatric and Treatment Program at the New York University Medical Center, ha. broken the course of the disease into five basic stages:

Stage 1 (May be the onset of Alzheimer's or may be due to depression.) Typically forgets what has just been read or discussed. Difficulty in job or social situations because of this. Unable to recall names. Difficulty choosing right word.

Stage 2 No recall of personal history and current events. Has difficulty handling money. Overwhelmed by new technology as simple as it may be. Difficulty doing simple arithmetic. Denies that anything is wrong.

Stage 3 Can no longer remember address or telephone number. Can no longer count backward from 20. Does not know what day, month or year it is. Has a hard time choosing clothing.

Stage 4 Forgets name of husband or wife. No recall of recent events and often patient does not know where he is. May have a fear of bathing. Urinary and fecal incontinence common. Psychotic and violent episodes can occur.

Stage 5 Ability to function physically is lost. Patient cannot walk, talk, or swallow food properly. Has to be totally cared for. Coma and death follow eventually.

Depending upon age, the course of the disease usually takes from three to fifteen years. The earlier the age of onset, the faster the disease moves. The average course for someone in his or her fifties is three years; for someone in the seventies, eight years.

No cure exists for the disease and there is no even partially effective treatment. However, some measures can be taken to alleviate the toll that the disease takes both on the victim and on the family. Any attempts at treatment should be made only under the strict care of a physician or psychiatrist. Tranquilizers may help calm the patient and lessen his or her anxiety. This medication can help the patient sleep; sleeping problems are common with the disease.

Probably the best thing the family of a victim can do is make life as simple as possible as the disease progresses. Everything that the patient needs in the daily routine should always be kept in the same place. Clocks should be large and in obvious places. Calendars should list one day at a time or be marked off. Take excess clothing out of bureau drawers and closets. The clothing that remains should be easy to put on and remove. Shoelaces, buttons, snaps, hooks and even zippers will become too complicated. Be thankful for elastic waistbands and Velcro. Eventually, caretakers will have to lay out clothing and supervise dressing and undressing.

Make food choices simple and easy to eat. As the disease advances, a victim's table manners will deteriorate and it will be increasingly hard for the patient to handle a knife and fork. Finger foods and sandwiches are best at this point.

Make the home safe. Take unnecessary furniture and obstacles out of passages from one room to another. Install grab bars in the bathroom and put a lock on the kitchen door (Alzheimer's victims are apt to forget to turn the stove off). Install gates across stairways. Make light switches accessible and obvious. Get rid of matches. Also, hide any dangerous liquids or medications.

As the disease progresses, victims often get lost, even in their own homes. The worst time is night. Wandering is common. A luminous tape, the kind that glows in the dark, will help guide a victim between bedroom and bathroom. If a person should go outside alone, getting lost is almost inevitable. Get a Medic-Alert bracelet (you can get a necklace but a bracelet is safer) stating that the bearer has severe memory loss and giving a toll free number to call. Medic-Alert application forms are available in many pharmacies and through local chapters of the Alzheimer's Disease and Related Disorders Association (ADRDA).

Taking care of an Alzheimer's victim is physically and emotionally exhausting. Just think for a moment of dealing with someone who asks you, perhaps continuously, "What day is today?" Those with Alzheimer's must always be watched for fear they will injure themselves or those around them or wander off. Though you may dearly love the victim, the amount of work required can wreck family life, be an enormous financial burden and be physically destructive to those responsible.

Support groups offer opportunities for those caring for Alzheimer's patients to exchange ideas, tales, tears and hugs. They are invaluable for lifting morale and restoring energy. Each of the 120 local chapters of ADRDA maintains a list of these support groups.

Another form of therapy that both victim and caretaker can benefit from is a day-care program such as the one described previously. It may help the victim maintain some degree of social functioning. Perhaps more importantly, it will give the caretaker some rest. Day-care programs for Alzheimer's patients, while not common, are increasing. Call ADRDA to find out if there is one near you.

Another way to get some respite is to hire a person to care for the victim, either full time or for a few hours now and then. Initially, the cost of hiring a person should not be great as he or she will act mainly as a companion; but as the disease becomes more severe, highly trained nurses may be required. Information about availability and costs can be obtained from ADRDA, a visiting-nurse association, your local mental-health department or office of the aging. Private nursing businesses can be found in the Yellow Pages.

When the patient reaches Stage 4 of the disease, the family may wonder what course to follow. At this point, the victim will probably be incontinent and may be prone to violent episodes, especially when he or she no longer recognizes family members and becomes totally disoriented. Violence may occur when family members are pointed out to the patient and he has no recollection of them, or when he is told that he is in his own house but has no familiarity with the rooms or furnishings.

The family must now come to grips with two unfortunate situations. The first is that the patient's condition will only deteriorate. It will not be long before he will require 24-hour-a-day supervision and will have little or no recall of people, places and memory of possessions. It will make no difference to him who feeds him his meals, assists him on the toilet or dresses or undresses him. Institutionalization, as heart-wrenching as it may seem, is probably the best course for both victim and family. But that decision brings up the second dilemma, one which doubles the tragedy of the disease—the cost of institutionalization. A nursing home with minimal facilities and trained staff will cost over $20,000 per year. That is the bare bones. A better-equipped and -staffed institution can run $50,000 a year, depending upon location. The harshest blow is that medicare, under most circumstances, pays nothing. Generally, medicare reimburses only those people over sixty-five who will recuperate within 100 days. There is no recuperation from Alzheimer's disease. Medicaid will assume costs of a nursing home (if the home accepts medicaid payments) but only after a patient's assets have been reduced to less than $3000. Some insurance policies, pension plans and supplemental income from social security will cover partial costs. The options, then, are brutal: a family can care for an Alzheimer's patient at home and risk emotional scarring and physical upheaval, or it can place the victim in an institution and watch its assets drain away.

By far the great majority of families with Alzheimer's patients choose the latter route. Consequently, most patients are on medicaid, their entire assets and often those of their families having been swallowed up. The tragedy is most severe if the family consists only of an elderly couple. If one member must be institutionalized, the well member, perhaps unable to support him- or herself, quickly faces poverty. That is the way the law reads. A legal specialty is growing to advise families of chronic-disease victims in ways of sheltering assets or of dispersing assets to family members so that the victim, technically destitute, will be reimbursed by medicaid.

Before considering which nursing home you might want to place a relative in, keep in mind that the better institutions have waiting periods that can last from two to five years depending upon how fast space becomes available. Thus, if a family member has to be institutionalized quickly, a lesser-quality nursing home with a shorter waiting period might have to do. When looking for a nursing home, first consider location. You will want a place that is close by family members. If religious considerations are important, the choice is still narrower. Then, visit each institution. Judge a nursing home by those criteria that would please or make life most pleasant for the patient.

Is the physical plant designed to be the least confusing possible for someone suffering from dislocation? Are the floors clearly marked, for example, by large numbers? Are there directional signs? Look at the floors themselves. Are they covered with shiny tiles that are hard on the eyes of elderly people? Is the furniture upholstered with a wavy-patterned fabric that might make a person dizzy? Be sure to notice how the staff interacts with the residents. Do nurses and doctors seem to respect the patients or do they treat them like children? Ask the administrator if there is any opportunity for patients to exercise. Are there art and music programs? Are children allowed to visit? (Alzheimer's victims usually relate extraordinarily well to children and receive enormous pleasure from their visits.) Under what circumstances are drugs and restraints used? Is there group therapy? Many, many questions can and should be asked but the best guide is to be intuitive and consider first what kind of environment would best suit the needs of the patient. A caveat: institutions make the final choice of whom they take and whom they do not take. Some institutions will say that they do not take Alzheimer's patients. If this is the case, it is just as well that you do not persist, because your relative, even if admitted, would probably not get adequate care. Other institutions are concerned about the stage of the disease. If a patient wanders, a nursing home may be reluctant to take him or her.

For more information about caring for Alzheimer's victims, two books are considered the bibles by Alzheimer's experts. They are: *The 36 Hour Day: A Family Guide to Caring for Persons with Alzheimer's Disease, Related Mental Illnesses, and Memory Loss in Later Life,* by Nancy L. Mace and Peter V. Rabins, Johns Hopkins University Press, Baltimore, 1981; and *Alzheimer's Disease: A Guide for Families,* by Lenore S. Powell and Katie Courtice, Addison-Wesley Publishing Company, Reading, Massachusetts, 1983.

Chapter 10

Retirement: The Golden Opportunity

You have to work on Ed Gartner to get the truth out of him. When I asked him what he did with himself now that he is retired, he looked me straight in the eye and said, "I skydive. Anytime you want to find me, look up in the air." Gartner (not his real name) is sixty-two years old. He has never skydived and has no desire to. He will also tell you that he was married five times and had two children with each wife. That's another jovial fib which he quickly retracts after the desired shock has been registered. He will tell you that he is a Bahamian citizen, too, that he consults a cobbler down the street when he gets sick and that he is going to get a job when he is eighty-five years old and for the next five years after that "give it all I've got" to make up for all the years he spent working and never enjoyed.

Beyond all the leg-pulling, Gartner looks and acts like someone around his age without too much on his mind. Tall and lean, with a full head of partially gray hair, he is in good physical shape with a terrific tan that he spends hours working on. He is a saltwater-fishing nut and carries rods and reels wherever he goes. He spends extensive periods each winter probing the shallow waters off Florida and the Bahamas in search of bonefish but flies back to New York frequently to see his wife of thirty-five years, whom he says he misses too much to be without for very long. His wife does not accompany him on these jaunts because she still works, in a high-pressured managerial position. When she retires in five years or so, Ed says that they will roam the tropics for bonefish.

In the meantime, his wife leaves him early each morning in their apartment in a Manhattan high rise. It is a small place, only one bedroom, and most noticeable for its ceramic dogs. The dogs lounge on the coffee table and sit panting on the thick carpet beneath it. Ed does not spend much time in the apartment. He is too busy making friends. Affable does not adequately describe this man. He is the kind of guy who feels a compunction to break down barriers of shyness and suspicion no matter who crosses his path. Gartner is a professional friend-maker; it is his principal retirement activity. He tells me that he could wander down to Macy's and find a bagel vendor on the sidewalk there whom he is on such good terms with that he invariably gets a free bagel out of his chatter. "People are more interesting to me than anything else in the world," he declares. "Just the sight of a person makes me interested in him."

He likes to call himself a contrarian, even in his retirement, going against the stereotype of drying up in an armchair. "I'm alive; I'm healthy," he says, standing up before me and showing off his physique. "I think young, I act young." With childlike bravado, he has run against the crowd for years. After college, he went to Honduras and lived for eight months in a peasant village as a gringo king. He has always made a point of not staying in the same job for more than seven years and disapproves of people who take their careers too seriously. He worked in his father's car dealership for seven years. Then he took two years off. He worked for seven years as a real estate broker. Then he took two years off. He worked for seven years as a stockbroker. And he took two years off. In 1972, he began an automotive supply chain with the profits he made in the market, three stores in New Jersey and one in Florida. He sold out after seven years and decided to retire.

"I never enjoyed working," he tells me, "and I never worked very hard. But now, I'm really living." In retirement, he defies the myth of withdrawal, loneliness, boredom and ill health. His days are full of activities which, while not what all of us might want in our retirement years, suit Gartner just fine. By eight on sunny summer mornings, he is on the roof of his apartment building soaking up the sun. He stays there until noon, sharing the pebble-strewn expanse with an eighty-six-year-old widow similarly inclined toward the sun. Afternoons find Ed somewhere in the city making friends with someone. And there are museums, movies, libraries and, invariably, younger women. Ed says his wife "does not strangle me," presumably meaning that she does not ask him too many questions about what he does with himself every day. On quiet afternoons, so this happy retiree tells me, he entwines himself in casual affairs with women half his age. "A man just was not meant to deny himself sexually. It's part of life. I don't think I am losing any points up there [motion heavenward] for doing this."

Gartner's formula for happy retirement is enviably simple, if not simplistic. "I believe in the three S's," he says, "sun, sex and the street." He has access to the sun year-round on his roof and on fishing trips. Sex he can get anywhere, anytime, he claims, and the street provides him not only with an opportunity to exercise by walking but also to strike up a conversation with anyone he fancies. "I would not trade my life for any other in the world. I may die poor but at least I'm living rich. How many people can say that?"

Gartner's values and interests notwithstanding, it is refreshing to meet such a retired person. There is nothing discernibly remarkable about him. He is not one of those eighty-year-old symphony conductors you hear about. He is just a regular person that one passes on the street every day.

Retirement is a bad word in this society, particularly, as it turns out, for those who have not yet retired. There is no doubt that it represents a major turning point in life. It is also a major opportunity. Common belief is that those who retire either shrival up on park benches or fritter away the rest of their lives playing bingo and shuffleboard in senior-citizen centers. These people, traditional thinking goes, are "over the hill," "used up," "fading fast," and "about to go down the drain." "Golden agers," it follows, are not living in their "sunset years"; they are living a day-to-day hell of feeling useless, unwanted and in the way.

And to reinforce these fears, we have all heard that retirement is a "killer." Anecdotes abound—the father of a friend, an uncle, a former boss—they all got sick, had an accident or died shortly after retiring. When Bear Bryant, who had coached the University of Alabama football team for twenty-five years, died of a heart attack in 1983, a month after retiring, much commiseration took the form of head-shaking exclamations: "See, that's what happens if you retire."

The fear is compounded by the inevitably increased medical costs that the elderly must bear. They can plunge a retired person deeply in debt. Thirty-three percent of the nation's annual health-care costs are charged to the 11 percent of the population over sixty-five. The sad fact is that the great majority of the elderly's medical costs are for chronic conditions that are not covered by medicare. Elderly people spend an average of 20 percent of their income on medical expenses—out of their own pockets. The consequences for those who suffer from chronic conditions such as diabetes or hypertension can be gruesome. A retired couple with a small but adequate income can find themselves on welfare in a matter of months if one of them develops a severe and lasting condition. It behooves the elderly to stay well. Obviously, not everyone can stay in good health. But the odds can certainly lean in one's favor if one eats properly and keeps in good physical shape.

Of the many studies that have been conducted on the effects of retirement, one stands out as perpetuating the myth of retirement as the first step to the funeral parlor. Conducted by a team led by British researcher W. Casscells and supported by a Harvard Medical School group, the late 1970s investigation came up with a tentative correlation linking retirement to an increased risk of heart attack. In 1980, the researchers presented their findings, which they acknowledged were very questionable, to a meeting of the American Heart Association. That evening and the next day, the media filled their pages and time slots with stories about the research findings. So doggedly did medical reporters pursue the purported link that several medical journals published articles urging caution in interpreting the findings. These reports and others pointed out that health problems are endemic to the elderly, not to the state of being retired. In fact, one quarter of those who retire do so for health-related reasons; they get sick *before* they retire, not after.

Certainly, studies have been conducted that show a connection between retirement and dwindling mental and physical health, lower self-esteem, and less happiness and life satisfaction. But under scrutiny, these findings turn out to be biased. In gathering the data, researchers asked retired people how they were feeling. Well, older people generally suffer more physical ills than younger ones. Yet, when the respondents informed the researchers that they were feeling just so-so and that they did not think too much of themselves now, investigators were quick to equate the problems to retirement rather than to age.

Retirement and Poor Health: A Doubtful Connection

Two recent but separate efforts have rectified this error by examining the findings of longitudinal studies that have followed individuals for years and screened out those people who were in poor health before they retired. Both efforts found that retirement poses no special danger to health, influencing it in only minor ways. One of the studies, conducted in Boston and based on 229 retirees and 409 people still working, found that even compulsory or unexpected retirement, often the most difficult ways to retire, had no effect on health. The study, led by David J. Ekerdt, warns, however, that the findings are not exhaustive. The Boston study does not consider, for example, how retired people who get a disease will deal with it compared to persons of the same age who are still working.

The other study, conducted by a research team headed by gerontologist Erdman B. Palmore, at the Duke University Center for the Study of Aging and Human Development, looked at the effects of retirement on income, health, activity and attitudes as reflected in six longitudinal studies. Like Ekerdt's study, the findings temper the traditional view of retirement's destructiveness. Income does decrease, of course; the earlier the retirement, the greater the decrease. The average reduction amounted to between 25 and 28 percent of preretirement income. Such a change affects people in different ways depending upon preretirement income and type of work. "Retirement is most severe on the lower middle class, those who are just above the poverty line to those with a medium income," Palmore told me. "White-collar workers earning high salaries will have accumulated savings over the years. But the middle-level worker is caught in the middle. He has few savings, and social security benefits do not approach his salary level. These people are the ones who are most apt to be unhappy."

But that does not mean that such people necessarily suffer heart attacks. Palmore found that retirement did affect health, but in very minor ways. It may be that those retirees whose health was poorer after retirement were suffering some undefined illness while they were working and that this may have been one reason that they stopped. Palmore also thinks that retirees may exaggerate their health problems as a way of justifying their retirement.

The study also found that retired people are far from inactive. As is borne out by Ed Gartner, retirees tend to spend more time making friends and socializing than working people. They also spend more time going to church and community organizations and functions. And the belief that self-esteem and self-satisfaction dwindle also lies on doubtful ground. Some studies suggest a slight degree of decreasing self-satisfaction; others a slight increase. Perhaps the message is that how you act in retirement and what you get out of it depend upon your attitude.

That early retirement has more pervasive effects than retirement at age sixty-five or seventy was one significant finding of the Palmore study. Early retirees suffer greater income loss; they are less satisfied with their lives; and they tend to be in poorer health. Researchers suspect that the last two traits occur both because health considerations force these people to retire early and because they have reached dead ends in their jobs. They have no place to go but out the door, and when they leave, they may not even get that bittersweet gold watch.

One of the reasons why so many studies reaffirm the myth that retirement is tantamount to death is that a generation ago data from longitudinal studies was less available. Rather than being able to follow a group of people on an ongoing basis, scientists relied on one-time surveys. If more retirees said that they were in poorer health and more dissatisfied with their lives than people who were still working, the message appeared clear that retirement was responsible. But Palmore thinks that many of these studies during the late 1960s were biased toward the work ethic. "I suspect that among middle-class academics who did these analyses, there existed a pro-work, anti-retirement bias. They projected their own fears of retirement on their respondents."

David Ekerdt suggests also that family physicians, people who are known to be loathe to retire themselves, foment much of the ill will toward retirement. Unconsciously, they may pass their dislike onto their patients. Ekerdt also points out a subtlety in

thinking about the effects of retirement; it focuses on the difference between an epidemiological and clinical view. Longitudinal studies involving thousands of participants suggest that
retirement has no ill effects, but a doctor's elderly patients are
almost necessarily in poor health. The doctor's own bias may
encourage thinking that retirement is a factor in declining
health.

Retirement is a largely mysterious and feared ritual, a major
life event and, many people think, a time of vulnerability. A
misfortune occurring to those who have just retired can most
easily be explained away by blaming it on the psychological
upheaval that the change caused. The work ethic that has
prodded and steered this country toward what it is today explains much of this feeling. We are a nation of workers and
strivers. Americans traditionally know no rest until the job has
been done, the fortune made, the reputation established. White-
collar workers are identified by what they do rather than by
who they are. And they spend much of their working life per-
fecting what they are. Occupation and ego become mingled.
Take occupation away and ego suffers. Retirement, with this
view in mind, *can* be a killer, especially for those who have spent
so many years doing one thing that they have not developed
other interests.

The Shortcomings

The bad reputation that retirement has is perhaps one reason
why fewer people are retiring today than a decade ago. Fifty-
seven percent of those over fifty-five are still working full time,
compared to 46 percent in 1974, according to a Louis Harris
poll commissioned by the National Council on Aging. Ironically, the older they get, the more they dislike the thought of
retirement. Eighty-one percent between sixty-five and seventy
years old and 85 percent between seventy and seventy-nine said
they did not want to retire. The 1981 poll also found that
Americans of all ages dislike mandatory retirement and do not
believe that older Americans should give up their jobs for
younger workers.

Once retired, though, people change their tune. Almost half
those retired people sixty-five and over told researchers that
they *had* looked forward to retiring when they were still work-

ing. Those who were earning the highest salaries looked forward to it the most and were the happiest afterward. Yet longings for the workplace remain very much alive. Most of those polled miss the money, the people they encountered while on the job and the work itself. They also miss the feeling of being useful, the excitement of the activity around them, the respect they received from others and the routine of a fixed schedule.

Retirement has a number of other failings, too, as outlined by Leland P. Bradford in an article in the *Harvard Business Review*. Bradford, one of the founders and the chief executive for twenty-five years of a small business, wanted to retire. He saw it as an opportunity to play golf and free himself from the stress of daily decisions. He even moved with his wife from Washington, D.C., to North Carolina so he could be closer to a favorite golf course.

As soon as Bradford walked through the firm's doors for the last time, he wanted to go back. More than that, he was hurt that no one called him for advice. He soon found that he got bored playing golf all day long, that the volunteer organizations he joined did not offer the challenges of running an organization, and that marital problems began to crop up, not an uncommon complaint among retirees. Among those of retirement age in the 1980s, the chances are that a woman runs the home and it is the man who is retiring. When he does retire and remain at home all day, both he and his wife find that he gets in the way. He tries to take over the management of the household. He is more apt to go shopping with his wife and they argue about what has to be purchased.

Leland Bradford alleviated his problem by writing a book called *Retirement: Coping with Emotional Upheavals*. One of the lessons it teaches is: If you have a choice of retiring or not, take no action until you have thoroughly thought the matter through. Consider the choice both from the viewpoint of the joys of being free and the disadvantages of not having a support group of colleagues or an "arena," as Bradford calls it, where you can show off your expertise.

The Corporation and Retirement Planning

Though more people fifty-five and older are working today than in the 1970s, the long-term trend is toward fewer elderly people working. In 1948, over 85 percent of the population between fifty-five and sixty-four worked. By 1982, the percentage had dwindled to 57 percent. Attitudes toward work are rapidly changing. No longer are people wedded to one job. We are mobile physically as well as occupationally. Second careers are as common today as second marriages. Fewer and fewer people identify themselves by their occupation. Interests are diversifying. The high-powered urban corporate lawyer of the 1970s may be more content today to live in the informal atmosphere that a small city offers, where he will have the opportunity to be a decent father, be on the boards of various cultural and educational institutions *and* practice law.

Following this trend that emphasizes human as well as professional values, enlightened corporations are offering their employees educational programs, sabbaticals, extended vacations and various early-retirement options, not all of which are designed to oust older workers to make room for younger and less expensive ones. Early retirement will probably become increasingly common. Numerous gerontologists and sociologists have noted, however, that the concept is a loaded issue. It means less money to retire on unless an employer offers an incredibly delicious carrot as an enticement in the form of severance pay or pension increase. Though the reward may be enough to enable the employee to continue with his accustomed lifestyle, the message is clear: "Your services are no longer needed." If one is under the delusion that his or her services *are* indispensable, the knowledge can be devastating. Even if a worker does not opt for early retirement, the fact that he knows the company wants him out is reason enough to feel depressed. "If a person is forced to retire and cannot find replacement work, or if there is a marked drop in income, he will be unhappy," says Palmore. "But this usually does not happen. Most people have the resources to find other employment and other sources of income."

Early retirement has a flip side. Called phased or gradual

retirement, it offers a flower-strewn educational path to the potential bliss of total retirement. Unfortunately, only a relatively few firms have adopted it, but necessity will undoubtedly persuade more organizations to do so. Mr. Bradford should have incorporated it into his own firm's policies before taking to the golf course. In phased or gradual retirement, an employee works less and less during a period of time, say, five years. This is usually accomplished by tacking on unpaid vacation time. The Polaroid Corporation has even adopted a plan that it calls "retirement rehearsal," whereby an older worker can take three months off, unpaid, to see what it is like not to go to the office each morning.

The danger here is that someone just beginning to "rehearse" will wake up in the morning and be at such a loss that he or she will skip right back to the office. Joseph S. Perkins, Jr., Polaroid's corporate retirement administrator, thinks that the best way to avoid this dilemma is to begin thinking about what you might want to take up as an avocation or second career when you are in your mid-forties. "A new career with its renewed stimulation, new interests and new demands could keep a person who might otherwise stagnate and opt for early retirement working well beyond retirement ages as we now know them," he told me.

Polaroid even offers pre-retirement seminars and coordinates meetings for retired employees to get together and discuss their experiences and problems. IBM partially foots the tuition for courses that employees considering retirement might want to take to prepare themselves for a new career. Connecticut Mutual Insurance Company in Hartford offers fully paid leaves to employees who will retire within two years so that they can take time to explore new life-styles and career possibilities.

There is another reason that some companies offer innovative retirement programs. Management at these firms actually wants some older employees to continue working when these people do not want to stay or want at least to slow the frantic pace that has been demanded of them. Why would an organization want to keep someone like this? The answer lies in the bursting of the baby boom following World War II. A labor shortage is on its way, and some farsighted organizations are preparing for it by trying out older workers on a reduced work schedule.

The labor force grew annually in the 1970s by a whopping 12.5 percent. But having babies was not so popular in the 1960s and families shrank in size. In the 1990s the working force will expand by less than one percent, according to Census Bureau projections. Though the coming shortage will not affect most employers for ten to fifteen years, it is already beginning to hit some high-tech firms that require large numbers of highly trained people. There, the employees who have gained years of valuable knowledge and experience on the job are being persuaded not to retire so that companies can both gain from their expertise and use them to train younger workers.

In general, though, such programs are in the minority. Much more effort is being devoted to getting rid of older employees in the kindest way possible. It is no secret that two young employees can be less costly to a firm than one older one. During recessions, cost-cutting measures are typical. One is called the "golden handshake." When DuPont offered full pensions and a bonus of a week's pay for every year worked to employees fifty-eight or older if they would retire, over 2000 accepted. The savings, tens of millions of dollars, allowed almost 3000 younger workers to keep their jobs. Everyone benefits—at least potentially. The organization comes out looking rosy because it has not laid off workers, an understandable cause of employee ill will and poor morale; younger workers keep their jobs; and those who have retired early walk away with a full pension and cash sticking out of their pockets, provided the deal that they have been offered is sweet enough.

The ultimate satisfaction for these workers would be if they could walk into another job (which frequently happens) or if they could pursue something that they have always wanted to do.

A New Life

Take David Weichman, a display artist for twenty-three years in the same graphics firm. One day in 1976, when he was sixty-three years old, the firm's owner announced that he had had enough. He was dissolving the organization and moving to Florida. Weichman took the news as an opportunity. For his entire life he had wanted to paint the flights of fantasy that crossed his mind, the European countrysides whose colors and shapes he remembered since childhood, and the devastation of war that he had seen in his native Poland. When news of the firm's closing spread through the industry, Weichman was offered a number of jobs; he had become a master of his trade. But now he had the chance to pursue a lifelong dream and that is just what he did.

Today, he lives with his wife in a small apartment outside New York. One of the rooms serves as his studio. It is full of the painting he has done over the past five years—brilliantly colored canvases of fanciful creatures romping in make-believe landscapes, impressionistic portraits and Biblical scenes. This slight, wiry man with sharp eyes is proudest of his biggest work, a wrap-around mural painted for the walls of the children's reading room in a nearby library. Children lie on the room's sky-blue carpet and gaze at scores of fairy-tale beings suspended around and above them. As an artist, Weichman is being taken seriously. A Manhattan gallery now represents his work; he has shows several times a year; families commission him to do murals for their children's bedrooms. He has never been happier. "You can't really look at me as an example of retirement," he insists, even though he is a wonderful example of what retirement should be all about. "I never had to go through all the mess that you hear retired people go through. I just took up something that I had always wanted to do. In a way, I unconsciously had been preparing for my retirement for years. When the moment came, I was ready."

Not everyone is as fortunate as David Weichman. But, while few people have the talent to become successful artists, everyone can prepare for retirement. It is wise to keep in mind that the state of being retired can potentially occupy a quarter of a century or a quarter of a lifetime, and that is a lot of time to be bored and depressed. Pension plans, insurance policies, individual retirement accounts and investments during one's younger and more lucrative years may make financial planning the easiest part of retirement.

People are not very good about preparing for retirement if the findings of the Louis Harris poll are any indication. Only 53 percent of those people sixty-five and over developed hobbies or other activities in preparation for retirement. Only eight percent took a course in retirement preparation; and only 64 percent had built up their savings over the years specifically for retirement. Those surveyed were most concerned about medical care. Eighty-nine percent of them said they had made the effort to have adequate medical coverage when they retired.

While good medical coverage is extremely important during your latter years, the best coverage comes from the benefits of years of exercise before and after retirement, as discussed in Chapter 5. Exercise to keep the cardiovascular system as young as possible, to keep joints flexible, muscles in shape and endurance up is really an inexpensive form of preventive medicine.

The most difficult part of retirement is the time. What does one do with all the days, the weeks, the months and the years with no job to fill them? You cannot read or watch TV all the time; you cannot fish or travel or constantly pursue those leisure activities that were formerly squeezed into weekends and two-week vacations. My father-in-law, a medical doctor, is currently dealing with the problem. At seventy-seven, he has just retired. Even though he plans to keep up his knowledge in his specialty, he knows the impetus to do so will disappear. While music, art and the origin of words and languages have long interested him, he cannot "practice" those; he can only continue to appreciate them and be curious about them.

Grandchildren have partially solved his dilemma by leading him to write children's stories, an avocation he began when his own children were small. His grandchildren now serve as the heroes and heroines of his writing, but the stories he has planned are for any child. Over the past year, he has become a student of children's literature. His appreciation of the difficulty of writing for children increases everytime he reads a story to a grandchild who does not greet it with instant fascination. Forethought has jolted this man into taking up a new discipline; love of his grandchildren is serving as the catalyst.

Many people are not so resourceful. I remember Jesse, a young looking seventy-year-old woman in Holyoke, a central Massachusetts mill town where I once worked as a newspaper reporter. I met Jesse in the crafts room of a senior-citizen center. Before her on a table was a figurine that she had made by filling a mold with plaster and baking it hard. She was removing some burrs with a piece of steel wool. Her hands were white with plaster of paris dust. Dozens of other figurines were jumbled up on shelves around the room. Jesse looked bored. I asked her if her figure was the first one she had made. "Lord, no; I've made about a dozen of them—statues, flowers, horses, dogs, whatever they've got, I've made. I could do it in my sleep, but it's the only thing I can do that's even slightly out of the ordinary. Let's face it, this is fill-up time here. These are projects that someone in some organization somewhere concocted for us old folk who have nothing else to do so we don't sit out in front of our houses and look dumb.

"There are a lot of sad sacks that come here, myself included. I get so bored I sometimes wish I would break a hip just because it would be something different for a change. If reincarnation really exists and I get the chance to come back as a person again, I would do everything I could to get good at something when I'm young that I can take up when I get old."

Like Jesse, too many retired people go to senior-citizen centers to fill up the years before they die. Others while away hours on park benches, at first chatting with fellow retirees but gradually finding themselves more and more alone as peers die off. Yet the world is not as closed to the elderly, even those who are not financially well off, as some people think. There is more to life than work, retirement and death, and the sooner the elderly as well as everyone else realize it, the better.

Look at the opportunities offered by Elderhostel. Martin Knowlton, a sixty-five-year-old eclectic who was most recently a professor of continuing education at the University of New Hampshire, but who was also an engineer, social activist and inveterate traveler, founded the Boston-based organization in 1975 after returning from a four-year-long backpacking trip through Europe. There, he stayed in hostels and pensions where he was struck not only by the informality and simplicity of the accommodations but also by the fact that Europeans, both young and old, travel as part of their continuing education. Once back, he discussed his observations with his colleague at the University of New Hampshire, David Bianco, who noted the empty dormitories and idle faculty during college vacations and in the summers. The idea of Elderhostel came to life—to offer summer courses to people over sixty to be taught on the largely empty college campuses both in this country and abroad. Ten years later, the idea is flourishing. During the summer of 1984, 80,000 elderly students attended programs on 760 campuses here and abroad. Each program lasts one week and usually includes three courses, ranging from marine biology to the history of the Pueblo Indians, all taught by college instructors. The cost is low, a maximum of $200 per week on campuses in the contiguous United States. The price includes tuition and room and board, with the understanding that one sleeps in college dormitories with shared bathroom facilities. Meals are served in college dining rooms, which usually means that the food is not very good. But the informality serves a very useful function: It forces the students together and encourages discussion and sharing of ideas and knowledge. Elderhostel students can theoretically spend several months of the summer traveling from campus to campus, taking different courses at each college. Costs in Hawaii and Alaska are slightly higher and package deals are arranged for abroad. You can get all the information by writing Elderhostel, 100 Boylston Street, Boston, MA 02116.

Volunteer programs, besides the traditional ones that museums, hospitals and nonprofit organizations depend on for much of their personnel, are springing up almost everywhere. They count on the knowledge, patience and general wisdom that the elderly have accumulated. Participants frequently become so valuable that they are offered a retainer. One program is called RSVP (Retired Senior Volunteers Program). Retired lawyers, doctors, teachers and musicians join it—any professional with a skill. They advise businesses, they consult and counsel, they teach and they perform. RSVP is not unique. There are many, many other such groups. The American Association of Retired Persons will provide information on a multitude of similar volunteer possibilities across the country. Write to the organization at 1909 K Street N.W., Washington, D.C. 20049.

Two other volunteer organizations, these specifically for retired business executives, are the International Executive Service Corporation, which places retired executives in small businesses abroad, and the National Executive Service Corps, for volunteers who want to work in domestic firms. So far, over 10,000 executives have found positions through these organizations. Other more exotic possibilities exist in the Peace Corps or VISTA, both on the lookout for elderly people with special talents.

It used to be that when someone said he was retiring, it meant that he had reached sixty-five. Now, mandatory retirement age is seventy, a time when an increasing number of people are still active, independent and resourceful. Fortunately, the pervasiveness of the law is beginning to lessen; federal employees, doctors and tenured college and university professors are exempt. Even so, the myth still persists that one loses the capacity to be productive at age sixty-five. Why does this supposedly happen to people at that age—why not at sixty or seventy? Sixty-five has been designated the end of useful life since 1935, when the Social Security Act was signed into law providing benefits to the retired. But choosing sixty-five as the time that benefits would begin was entirely political. In 1935, right after the Depression, there was 25 percent unemployment. The cry was to get rid of the older workers and let the younger workers have the jobs. At that time, half a century ago, sixty-five was truly old. Now, it is barely the beginning of old age. Yet sixty-five as the cut-off point that we hold to is persistent, just as is the myth that thirty marks the end of youth.

Signals come from all directions. Management sends you a brochure on your retirement benefits. Your neighbor asks you when you are taking that trip to Greece that you have always talked about. Or you look at yourself in the mirror in a new light, one that emphasizes the wrinkles and the gray hair rather than the fire that may still dance in your eyes. The elderly themselves are in part to blame. No one who is sixty-five and in good health should mope and be depressed about getting old. Such people should be out showing the world how young they are.

Examples of people over sixty-five, even seventy, who are in positions of power certainly do not stop with Ronald Reagan. People over eighty are still running marathons, painting magnificent art, chairing board meetings, helping disabled people and teaching youth. But most of this talent goes to waste. Both individuals and society should realize that people stay healthier mentally and physically for a much longer time than they did even ten years ago. If educators have awakened to the benefits to society of introducing mere three-year-old minds to the joys of learning in preschool programs, society and the elderly themselves must awaken to the realization that people closer to the farther end of life also have minds that are alive and inquisitive, with a long and productive future awaiting them.

Chapter 11

A Friendly Retreat

The people of Crestwood in southern New Jersey are the first to say that they live in unnatural circumstances. They will exclaim about the community's friendliness and security in the same breath that they will talk about those living there who go "buggy." They worry about the "hibernators," people who never leave their houses, while marveling at the activities that Crestwood offers. They maintain that they do not miss the presence of children, but they quickly show a visitor a huge storeroom full of cribs, playpens and strollers for visiting grandchildren. When they see an ambulance or first aid car with lights flashing in front of a home, rather than commiserate that another resident has been struck down, probably by stroke or heart attack, they proudly point out that the community has its own emergency vehicles. The awareness that death lurks close by does not lessen the spirit of this retirement village—built very much on the premise that the time left is short and people should get as much out of their lives as possible.

With a population of 15,000, Crestwood is the largest retirement community on the East Coast. It is just one of 2000-plus that dot Florida, California, Arizona, Texas and, more recently, New Jersey. The largest in the country is Sun City, Arizona, with 50,000 residents. Close to one million people live in these centers and sociologists, intrigued by the increasing numbers of people moving into them, point out that they offer a new way of life during the ever-lengthening span of years between retirement and old age, when incapacitation can bring

246

independent living to a halt. Until twenty years ago, this postretirement period was nonexistent or was compromised by ill health. Now, it can last fifteen to twenty-five years and offers opportunities that Americans are just beginning to explore.

New Jersey is the fifth most popular retirement state. Much of the building of communities for the retired is taking place in the south-central part of the state, long a poverty pocket whose towns hovered on the edge of bankruptcy. Ocean County, a wedged-shaped flatlands of scrub pine and oak, is already heavily populated with both retirement villages and older people. Beginning in the early 1960s developers moved in, attracted by low land prices and proximity to both New York and Philadelphia. They were generally welcomed by town governments, who knew that the people who would live in the developments were not going to cause social problems and would put tax money into dwindling coffers. Ocean County now has forty retirement communities, according to the Ocean County Planning Board, with more than 40,000 dwelling units. While these communities were being built, the county's population began to grow. Between 1970 and 1980, it increased by 66 percent and its sixty-five-plus population more than doubled. Now, over 25 percent of its population is elderly.

For those who are considering living in retirement communities, New Jersey's offer bargains unheard of in Florida or in Arizona. Average dwellings sell for $60,000. In other states, the price is $20,000 higher. Property taxes in Ocean County are incredibly low, generally under $3 per $100 valuation. The other appeal is proximity to offspring. Almost all the people who live in New Jersey's retirement communities moved from New York City, northern New Jersey, Trenton or Philadelphia. Many have children still living in these areas. If these people had chosen to move to Florida or other Sunbelt states, weekend visits would be impossible. One reason why people in retirement who have settled in faraway communities move back is to be closer to their children.

Two days after I met Naomi Rice, a resident of Crestwood for sixteen years, she took me to the cemetery, which she thinks is one of the most beautiful spots in the community. The cemetery is a huge rectangle carved out in an area of pine and oak trees. Only half the area has been developed, planted over in lush lawn grass indented by hundreds of headstones depressed an inch or so below the surface. Vases, some containing real flowers but most with bright plastic ones, stand on the markers. As Naomi drove me around the perimeter, she cheerfully commented on how bright and pretty and well-kept the place is. She pointed out with equal cheer where she and her husband, John, are going to be buried. I asked her why there are no upright gravestones. She replied that it would be too difficult to mow around them and that the cemetery would not look so nice if the grass were not evenly trimmed everywhere.

The community's manicured lawns are a symbol of its attempts at a perfection not seen in the real world. Even at summer's end, when most lawns look frayed and ragged, Crestwood's grass spreads with blinding greenness up to the foundations of homes, along streets and around its ten clubhouses. Flower beds with perfect borders interrupt the flow from time to time. The little trees that dot the grounds—indigenous scrub pines as well as white pines, cherry trees, dogwoods and cutleaf maples—are perfectly shaped, as if in a showcase rather than part of a natural beauty.

The community's 9000-plus homes complement the landscaping with a perfection of their own. The newer homes sparkle so much that they look like an artist's rendering of a planned community rather than like a place where people really live. Their short blacktop drives contrast startlingly with the green grass and the gray-white concrete walks leading to front doors. Trash bags, gardening tools, boots beside the back door and open garages are rarely seen.

The exteriors of the houses are aluminum siding that looks like clapboard. Buyers can choose blue-gray, light green, light yellow, white or beige. Houses in the older parts of the community are faced with brick, but even those twenty-year-old homes sparkle. So do the mobile homes in Pine Ridge, an area reserved for dwellings that Crestwood residents call "manufactured homes," even though there is no getting around the fact that they arrived on wheels which are now concealed in concrete foundations. There are about 1000 mobile homes in Pine Ridge. While residents of the brick and aluminum-sided houses may hint that those who live in Pine Ridge are not quite as well off as those in other parts of the community, the lawns and manicured trees and flower beds are just as dashing.

Like the houses and grounds, the residents of Crestwood have a sparkling similarity to one another. Their day-to-day dress has a certain uniformity. For both men and women, light-colored pants and shoes seem obligatory in warm weather or indoors. Women favor loose-fitting multicolored and flowered blouses, while men's shirts are likely to be of a solid color. The dress for the community's frequent dances is more elaborate. Men retain light shoes but switch to darker pants and white shirts, often decorated with a string tie. The women wear knee-length dresses or skirts fluffed out by numerous petticoats that bounce up and down to the faster music like cotton balls and sway and swirl in rhythmic continuity to the slower beats.

The women pay an enormous amount of attention to their hair. Two styles are favored in the community's six beauty parlors. The more popular is frizzed with tight tresses descending the back of the neck. The other is more sporty—a shaped cut that closely follows the head's contours. For a community where "activity" is the key word, it seemed strange to me that more women did not go for this crisper, get-up-and-go style.

Good cheer is another prerequisite. Hail-fellow-well-met, the ability to take as well as to give a light ribbing, gay laughter and general enthusiasm are all badges of Crestwood life—the social ambiance from one retirement community to the next is much the same. At a Kiwanis Club meeting I went to with John Rice, the enthusiasm and cheer reminded me of college fraternity life, with the president of the chapter inundated by friendly hisses or applause at virtually anything he said or did. Residents who do not show such outgoing traits are clearly worried about.

One afternoon, Naomi took me to a cancer-dressing meeting, the purpose of which mystified me until I saw what eight women in a basement room in Friendship Hall, one of the clubhouses, were doing. They were painstakingly stitching together diapers from old sheets, to be used by cancer patients in local hospitals. A great pile of diapers in a variety of colors lay on a table in the middle of the room awaiting final stitching. This was volunteer work at its most unsung. The women smiled and gossiped as they stitched. Miriam, the head of the group and a tall, slim, healthy-looking woman, explained in detail, punctuated by bright laughter, how the diapers were assembled. After we left, Naomi told me that Miriam's husband had died of cancer, as had the husbands of three other women in the group. Three of the women had cancer themselves.

To some extent the cheer is contagious, By the second day of my visit, I found myself as smiling and cheery as the residents I met. Part of this attitude must have to do with the proximity of death. Conversations frequently touch upon one resident or another who has been hospitalized or moved into a nursing home. There is an awareness here that time is limited. Most of what is going to happen in one's life has already occurred. The time for competing and excelling is past. Now is the time to do what you have always wanted to do. You see this attitude in the unhurried way the people move, a casualness that cannot be attributed to age alone; in their cordiality; and in the small, daily sacrifices they are willing to make for each other. There is a sense of rediscovering a quality of life— a basic caring for your neighbor—that has vanished from urban environments.

Another reason for the prevailing social attitude is selectivity. Prospective buyers ill-disposed toward basic optimism and cheer can certainly sense that they might be moving into the wrong neighborhood. "When you buy here, you don't just buy a house, you buy a way of life," Jill Roy, a resident for nine years, told me. "And if you can't make it here, you are ready to be planted."

Crestwood is by no means unique. Retirement communities everywhere in this country develop a similarity of spirit, dress and activities. Adherence to a status quo in each community has led to sharp criticism mixed with ridicule. "They're places you go to play golf and shuffleboard before you die," is a common reaction. While residents may look the same and carry themselves with a similar demeanor, these visible superficialities have little to do with what people really think or do. At Crestwood, Anthony J. Thompson dresses just like the other men and shows the same courtesy they do, but there he stops. He worked for General Electric for thirty years in "production." He had always wanted to work for a newspaper. When he moved to Crestwood, which had no newspaper, he saw his opportunity. Now Thompson is the editor of the monthly

Crestwood Village Sun, which usually runs to eighty pages and has become the voice of the community. Another man makes exquisite birdhouses which he sells at fairs up and down the East Coast. Bob Briand worked as a band leader and now leads a five-piece swing band that plays for Crestwood's many dances—but he is also a would-be architect. Though he has no formal training, he has built up a little business as a designer. Andy Dudas plays the ukelele with such expertise that he draws crowds throughout southern New Jersey. Jill Roy was a widow when she moved into a mobile home in Pine Ridge. A retired teacher, she now writes a weekly gossip column for the *Advance News,* a newspaper in nearby Lakehurst. She tells me that she avoids writing about "unhappy situations." "They just produce panic and that produces stress and stress makes people sick. So I stick to happy news." To think that life stops in retirement communities and is replaced by a purgatory of cheer and golf and club activities is to turn a blind eye toward a more durable side of humanity—the creative, dreamy side frustrated for years and finally let loose. As Frances Fitzgerald observed in her profile of Florida's Sun City Center in *The New Yorker,* retirement communities offer an extended, worry-free period of time for people to do what they have always wanted.

How and why Naomi Rice and her husband came to Crestwood is typical of its residents. For years they had lived in Trenton, forty miles away, in a house they had bought that was big enough for raising two sons. John had worked most of his professional life as a communications technician at McGuire Air Force Base. When their sons grew up and moved elsewhere to raise their own families, John and Naomi were left with a big empty house. "We almost sold the place and rented an apartment," John told me one day, shaking his head as if he might have been on the verge of madness to have considered renting. Now sixty-eight, he is tall, straight and lean, with elegantly swept back gray-black hair. His bearing is that of someone who has all the time in the world. He likes to deliberate over questions for long, silent seconds before producing what are often profound answers.

Relatives of Naomi lived near Crestwood and on a visit to them the couple stopped in to look over some of the models. They immediately liked what they saw and for $14,000 purchased a two-bedroom cooperative apartment in a one-level,

brick-faced duplex. When they moved to Crestwood after selling their home in Trenton for many times what they paid for
it, their financial situation had never been better, especially since
John continued to work until 1978. "Elderly people who have
rented all their lives are finding themselves in trouble," John
observed to me as we went together to one of Crestwood's
endless stream of activities and social functions. "They can't
move here or to any other retirement community and they can't
continue to pay their rent. The key to being able to live in a
place like this is to have another house to sell so you can have
enough capital to buy a smaller place and still have plenty left
over."

The houses are not, all things considered, expensive, and for
the money they are attractive. For $54,990 (1984 prices) you
can purchase the Wessex, the least expensive home. It is a
compact aluminum-sided dwelling with two bedrooms, living-
dining area, kitchen, one bathroom, utility room, patio with
sliding doors and attached garage. The master bedroom measures 11'6" × 14'1", which is not a bad size, and the living-
dining area is 12'1" × 22'9". The price includes a finished
bathroom and all kitchen appliances except a dishwasher.
Monthly maintenance fees average around $135, with another
$150 or so for electricity if you choose a monthly equal-pay-
ment plan. (All the homes are electric-heated.)

Prices begin climbing from the Wessex, through the Edge-
mont, the Fairfax, the Sherborne, and the Yardley (fourteen
models in all) to the Hallmark, the top-of-the line dwelling,
which goes for $89,990 with monthly maintenance charges of
around $213. Like all the homes, this one has two bedrooms,
but has such additional amenities as a separate dining room,
two full bathrooms, a foyer, a pantry, and central air-condi-
tioning. This model is not much in demand and not many have
been built. The most popular houses are the Lynnewood (a
cooperative apartment) at $74,490, and the Yardley at $76,990.
Both are higher-priced models, an indication that residents are
willing to pay a slight premium for their new homes.

When the Rices moved to Crestwood, Naomi had only recently quit her job as a museum curator's assistant at Princeton
University. A short, energetic woman who even now, at sev-
enty-one, finds it hard to sit still, she had nothing to do when
John left for work every morning except take care of her two

toy poodles. "I knew I would get fat as a cow," she told me during one of her frequent rapid-fire comments about Crestwood, "so I began decorating our home. One day Mike Kokes [Crestwood's principal developer] came over and saw what I had done. He offered me a job as a decorating consultant for the models he was showing customers. I have never had a moment of regret since then. You have to get involved if you live here. You can't become an island."

Residents of Crestwood, which its developers have dubbed Crestwood Our Town, proudly inform visitors that twenty years ago only pine trees and twenty-six houses stood where the community sprawls today. The place was a frontier town when the initial 500 units were completed in 1965 and retired couples, widows and a few widowers tentatively put their money down for cooperative apartments. All the apartments then were either in single-level duplexes or in four-unit buildings— "quads," the residents call them. They cost $7500. "You should have seen it," exclaims John Rice, who moved in three years later. "There were no paved roads. The only place to buy food was a little general store in Whiting. We didn't even have telephones."

"We were all pioneers," confirms Miroslav A. Kokes, whom most people call Mike. "The first winter we were open I plowed the roads and driveways myself and the first summer I cut the lawns." Kokes came to Whiting, the hamlet in Manchester Township where Crestwood is located, in 1964 to develop 120 acres that a friend had purchased. He had a retirement community in mind. The then-mayor of Manchester Township was all for the development and he told Kokes that it would put his town on the map. But the people who lived in the twenty-six homes in Whiting, the "pineys" immortalized by John McPhee in his 1967 classic *The Pine Barrens,* were apprehensive. Pickers of blueberries and harvesters of cranberries, they had lived all their lives among the almost million acres of sandy soil that makes up the barrens, an area that looks so much the same that, in undeveloped parts, a stranger can get lost in minutes. You can still see the untouched pinelands around the perimeters of Crestwood—a dense, undulating blanket of scruffy oaks and pines growing out of a sea of sand hidden by blueberry bushes. It stretches for miles in all directions, and fortunately, it will stay that way because of recent preservation legislation. But in the 1960s, the people of Whiting believed that their blueberry bushes and cranberry bogs were about to disappear forever under Kokes's bulldozers. Even Ocean County planners wanted to condemn the scheme lest it turn into a rural slum the way some other developments had.

Kokes did not come to Whiting without experience. He had already constructed a number of smaller developments in Jackson Township to the north, "build, service and good-bye developments," he says of them. Now he wanted to create something more meaningful to both himself and buyers. "I always had a good relationship with the elderly," he told me simply in his office at Crestwood. "I have cared about the people here and I think they appreciate it." His behavior in the community and his obvious attachment to it lead one to suspect that he came to Crestwood to nurture a dream instead of to build a development. "I will stay here as long as I am needed," he says.

He arrived in this country in 1949 from Czechoslavakia, a refugee from Communism. When he got off the boat in New York, all he had, he says, was "one wife and two children and we each had a shirt and two changes of underwear. A Catholic agency gave me twenty dollars on the docks, five dollars for each of us, and told me to pay it back when I could." Kokes's story of finding a place in mainstream America is similar to those of hundreds of thousands of other immigrants. Friends got him a job as an assistant to a contractor. He went to night school three times a week to learn English. Eventually he moved out of the city and began building on his own in New Jersey suburban towns. Now in his sixties, he is the king of Crestwood, though he assumes the role with an unassuming modesty.

Crestwood was initially advertised as a gracious country retreat for the retired, away from the dirt and hassle of urban life. When, after he had finished the first 500 units, Kokes announced that he was going to start on another 500, there was grumbling from the residents that he might never stop building, fears that Crestwood would turn into the very sort of urban environment that people had wanted to leave.

Mike Kokes usually gets what he wants and he does so in a gentlemanly way. "You know," he told me, "I always believe in negotiation. My wife taught me to negotiate. People always have problems; someone is always complaining. My wife is a very hardheaded woman. When she used to get mad at me, she sometimes wouldn't talk to me for three days. That's three days wasted. So I learned to talk, to negotiate. I find that that is the only way to operate."

He has the look of a law professor, not only in the way he sits and adjusts his spectacles from time to time but in his habit of glancing up in the air when considering the answer to a question. And when he does respond, morality seems to emanate from him. His brow is often furrowed with concern about how he can best serve the community. Though he does not live there (he lives in a town twenty minutes to the north), he spends fourteen hours a day at Crestwood in a series of meetings with managers and residents. As far as residents are concerned, at least the ones I sought out and others who made their opinions known to me, almost everyone feels that he is crucial. Talk to anyone at Crestwood and Mike Kokes's name is mentioned in the first three minutes of conversation.

"I always try to come up with new ideas to help the people," he tells me. One of the things he quickly realized after the first 500 units opened was that some lonely people were moving in. Perhaps because of Kokes's own background, many of the early buyers were immigrants, including a large contingent of Germans from northern New Jersey, Italians from Brooklyn and numbers of Irish and Scandinavians. Most of them had been skilled workers or employed in low-level administrative roles in production departments, in offices, in warehouses and in parts departments. There has been little change in professional background, although a scattering of lawyers, doctors and business executives have moved in. One resident informed me: "Plumbers, electricians, nurses and seamstresses are the most highly prized people we have. Intellectuals are not much in demand."

Kokes worries about how new residents will adapt. He wants to make them feel wanted. Initially, he asked older residents to introduce the newer ones to activities or to take them shopping. Now he even includes residents in the planning and growth of the community, making them feel an integral part of Crestwood. When he thought an arts and crafts club was needed, he asked a resident to found one. When a resident inquired about when construction would start on a clubhouse, Kokes sized up the man and appointed him head of the building committee. Such diplomacy also pays off in increased sales. Between 60 and 65 percent of the residents heard about Crestwood through word-of-mouth.

The community now encompasses 2000 acres and is still growing. The early residents' fears that they had invested in a rural retreat that was on its way to urban blight have faded, and Kokes has won awards for the assistance he offers potential buyers. According to his marketing manager, David S. Wolff, "You get on the Garden State Parkway and pass all those little towns that are full of little houses that people bought years ago for forty thousand dollars and are now all paid off. The people who live in those houses are the people that we are after. Between Boston and Philly, you have a lot of gray-haired folk. They're swimming in frozen assets in those houses. We show them all the techniques so they can get their money out of their house in the best way possible."

The marketing and salespeople use seminars and elaborate brochures to talk up attractive gimmicks like Crestwood's "no risk" program, which is directed toward people who are tempted to move to Crestwood but are held back by their fear that they will not be able to sell their present home. The community's salespeople tell them not to worry, just to choose the house in the community that they want and put down a deposit with the guarantee that if they cannot sell their house by the closing date on their new purchase, all the deposit money will be refunded.

After the second 500 units were built, Kokes assigned to the collection of 1000 homes the pedestrian label Village I. Then he started on Village II, and after that on Village III. Now he is finishing up Village VI. (Pine Ridge, the mobile-home community, and another community, Whiting Village at Crestwood, which was begun about the same time as Village VI, make a total of eight villages.) Kokes also put up two shopping centers at either end of the community, both of which he owns and leases out space in. The larger shopping center, which dominates the clutter of ramshackle houses that used to make up the hamlet of Whiting, supports a huge A&P, four restaurants, a health-food store, men's clothing store, gift shop, pharmacy and various lawyers', doctors' and insurance agents' offices. So comprehensive is it that Crestwood residents complain that younger people use it, some coming from Toms River, ten miles down Route 530.

The smaller center, called The Marketplace by the residents, has fewer stores and offices but is no less appropriate to the needs of the people of Crestwood. Kokes built it in 1974. Interest rates on construction loans were then 13 percent, higher than Kokes could afford. He negotiated with residents, telling them that if they would buy shares in the company specifically to raise capital for construction, he would pay them an interest rate of 10 percent. Ten percent in those days was unheard of. The residents bought shares and enough capital was raised. But Kokes could not do that again. Most of the people at Crestwood are frugal; they like to put money away. New Jersey banks have realized that. Since the shopping center went in, eight banks have opened branches in the community. One effect of Kokes's comprehensive marketing technique is that people who move there have cash from the sale of their old house. The competition between banks that offer gifts and cash rebates for opening savings accounts is a sure sign that they smell money. The residents are proud of their banks, quickly citing the number as evidence that the elderly are not necessarily poor.

Money and independence are close bedfellows at Crestwood. Residents feel that they have challenged and bested the myth that the elderly are a poverty-stricken and abject lot. They have scrimped and saved, just as Reaganomics dictates. And what they can show for their efforts is there for everyone to see. Most important, they maintain, is that they did it themselves. And in their small world, this is true. If money is needed for an activity, residents raise it themselves. Village I residents formed their own maintenance company. Anthony Thompson began the newspaper. President Reagan epitomizes the attitude that getting the job done yourself is the best way. And, residents vehemently believe, he cannot be blamed for the threat to social security in 1982; that was Congress's fault, it wanted the cutbacks. Besides, the feeling goes, social security should not be considered a source of income; it is merely an insurance policy.

The residents say nothing about the fact that Kokes built their homes, the banks and the shopping centers. They do not mention that he installed his own water and sewer lines or founded a maintenance company to cut lawns, plant flowers, plow snow, collect garbage and make repairs to the exteriors of the co-ops. Kokes also built three medical centers and he formed his own cable television company to serve the community. In the next phase of development, he plans to erect another mobile-home village; another "stick-built" village as he refers to dwellings that are constructed at their sites rather than prefabricated; and eventually a life-care center for residents who need constant medical supervision and meals served to them.

"Everybody complains that Mike Kokes owns everything around here," he exclaims. "I had to in order to attract people. But I also have to be very careful not to overdo." Now, as the first residents enter their eighties, there is a need for a nursing home. Kokes was sorely tempted to build one but decided against it. "This is an area that we really know nothing about. We are real-estate people. Nursing homes are a medical matter and there are a lot of outfits with expertise in the field," he told me. So for the first time ever, Kokes bowed out of a project intrinsic to the development of Crestwood as a complete retirement community. Instead, he sold five acres to a specialist in the total-health-care business. Though the home will undoubtedly benefit residents of Crestwood, it both marks the maturing of the community and suggests that it has grown too large for Kokes's family enterprise to handle alone. (Kokes is president of Crestwood Village, Inc. His two sons, Jan and Jerry, are vice presidents.) Another family is also a principal.

The administration of each village is under Mike Kokes's influence. A series of Kokes-conceived bylaws include stipulations against laundry hanging on outdoor lines, visible TV antennas, trash placed outside of homes, cars parked in the streets, driving faster than twenty miles per hour and, as in most retirement communities, residents under fifty-five and resident children under eighteen years old. The crucial bylaw, though, is that each village's affairs are determined by a board of seven trustees who, with few exceptions, live in the village and are elected for two-year terms by its residents. Kokes came up with the number seven. It had to be odd so that ties could be broken. A smaller number would have meant too much work for each trustee; a larger number would have led to factions and strife. Kokes is very proud that residents have sought him out over the years to run for office. He believes the invitations are as great a sign of his success as his actual building of the community. He has been on every village's board at one time or another and he is now a trustee of Village VI, the newest. In Village I, he proudly tells me, he received the second-highest number of votes. In Village III, he received the highest.

The villages at Crestwood are not really villages. They are clusters of homes (co-ops in Village I through IV and fee-simple dwellings in the other villages) that were built at more or less the same time. They have no separate identities or personalities save for Pine Ridge—and Village I, whose abundance of elderly residents gives it a reputation as a seat of wisdom; most people there are in their seventies. Insofar as any distinction can be made between villages, it lies in the actions of the boards of trustees and the activities in clubhouses. Village I is often identified, for example, as the village whose trustees moved to initiate its own maintenance service rather than to rely on Zimko, the company set up by Kokes. In a spirit of independence, the residents voted to assess themselves $100 per home for the construction of a maintenance building and the purchase of equipment. Monthly fees have thereby been reduced, and people in other villages look up to these original settlers with a mix of admiration and envy.

Village II and III stand out because their boards decided to fire Zimko and bring in another maintenance firm. This decision followed complaints that insulation underneath the floors of homes had been installed backward. A class-action lawsuit and bad feeling resulted. The suit was settled when Kokes agreed to replace the insulation. But the bad feelings remained, alleviated to some degree by the hiring of a new maintenance firm at cheaper prices.

Activities are the linchpins of happy retirement-community living. Flip through the pages of the *Crestwood Village Sun* and look at the offerings residents can pursue. On Mondays, those in Village V can meet at Hilltop, the village's clubhouse, for aerobics classes, chess games, quilting and bocce—an outdoor game in which players toss steel balls with the object of coming as close as possible to a lead ball; on Tuesdays, for arts and crafts, beaded-flowers classes, camera club, cards and games, men's exercise, travel club and line dancing; on Wednesdays, for aerobics, ceramics, coin and stamp collecting, women's exercise, singing and golf (there is only one nine-hole course in the community but residents often play on nearby public courses); on Thursdays, line dancing in the afternoons and social dancing in the evening. Each village has similar offerings. And then there are dozens of intervillage activities, clubs and trips, such as a twelve-day bus tour through the South and a winter's cruise from Los Angeles to Port Everglades via the Panama Canal.

You can dance every night of the week somewhere in the community, one member of Village V told me with glee. "We have square dancing, round dancing, and line dancing," he said. "Take your pick; and we don't shuffle around, we kick up our heels." Line dancing is the favorite because of the preponderance of women. A line of thirty women whirling and swirling in harmony along the length of one of the community's clubhouse auditoriums is a stirring sight.

There are also "special events" each month. Many of these are dances, concerts given by singing groups made up of community members, and bazaars where ceramics, quilts and jewelry are sold. One of the most popular is the monthly Resident's Club meeting which, as might be expected, is a meeting of all the residents of a village. I went to one in Village V with John Rice who, though not a resident of that village, likes to keep his eye on what is happening throughout the community. We arrived fifteen minutes early. The club's huge auditorium, with a vaulted ceiling supported by graceful laminated wooden arches, was swarming with gaily dressed residents milling about and chatting with neighbors as they munched cookies and cake and sipped coffee. Cookies, cake and coffee are obligatory at any Crestwood meeting. At a table with a round wire cage on it, people were selling numbered tickets for a dollar apiece. Each ticket had two parts; one was given to the purchaser, the other put in the cage. This was "50–50," another understood part of every Crestwood social activity. At the end of the evening, the money would be divided into three or four lots, the cage spun and tickets drawn for the lucky winners.

John introduced me to some of his friends, people dressed more informally than he. John rarely goes anywhere without coat and tie, a dress that many men from Village I have adopted to set them apart from their younger colleagues in the newer villages. The drift of conversation following introductions is predictable. Over and over, the number and range of activities

are recited for my benefit. The enthusiasm is electric. A former Grumman Aerospace engineer, who moved to Crestwood
five years ago, began telling me about bowling—the clubs, the
events, the competition and so on. A man who used to work
for an adhesive manufacturer in northern New Jersey joined
in with accounts of the impressive arts and crafts produced by
residents. Some of them were to be sold over the coming
weekend at one of the many bazaars. All the conversations invariably end with indignant comments on the way the outside
world looks upon retirement communities, this community in
particular, as places to die. As one happy two-year resident said
to me, "Some people think that this must be like living in a
graveyard. But I think it's like dying and going to heaven."

The meeting, started off by the pledge of allegiance to the
flag, which is how Crestwood meetings always begin, was far
from the New England town meeting I had envisioned. It was
instead a lengthy series of reports and announcements by the
heads of clubs. Controversy and discussion are evidently not
part of these monthly gatherings. I got the impression from
the reports that the activities whirl on year after year, interrupted only by pleas for members to pay dues, pleas for more
residents to join clubs and proud announcements of club accomplishments. The only wrangling that took place during this
meeting concerned the redecoration of the auditorium. One
of the plans to be voted on at a later time called for flower
boxes to be placed under the clubhouse's windows. As Charles
Smythe, the president of the trustees, described the plan, a
woman jumped up and grabbed the microphone to protest that
the plan had never been approved by the Resident's Club. A
stunned silence followed. Smythe stared at her as if she had
struck him. But he retained his composure and pried the microphone from her hands and spoke into it in a hurt but firm
voice. "I would never, *never* do anything that the Resident's Club
had not approved; never!" The woman looked at him with
mouth wide open in surprise. Tears began to course down her
cheeks. She hung her head and slunk back to her seat. The
silent audience stared at her. Then murmurs rippled through
the auditorium while another report was read. Within moments, equilibrium was regained. It was as if the uncharacter-
istic event had never occurred or, if it had, it was just as well
to ignore it.

There was no ignoring the Ocean County Swells, a barber-shop quartet brought in for entertainment. To wild applause, the singers crooned such pointed lyrics as, "Life is really what you make it/Stand up and show that you can take it." Another went: "Down our way/You know everyone and they know you." But the residents saved their greatest applause for a joke told by the lead singer. Clara and Clarence, it went, lived in a nursing home. They decided to get married. The news excited the women residents and gave them all sorts of nice fodder for their gossip. After the wedding, the couple went off on a honeymoon for a week. When they returned, the nursing home was abuzz. "Well, Clara," the women exclaimed, "what was it like?"

"Oh, it was wonderful," Clara replied. "Clarence and I had a just wonderful time."

"No, Clara, you know what we mean. What was *it* like?"

"Oh, *that*. Well, we did it almost every night."

"Almost every night?" the women gasped.

"Yes, we almost did it on Monday night, and we almost did it on Tuesday night, almost on Wednesday, almost on Thursday . . ."

The audience loved it. They laughed, they applauded, they howled with delight in recognition of a plight that they either have experienced or feared that they would experience.

There are those in the community who do not attend such meetings or join in the activities. Instead, they hibernate in their little homes. Loneliness is one of the community's greatest problems. Alcoholism is another. Drug addiction is still another, though it must be separately categorized because it often occurs when doctors prescribe different medications.

A story circulates about a woman who moved into the community several years ago and still has not unpacked. Her home is crammed with cartons and she makes her way from room to room along narrow passageways. The neighbors rarely see her. When someone comes to her door to ask how she is, she replies that she is busy and shuts the door. And then there are the people who go "buggy," perhaps out of sheer loneliness or perhaps because of the paranoia that is characteristic of the early stages of Alzheimer's disease. They constantly call on their neighbors, sometimes to report that they have been burglarized, sometimes to accuse another neighbor of robbing them. There has been only one case of burglary in the community and the thief, who was not a resident, was caught.

People who have unwillingly moved into retirement communities have the worst adjustment problems. In most such cases, they are put there by their children who no longer want to take care of them. Voluntary residents of Crestwood express outrage at such treatment and look upon the victims with great pity, knowing that their families, the link to the greater world, have abandoned them. Most glaring of the stories about these people is the one about a woman in a neighboring retirement community who died in her house and was not found for several days.

While expressions of compassion greet accounts of loneliness, residents also adopt the stony-hard view that some of the people in these situations are there by their own making. Get Naomi Rice on the subject of people not benefiting from all that Crestwood offers and words pour out of her mouth. "It really bugs me when I hear people who live here say that this is a place to die in. This is a place to live in. The kids are gone; we still have some good health left. There are hundreds of things to do and hundreds of people to do them with. People are not going to ring everyone's doorbell. It's up to the new residents to get involved."

But to the embarrassment of all, some people do become islands. When Naomi Rice heard the story of the woman who lived in the houseful of boxes, she lay awake thinking about her. "At three in the morning, what I was going to do about this kind of thing suddenly hit me." The next day she went to Kokes and talked over her idea—the building of an entire center devoted to reaching out to residents of the community who needed help. The program would provide everything free of charge, from crutches and wheelchairs to counseling services. There would be a meals-on-wheels program (for a slight charge) and an employment service. Kokes liked the idea and provided an office and supplies. Naomi set up shop and called her innovation C.A.R.E.S. (Crestwood Assistance Referral and Employment Service).

Six years later, in 1980, C.A.R.E.S. had outgrown its office and Naomi went back to Kokes with plans for a larger program. Kokes donated $30,000 worth of land for a new building. But it was up to the organization to raise the money for the structure. It was to be comprehensive with space for all the equipment necessary for the disabled, as well as offices, counseling rooms and meeting rooms. By this time, John Rice had retired, and he and Naomi set about raising the money from residents and from the local business community. They found the task easier than they had anticipated. Within a year and a half, they had raised a quarter of a million dollars. Naomi is now the C.A.R.E.S. executive director and John its president. She oversees a volunteer force of 350 residents who spend much of each day in the villages with those who need help. They transport the disabled to the shopping centers; they deliver meals; they visit the lonely and they counsel those who want to talk about their problems.

So far as I am aware, no other retirement community on the East Coast offers such a service. C.A.R.E.S. has put Crestwood in an enviable position. Naomi finds herself receiving representatives from other retirement communities who want to follow her lead. "We couldn't have done this if everyone had come here merely to die," she told me in her office as one of her toy poodles paced back and forth on her desk. "C.A.R.E.S. exemplifies what this community is all about. We got C.A.R.E.S. going because the people here hope that this can be an even better place than it already is. And we did it ourselves. No one gave us the money to put up this building. These, to me, are signs of life and health."

Crestwood and other planned retirement communities are not for everyone, no matter how outgoing they may be. A truly independent person might find it difficult to avoid the obvious pressures to join, join, join that seem endemic. But these communities are a remarkable phenomenon, a battering ram smashing down the gates that have imprisoned the elderly for decades. Visit one and you can suddenly see aging held in check or at least avoided for several additional years. At last, those people who have planned for later years have a choice. They can live in youth-oriented everyday society or they can seek refuge on islands such as Crestwood, where they can hold their heads high and scorn the baleful eye of the outside world.

Another Way of Living

Retirement Communities

There are about 2500 private retirement communities scattered about the country and the number is rapidly increasing. Almost one million people live in them. The majority of the communities are in the Sunbelt states from Florida to California, though they are also springing up in New Jersey and Pennsylvania and close to urban centers. Some 90 percent of them have a population of under 500. The largest is Sun City Center with 50,000 people.

Most communities have a minimum age requirement of fifty-five and do not permit children under eighteen years of age to reside in them. The cost of a house, cooperative apartment or condominium varies enormously, roughly from $40,000 to $250,000. Prices in mobile-home communities are far less, generally ranging from $20,000 to $30,000. The least expensive housing is in New Jersey and Pennsylvania, the most expensive in Florida and California.

In selecting a community, you have to keep in mind that you will be buying a way of life, not just a place to live. You should, of course, visit a lot of communities. Pay attention to the type of people living in each one, the most popular activities and the possible social pressures. You should question residents. Ask them about the housing. Are the dwellings well built? Are the grounds decently maintained? Are there any hidden costs? Is management reliable? How much is a home likely to appreciate over a given number of years?

If you are interested in a long-term commitment, check on continuing care facilities that offer medical supervision and eventual nursing capabilities. If a retirement community that you are interested in has this arrangement, check on the cost as well as on the waiting period for the nursing home. Some charge a hefty entrance fee, and monthly costs might be too high for some budgets. If a community does not have continuing care, check on the availability of local nursing homes.

The literature on retirement communities is still meager, but three books have recently been published. They are:

Changing Properties of Retirement Communities, by Robert W. Marans, published by the Institute of Gerontology at the University of Michigan, 1984.

Continuing Care Retirement Communities, published jointly by the American Association of Homes for the Aging and the American Association of Retired Persons, 1984.

Continuing Care Retirement Communities: An Empirical, Financial and Legal Analysis, published by the Wharton School at the University of Pennsylvania by Richard D. Irwin, Inc., 1984.

You can get further information by contacting:

The American Association of Homes for the Aging, 1050 17th Street N.W., Washington, D.C. 20036.

The American Association of Retired Persons, 1909 K Street N.W., Washington, D.C. 20049.

The National Council on the Aging, 600 Maryland Avenue S.W., West Wing 100, Washington, D.C. 20024.

Shared Living

A variation on a retirement community, "shared living" is an arrangement in which a group of unrelated people, often no more than five and not necessarily all elderly, live in a house and share the kitchen, dining room and living room. Most bedrooms are single with private bath. Residents are responsible for cooking joint meals and for cleaning. Most of these arrangements occur in urban areas and they are restricted to people who are healthy and independent. For single elderly people, they offer an environment easier to manage than one's own house and with less social pressure than in a retirement community. Many of them are limited to five residents because of zoning regulations that permit no more than five unrelated persons to live in a single-family house. Another advantage is that not all of them are age-segregated.

Most shared-living arrangements are under the auspices of social service agencies, churches and community groups. Personnel from these organizations maintain the buildings, screen applicants, help new residents adjust and handle the unpleasant task of informing established residents who have become ill that they must move into a total-care facility such as a nursing home. Shared living is very inexpensive compared to a nursing home and, of course, does not involve the financial commitment of purchasing a dwelling as in a retirement community. Monthly fees average around $200.

For further information, write:

The American Association of Retired Persons, 1909 K Street N.W., Washington, D.C. 20049.

Shared Housing Resource Center, 6344 Greene Street, Philadelphia, Pa.19144.

Chapter 12

Resurgence of the Elderly

*I*t is fair to say that this is the most exciting time to be growing old that the world has ever witnessed. While those who are over seventy-five will probably not benefit from the tremendous surge in knowledge about the aging process, those in their forties and fifties are likely to. The enormous increase in the over-fifty-five population is, at the same time, having a marked effect on the way this society views the elderly and those growing old. Being old is increasingly more a state of mind than a biological marker. Those over sixty-five are no longer so readily looked down upon for being elderly unless they fulfill the stereotypical image—frail, retiring, forgetful and in poor health. These misfortunes occur to fewer and fewer people in their sixties and seventies and are increasingly becoming the burden of the so called "old old," those over eighty-five.

For those younger and in good physical and mental health, something profound is occurring. They are being welcomed back into society, a change from the more youth-oriented 1960s and '70s during which they were pushed into obscurity. Given their growing numbers, it is understandable that politicians are listening to them. The advertising industry is also realizing that they are not only consumers but that they can sell products. No longer are the elderly ridiculed on television commercials. Gray-haired actors and actors with hair dyed gray now advertise hamburgers, coffee makers, airlines and Caribbean islands. Only five years ago, these jobs were restricted to much younger people who were talking primarily to their contemporaries.

The messages that the elderly are sending via the advertising industry are primarily for a certain segment of the burgeoning older population—the well, the healthy, the active and the financially stable. After abandoning and ignoring its old people for decades, American enterprise is now telling them, "You're okay, provided that you can still consume." That, incidentally, is similar to the message that the elderly receive from their offspring: "We love you but don't get sick and be a burden to us." The other elderly, the poverty-stricken, the disabled and the lonely are just as ignored as they ever were.

How many of these "unacceptable" elderly there are is uncertain, but their numbers are increasing. The elderly are not as badly off as some would believe. They certainly have more money than they did twenty years ago. The median income today for those over sixty-five is $12,500 per year. Almost 75 percent of these people own their homes. Their living expenses are lower because they no longer have to support children; they also consume, and thus buy, less food. They are also apt to participate in a sprawling underground economy that uses skills honed during their younger years and pays in cash. Thousands of retired consultants, teachers, technicians and craftsmen keep right on consulting, teaching, repairing and creating. How much money they make is unknown, much to the frustration of the Internal Revenue Service. A seventy-nine-year-old former building superintendent turned house painter told me that he had not even touched the substantial sum of social security benefits that he had accumulated since his retirement at sixty-five. The monthly checks went right into a money-market account that his son had set up for him to draw upon when he got too old to paint. But he did not foresee this day. Working on his own in a neighborhood of New York City, he was able to underbid younger painters for jobs and was so popular as a result that he was booked, as he says, "until I paint myself into the grave."

Yet tens of thousands of older Americans still live in poverty. One out of seven are below the poverty line of $5000 per year, a big improvement since 1970 when one quarter of those over sixty-five hovered in poverty. About half these poor elderly live in large cities, the other half in towns and rural areas. In towns, at least you know your neighbors, and the chances are that someone will look in on you to make sure that you are all right. And in the country, expenses are relatively low. But $5000 in a large city does not go far—about half for rent and half for food. Blacks fare the worst, especially single or widowed black women; just under 43 percent live in poverty. The figure for black men is almost 32 percent. Elderly single white women are considerably better off: 17 percent of the country's 16.4 million are under the poverty line. Of all the possible groups, white males are the best off. Only just over eight percent of their numbers live in poverty.

While the present administration tells us that social security is safe through the turn of the century, at least through 1988 if President Reagan holds to his campaign promises, the future of medicare is not so secure. Medicare is essential, paying about 45 percent of medical costs for the elderly. If legislation had not been approved early in 1983 that limited the amount hospitals could be reimbursed for medical care, the system would have been bankrupt by 1988. Previously, hospitals could charge whatever they wanted and the government would pay, an incredible flaw in the initial design of medicare. With the new legislation in place, hospitals are being forced to be more cost-conscious. Their reward is that, if they can provide a specific service for under what the government will reimburse, they will be paid the full amount and can keep the difference. By the end of 1984, the change was beginning to pay off. The annual increase in hospital costs had declined five percent.

Even though the new legislation helps, it only delays medicare's eventual financial problems. Projections show that by the year 2000 the trust fund that pays medicare's bills will be $150 billion in debt. Further surgery is inevitable and will initially come in a reduction of the amount doctors are reimbursed for treating the elderly. But while the system is trying to avoid bankruptcy, it is also beginning to feel a strain that it will not be able to survive unless some radical changes are made. As the population gets older, chronic diseases like Alzheimer's, diabetes, kidney failure and stroke will become more common. Heart disease, cerebrovascular disease and cancer are the most frequent chronic conditions and the three leading causes of death among the elderly. In many instances, these diseases do not require prolonged hospitalization, the very cost that medicare was designed to cover. Instead, victims are either cared for at home by custodians or they are moved to nursing homes, neither of which medicare will pay for except in limited situations. The financial burden on individuals and families is enormous, often sending them into poverty.

The question of how to handle this burden is one of the most awkward that those interested in improving the nation's health-care system have ever faced. Planners and politicians have consequently ignored the problem. But the increasing numbers of the elderly are soon going to force an end to this attitude. Just look at the growing political clout of the eighty-five-year-plus age group, the fastest growing in the country. In 1900, there were a mere 123,000. Now, there are about 2.5 million. By 2050, there will be 16 million people age eighty-five or older, five percent of the population. And there are plenty of people coming along who will undoubtedly enter the ranks of the eighty-five-plus group. Almost 8 million people are now between seventy-five and eighty-four years old, just 10 times more than there were in 1900. By 2050, the Census Bureau predicts that there will be over 20 million, almost seven percent of the population.

For the first time ever, it is becoming more commonplace for a middle-aged person to have parents and grandparents to watch over while at the same time seeing some signs of aging creeping up in her- or himself. In the 1940s, someone in his or her mid-forties would remember grandparents only from the dreaminess of childhood memory. And their parents would be likely to die within the next few years. Now, and increasingly so in the future, families in which the majority of members are middle-aged or older will be the norm.

Chronic diseases affect over 50 percent of those over seventy-five years old and force 22 percent to alter their lives to some extent. By 2000, over 50 percent of the people in the seventy-five-and older bracket will have to change their lives because of compromises forced upon them by chronic disease. Already 35 percent of those eighty-five and older need some kind of assistance, whether it be help in walking, bathing or eating. Over a million live in nursing homes. With their numbers increasing rapidly each decade, there will be two million by the year 2000 and a whopping five-and-one-half million by

2050. If Census Bureau projections are correct, the nursing-home business will be a big business. While medicare reimbursed the elderly under $500 million in 1981 for nursing-home costs, individuals, pensions and private health insurers paid almost $10 billion to nursing homes.

Health policy planners who hope that the problem of escalating medical costs for the elderly will just go away like to cite a paper published in 1980 in *The New England Journal of Medicine* by James F. Fries, a gerontologist at the Stanford University Medical Center. It questions whether the elderly of the future will really need the kind of medical care that they are now receiving. One of Fries's theses, the one that is most attractive to ax-wielding health-care policy planners, is that medical technology has largely eliminated the acute diseases that killed so many people before the middle of this century. We do not worry much today about dying from infectious diseases like smallpox, diphtheria, rheumatic fever, polio and tuberculosis. But in the early years of this century, death from these diseases and many others were common.

Since infectious diseases can now be controlled, says Fries, chronic diseases are the main killers of the elderly. These diseases have always been present, of course, but until the infectious ones could be alleviated or cured, the chronic ones were not so evident. The acute infectious diseases killed us first.

Not so much is known about the chronic diseases as about the infectious ones. The linchpin of Fries's argument is that if we take care of ourselves, we can put off the onset of many of them. Eventually, then, we will die of old age. Fries calls upon what he refers to as the "plasticity of aging"—the ability to influence our cardiovascular system, for example, by exercising, and he stresses the aptness of the trite adage, "Use it or lose it."

Maintaining ourselves to fend off chronic disease together with the reduction of death from acute illness (the exception being pneumonia, often the last stage of chronic disease) would act to compress morbidity, epitomized by the stereotypical sick and helpless old person, into the very last years of life when the body has so little reserve that it quickly succumbs to whatever attacks it. While Fries does not specifically suggest how chronic disease should be discouraged, his implications are clear. A use-it-or-lose-it ethic should be instilled in the population, an ethic of bodily and mental maintenance that will prevent chronic disease and allow the elderly to live a long and vigorous life until they arrive at death's doorstep, at which point death will take over quickly and efficiently and charge very little for the effort. So worn out will be the body that no amount of expensive medical technology and hospitalization will save it. Untold years of sickness and family suffering will be forgone, to say nothing of the dissolution of family finances.

The National Institute on Aging would like to see Fries's theories become reality. It even stated as much in its National Plan for Research on Aging, issued in 1982. The goal of gerontology was to promote "health and well-being by extending the vigorous and productive years of life." A few years ago, Dr. Gairdner Moment, a gerontologist at the National Institute's Gerontology Research Center, told me: "Gerontologists want people to live the best they can and then go *puff* at the end rather than into a nursing home." Most people want to do just this. They want to live long lives, but only if they can remain healthy until they die. Mental and/or physical incapacitation is more frightening than death itself.

While Fries's ideas are logical and possible, they are ahead of their time and, as a result, he has been soundly criticized by gerontologists who are dealing with the health problems of the elderly right now. Dr. Robert N. Butler, head of Mount Sinai School of Medicine's Department of Geriatrics and Adult Development, told me, "We have more disease and more disability in every decade of life. I think Fries is defining an aspiration that we all have, but we are not there yet."

Not yet. But the prospects have never been brighter to live to a much greater age than we now do and suddenly die, go "puff," rather than to suffer a lingering death. Though it is difficult to find a person over seventy who does not suffer from one physical or mental ill or another, a thought that makes us want to shrink away from the inevitable process of aging, there is a new way to think about aging. The most exciting finding that has come out of recent gerontological research is that we exert far more control over our own aging than we ever imagined we could, even five years ago. While heart disease may be the country's leading killer of the aged, diet and exercise can make the difference between living and dying. And while scientists have not discovered why certain people get Alzheimer's disease, funding for research into its cause and management has increased from $500,000 per year in the 1970s to over $37 million today.

It may turn out that preventive measures *are* the most important key to ameliorating the effects of old age. Most of gerontological research is still in the exploratory years. Though scientists have dissected, analyzed and measured the human body and all its parts and all its functions for years, they never learned much about the reasons why it aged. Now, gerontologists are going back for a fresh look. They are science-fiction astronauts revisiting a planet whose first explorers never looked for its most valuable treasure—the key to its mortality. Whatever they find, and it will not be just one key that fits a hole marked "on-off," not too many more years will go by before humankind begins to benefit from knowledge about the biochemical intricacies of aging. That knowledge, together with an increased awareness of how we can slow the aging process by strengthening ourselves, should result in our living far beyond our present years.

Glossary

Acetylcholine—A neurotransmitter important for memory and muscular control. The symptoms of Alzheimer's disease are closely tied to diminishing levels of this substance.

Adrenal glands—Perched on top of each kidney, the adrenals are hormone factories, manufacturing over 50 hormones, including all the steroids.

Adrenaline—See epinephrine.

Adrenocorticotropic hormone (ACTH)—A hormone secreted by the pituitary gland during times of stress which travels to the adrenal glands to alert them to secrete other hormones that will prepare the body for an emergency.

Aerobic exercise—Exercise that promotes cardiovascular fitness by sending a continuous and large flow of blood through the heart and muscles. Swimming, jogging and bicycling are examples of aerobic exercises. Tennis and basketball are not because the body is not constantly being exerted.

Age spots—See lentigines.

Alzheimer's disease—A form of dementia in which mental functions, beginning with the ability to remember recent events, deteriorate over a course of years due to the decline of levels of the neurotransmitter acetylcholine. Eventually, there is a complete loss of memory and awareness; loss of muscular control, including incontinence; and loss of the ability to speak and to swallow. An estimated two million people in this country have the disease.

Amyloid—A fatty waste product that makes up the senile plaques of Alzheimer's disease victims. Some researchers theorize that it may be the cause of the disease. Amyloid also collects in the heart, kidneys and other organs and may be a cause of some aspects of aging.

Androgens—Male sex hormones.

Antioxidant—See free radical scavenger.

Arteriosclerosis—An arterial disease in which artery walls thicken. See atherosclerosis.

Artery—A blood vessel that carries blood from the heart to different parts of the body.

Arthritis—A catchall term, like rheumatism, that refers to aches and pains in the joints. Whereas arthritis affects only the joints, rheumatism affects tendons and muscles as well as the joints. Osteoarthritis is the most common kind of arthritis. Virtually everyone gets it to some degree as he or she gets older. It begins with pitting and cracking of the cartilage that serves as a cushion between joints. The eventual result is that the bones of the joint grind against each other. In their attempt to repair the damage, bones grow spurs and knobs which make movement painful. Joints that bear weight are most commonly afflicted but fingers are often affected also. Rheumatoid arthritis, which can be more serious than osteoarthritis, is not a disease of the elderly, but an elderly person with it may develop extremely painful symptoms. It is thought to be an autoimmune disease.

Atherosclerosis—A specific kind of arteriosclerosis, though the two terms are often used interchangeably, in which the thickening of an artery is due to the accumulation of plaque (see atherosclerotic plaque) on its inner wall, thus reducing its diameter and impeding the flow of blood.

Atherosclerotic plaque—A deposit consisting of fat, cholesterol, calcium and red blood cells that accumulates on the inner walls of arteries, especially where the walls have been irritated.

Autoimmune disease—A disease that occurs when the body makes antibodies that attack itself. This happens more frequently among elderly women than among any other age group. Examples of the disease are rheumatoid arthritis and systemic lupus erythematosus.

Axon—An arm of a neuron through which neurotransmitters pass to other neurons.

Basal nucleus—The part of the brain just above the point where the spinal column joins the skull. Neurons that produce acetylcholine are in abundance here. The basal nucleus is of great interest to those researching Alzheimer's disease.

Blood pressure—The force that blood exerts against artery walls. Two measures of the pressure are commonly taken, the systolic and the diastolic. Systolic pressure (the upper number of the fraction) is the force with which blood flows through the arteries when the heart contracts. Diastolic pressure is the force when the heart is relaxed.

Calcium—A mineral crucial to bone growth. The loss of calcium is the main reason for the bone weakness typical of the elderly. This can be prevented by consuming the mineral in sufficient quantities and by exercising.

Calculus—See Tartar.

Cardiovascular disease—A broad term commonly applied to all diseases caused by changes in the heart and in blood vessels. Most such changes are caused by atherosclerosis, and the most common diseases that result are heart disease, hypertension and stroke.

Cataracts—A loss of transparency of the lens of the eye. The condition is remedied by removing the lens and correcting vision through special eyeglasses, contact lens or implantable lenses.

Cholesterol—A fatty substance found in animal tissue and essential as a building block of cell membranes, bile, nerve insulation and some sex hormones.

Chromosome—A threadlike structure made up of DNA. Each species carries a specific number of chromosome pairs in its somatic (body) cells and half that number in its sex cells. Humans have 23 pairs of chromosomes.

Climacteric, female—See menopause.

Climacteric, male—A psychological crisis that strikes usually in middle age when a man realizes that his youthful energy has passed, his responsibilities are enormous and his opportunities limited. The symptoms are loss of libido, depression and fatigue. Understanding the physical processes of aging is one way of extricating oneself from the dilemma.

Collagen—One of the principal ingredients of connective tissue, giving it body and elasticity. In childhood and youth, its fibers are in parallel alignment, the main reason why young skin is smooth, firm and bouncy. As we get older, collagen fibers cross-link—attach themselves to neighbors in a helter-skelter way—thus losing their tensile strength and elasticity.

Corticotropin-releasing factor (CRF)—A hormone secreted by the hypothalamus in times of stress. It travels to the pituitary gland.

Cortisol—One of the major stress hormones secreted by the adrenal glands. In elderly rats, its secretion never stops, thus keeping an animal in a constant state of stress.

Creutzfeldt-Jakob disease—A rare and fatal neurological disease caused by a slow virus.

Cushing's disease—A disease usually caused by a tumor in the pituitary gland which stimulates the gland to secrete hormones associated with stress so that the body is on constant alert. The condition often results in the development of osteoporosis, diabetes and atherosclerosis. Some researchers cite the disease as an example of what can happen to people under long-term stress.

Cytoplasm—The substance of a cell excluding its outer membrane and its nucleus.

Death hormone—See Decreasing consumption of oxygen hormone.

DECO—See Decreasing consumption of oxygen hormone.

Decreasing consumption of oxygen hormone—Commonly called DECO and sometimes death hormone. A hormone secreted by the pituitary gland beginning in early adulthood that blocks thyroxine, a hormone that governs metabolism. One theory maintains that life expectancy would be increased if the secretion of DECO were reduced.

Dehydroepiandrosterone (DHEA)—A hormone produced in the adrenal glands that may inhibit metabolism and thus indirectly encourage disease. DHEA levels diminish with age.

Dementia—A catchall term for a group of diseases affecting mental functioning.

Dental plaque—Sticky film on the teeth consisting of gum secretions and saliva in which bacteria breed.

Diabetes—A disease common in the elderly caused by an insufficient production of insulin. Insulin is the hormone that directs cells and tissues to store and release glucose, a form of sugar that the body uses for energy. Juvenile or Type I diabetes is usually diagnosed in childhood. The far more frequent Adult Onset or Type II diabetes is usually diagnosed after age thirty-five. It is the leading cause of blindness and can cause severe circulatory problems that can result in impotence in men and to a loss of sensation and the eventual need for amputation of the lower limbs. Though hereditary factors play a role in who gets it, diet is also an important cause. Overweight people are common victims.

DNA—Deoxyribonucleic acid, the chemical responsible for inheritance. It consists of molecules known as nucleotides. DNA's ability to duplicate itself is crucial not only for the perpetuation of a species but for good health. One of the major theories of aging is that DNA loses the ability of duplication and makes mistakes which result in cancer.

Dopamine—A neurotransmitter whose levels are greatly diminished in victims of Parkinson's disease. It is produced in the brain and in the adrenal glands. Hope for sufferers may lie in transplanting adrenal tissue to the brain.

Dowager's hump—A characteristic sign of osteoporosis (see osteoporosis) in which collapsed vertebrae force the upper back into a hump. So named because osteoporosis used to be a disease primarily of the wealthy class whose women were not apt to exercise.

Exercise is thought to help prevent the disease.

Dyspareunia—A condition occurring in many postmenopausal women in which the vagina shrinks in depth, its walls lose elasticity, and intercourse becomes painful because of dryness. Women who maintain sexual activity usually do not suffer the condition.

Epinephrine—A hormone also known as adrenaline. It is one of the major stress hormones, secreted by the adrenal glands to ready the body for an emergency.

Estrogen—One of the principal female sex hormones. Its sharp decline at menopause is thought to be at least partially responsible for the pronounced calcium loss in postmenopausal women who do not consume sufficient calcium and who do not exercise.

Face lift—A surgical procedure done primarily for cosmetic reasons whereby the skin and underlying tissues of the cheek are tightened to make wrinkles disappear. A similar procedure can be done to remove folds around the eyelids and around the throat.

Fibroblast—Connective tissue cell that forms collagen.

Fluoride—A trace element that is being used experimentally as a treatment for osteoporosis.

Free radical—Atoms and molecules that are formed during the course of metabolism. They have one unpaired electron and are thus attracted to the electrons of other molecules, a union that causes damage to both the molecule and the cell of which it is a part. One theory is that the damage done by free radicals causes aging. Damage may be exacerbated by ultraviolet light from the sun, diet, ozone, petrochemical pollution and the breakdown of fat. The greatest generator of free radicals, however, is the passage of oxygen through cells.

Free radical scavenger—A compound that has the ability to attack and destroy free radicals. Common ones are vitamins C and E, selenium and the food preservative BHT.

Gene—A sequence of DNA that codes for a specific protein. We have about six million genes in each of our cells. Each gene has a fixed location on a particular chromosome.

General adaptation syndrome—The name the pioneer stress researcher, Hans Selye, gave to stress in the 1930s.

Genome—All the genes on one half of a species' chromosomes and that contribute to a complete set at fertilization of an egg by a sperm.

Gingivitis—Inflammation of the gums.

Glaucoma—Gradual deterioration of the optic nerve because of high pressure in the eyeball. A major cause of blindness in the elderly.

Glia—A cell in the brain that acts to support the brain's mass.

Hardening of the arteries—See atherosclerosis.

Hayflick limit—The theory, named after its initiator, the gerontologist

Leonard Hayflick, that the life span of a population of cells is limited to around 50 divisions, at which point it dies out.

Heart attack—The death of heart muscle (myocardium) because of an obstruction in a coronary artery so that blood and oxygen cannot reach it. A heart attack is fatal or not depending upon how extensive the damage is to the heart muscles. Myocardial infarction, infarct and coronary are other names for heart attack.

Hela cells—A line of cancer cells taken from a cancer victim named Henrietta Lack that are widely used in laboratory research because they are immortal.

High blood pressure—See Hypertension.

High density lipoprotein (HDL)—A term that describes the way cholesterol is packaged by proteins. Some proteins remove cholesterol from blood and return it to the liver, where it was manufactured. High density lipoproteins are thought to do this and are thus thought to be beneficial.

Hippocampus—A little-known part of the brain thought to be responsible for short-term memory and learning.

Hypertension—Persistently high blood pressure. The cause is not clear but is related to stress, diet and kidney disease. It is one of the main causes of atherosclerosis and can result in heart attack and stroke.

Hypothalamus—A small mass of tissue in the center of the brain that is largely responsible for hormonal flow. Its secretions "tell" the pituitary gland which hormones to release. The hypothalamus is also the control center of our temperature, libido, hunger, pain and pleasure.

Hysterectomy—A surgical procedure to remove the uterus. The operation should have no effect on sexual desire or ability.

Kuru—A fatal neurological disease, once common among New Guinea tribesmen, and discovered to be caused by a virus transmitted by cannibalism. The damage to the brain has vague similarities to that seen in Alzheimer's disease.

Lecithin—A natural substance found in egg yolks, meat and fish that is indirectly a precursor of the neurotransmitter acetylcholine. Some health-food faddists believe that if you consume lecithin, available in health-food stores, you will improve your memory. There is no evidence for this, however.

Lentigines—Clusters of highly pigmented skin, usually appearing on the most sun-exposed areas of elderly people. Also called age spots or liver spots.

Libido—The desire to fulfill biological needs, prime among them being the sexual drive.

Lipid—Fatty substance found in the blood. Cholesterol and triglycerides are examples.

Lipofuscin—A yellow-brown pigment that accumulates in some cells as a waste product. Its buildup over the years may damage the ability of cells to function, though there is no evidence for this.

Liver spots—See Lentigines

Longitudinal study—Long-term scientific study that follows a group of subjects and assesses changes in them over time. Study samples are usually large. A longitudinal study is in contrast to a cross-sectional study, which gathers information at only one time.

Low density lipoprotein (LDL)—A term describing a form in which cholesterol is packaged by proteins. This is the "bad" form in which proteins carry cholesterol from the liver, where it is manufactured, to different parts of the body. For an unknown reason, the LDL combination results in atherosclerosis.

Lymphocytes—White blood cells crucial to the immune system. We have about one trillion of them. Half of them mature in the thymus gland and then circulate in the bloodstream or settle in the spleen, tonsils, appendix and lymph nodes to await foreign particles like viruses. The other half matures in the bone marrow before circulating in the bloodstream or settling in the lymphoid tissues.

Lysosome—Structure within a cell that is partially responsible for cellular digestion.

Major histocompatibility complex (MHC)—A cluster on the sixth chromosome in man that may influence immunity, life span and the generation of free radical scavengers.

Menopause—The cessation of menstruation, typically occurring during the mid-forties to the early fifties because of the halting of hormonal production by the ovaries. Most women are not affected physically or emotionally by menopause except, of course, that they are no longer fertile and they no longer menstruate. Some women experience, however, hot flashes and dull pains in the pelvic region. They also may be irritable. Some women may feel that menopause marks the end of their sexual attractiveness and activity, a fear with no physiological basis.

Neurofibrillary tangle—Filaments within neurons that become ensnarled, a characteristic of Alzheimer's disease and other neurological disorders.

Neuron—Nerve cell in the brain.

Neurotransmitter—A substance that carries chemical messages between brain cells. Acetylcholine and dopamine are two examples.

Norepinephrine—A neurotransmitter secreted by nerve endings during stress. Its levels in the body can be measured as a marker of stress.

Osteoporosis—Severe loss of calcium from the bones, leaving them porous and fragile. Fractures often occur in the vertebrae, hips and wrists of victims. Postmenopausal women are most at risk.

PABA—The full name is para-aminobenzoic acid, a free radical scavenger that is the main ingredient in good sunscreens.

Parkinson's disease—Caused by the decline of the neurotransmitter dopamine. Symptoms include tremors, a shuffling walk and a fixed stare. The condition can be partially alleviated with the drug L-dopa.

Peptic ulcer—A raw sore in the stomach lining or more commonly in the section of the intestine closest to the stomach. The ulcer is caused by digestive juices attacking the lining. Stress is thought to be an important cause, but the mechanisms are not known.

Periodontal disease—The gradual destruction of the gums, tissues and bones that hold the teeth in place. It is also known as gum disease.

Physically fit—The state you will be in if your heart beats at least 70 to 85 percent of capacity for twenty minutes three times a week. The benefits to the cardiovascular system are enormous. Recent research indicates that physical fitness can extend life expectancy.

Pituitary gland—A pebble-sized part of the brain that hangs from the hypothalamus on a stalk. It is the master gland of the endocrine system, responsible for the secretion of hormones that control growth, development, stress and sex.

Placebo—An inactive substance given to subjects in medical or psychological experiments. Placebos are used as a way of controlling experiments. Those given the placebo can be compared to those given an active substance to assess change.

Presbyopia—An eye condition typical of middle age characterized by increasing lack of ability of the lens to change shape. Farsightedness is the result.

Prion—Infectious agent that some researchers theorize could be the cause of Alzheimer's disease.

Prostate—A gland that encircles the urethra just below the bladder in males. It contains the milky fluid that helps transport sperm during its passage toward fertilizing an egg. The prostate begins swelling in most men during middle age (see Prostatitis).

Prostatitis—The condition that results when the prostate gland swells and constricts the flow of urine from the urethra. Symptoms can range from a constant need to urinate to bladder and kidney infection. If infection occurs, part or all of the prostate may have to be removed. Most of these procedures do not cause impotence.

Scrapie—A fatal disease common to sheep and goats and caused by a slow virus. The disease is so called because infected animals constantly scratch themselves. The brains of victims have plaques resembling those found in victims of Alzheimer's disease.

Senile plaque—Distended parts of a neuron caused by a fatty substance called amyloid. Senile plaques are characteristic of the brains of Alzheimer's disease patients as well as victims of several other neurological disorders.

Senility—An obsolete term referring to the mental slowing down and fuzziness once assumed to be characteristic of the elderly.

Skin cancer—A form of cancer that most frequently appears on the face, lower arms and back of the neck. It is thought to be caused by the sun's ultraviolet light. Most typically, light-skinned people who do not protect themselves from the sun get it. The cancer takes three forms:

1. BASAL CELL CARCINOMA—Begins as a small nodule with raised edges, developing a crusted ulcer in the center. It rarely spreads, but the nodules should be removed.

2. SQUAMOUS CELL CARCINOMA—Begins with the growth of rough spots of thickened skin called solar keratoses that can grow to a large size. This cancer is more dangerous than basal cell carcinoma because cancerous cells can spread to lymph nodes and then to other parts of the body. Solar keratoses should be removed.

3. MALIGNANT MELANOMA—Extremely dangerous and fatal to 50 percent of those who get it because cancerous cells rapidly spread to other parts of the body. If an existing mole begins to grow or to change color from black to purple, you should have a doctor look at it.

Steroids—A class of organic compounds that include cholesterol and many hormones, including the stress and sex hormones.

Stratum corneum—The outermost skin layer, the only one that can be penetrated by cosmetics, save those that contain cortisone, which will penetrate to deeper layers. Moisturizing creams will swell up the cells of the stratum corneum and temporarily conceal roughness and small wrinkles.

Stroke—Death or damage to part of the brain due to one or more of the following reasons: a blood clot forming in a cerebral vessel; a blood clot or atherosclerotic plaque that flows into a cerebral vessel from another part of the body and lodges there; and pressure on a cerebral vessel from a tumor.

Superoxide dismutase—A free radical scavenger.

Tartar—Dental plaque that has hardened and pushed its way under the gums. It must be chipped away by your dentist. Calculus is another name for it.

T-Cells—Lymphocytes (white blood cells) that are processed in the thymus glands before being able to defend the body from foreign substances like viruses and bacteria.

Testosterone—The principal male sex hormone. It is produced in the adrenal glands of both men and women and in the testicles in men. The hormone is responsible for male characteristics such as deep voice, hairiness and muscular development. Until recently, researchers assumed that its levels dwindled with age. This has now been disproven. Maintenance of testosterone levels depends to a great extent on physical and psychological health.

Thymus—A small gland behind the breastbone that is important for immunity. Beginning in one's adolescence, the gland starts to shrink and by adulthood is only 10 to 15 percent of its former size.

Triglyceride—Fatty substance found in animal tissues. High levels of triglycerides in the blood are associated with atherosclerosis.

Type A Personality—A heart-attack-prone personality type characterized by aggressivity, ambition, competitiveness, hostility, guilt and inflexibility.

Type B Personality—A personality type characterized by passivity, calmness and lack of urgency. Type B individuals are far less likely to have heart disease than Type A's.

Ventricle—A pumping chamber in the heart. There are two of them. The left ventricle pumps oxygenated blood to the arteries. The right ventricle pumps blood from the heart to the lungs.

Sources

Chapter 1

Aloia, John F. "Osteoporosis: Alternatives to Prevention and Treatment—The Role of Exercise." Presentation at the Seventh Annual Brookdale Medical Conference on Aging, Mount Sinai School of Medicine, New York, Dec. 2, 1983.

Arenberg, David. "Differences and Changes with Age in the Benton Visual Retention Test." *Journal of Gerontology*, Vol. 33, 1978.

Bishop, Jerry E. "Scientists Are Firming Link to Cholesterol with Coronary Disease." *The Wall Street Journal*, Jan. 10, 1984.

Brewerton, Derrick A. "Rheumatic Disorders," in *Clinical Geriatrics*, 2nd edition, ed. Rossman, Isadore. Philadelphia: J. B. Lippincott Co., 1979.

Brody, Jane E. "Debilitating Bone Condition Can Be Prevented." *The New York Times*, Jan. 11, 1984.

———. "Lowering Cholesterol in Blood." *The New York Times*, Jan. 18, 1984.

———. "Personal Health." *The New York Times*, Dec. 19, 1984.

Caplan, Louis R. "Neurology," in *Health and Disease in Old Age*, ed. Rowe, John W., and Besdine, Richard W. Boston: Little, Brown and Co., 1982.

Castelli, William P. "Natural Disease Investigation: Atherosclerosis, Blood Cholesterol, and the Environment." *The American Journal of Forensic Medicine and Pathology*, Vol. 3, Dec. 1982.

"Consumer Expenditure Study." *Product Marketing*, Aug. 1984.

DeFronzo, Ralph A. "Glucose Intolerance and Aging." *Diabetes Care*, Vol. 4, July/Aug. 1981.

"Diabetes and Aging." National Institutes of Health pamphlet, 1979.

Eden, John. *The Eye Book*. New York: Viking Press, 1978.

Gallagher, John C. "Osteoporosis: Alternative to Prevention and

Treatment—The Role of Pharmacological Therapy." Presentation at the Seventh Annual Brookdale Conference on Aging, Mount Sinai School of Medicine, New York, Dec. 2, 1983.

Giansiracusa, David F., and Kantrowitz, Fred G. "Metabolic Bone Disease," in *Health and Disease in Old Age,* op. cit.

Gilchrest, Barbara A. "Skin," in *Health and Disease in Old Age,* op. cit.

Goldman, Ralph. "Decline in Organ Function with Aging," in *Clinical Geriatrics,* op. cit.

Goleman, Daniel. "The Aging Mind Proves Capable of Lifelong Growth." *The New York Times,* Feb. 24, 1984.

Gordon, Tavia, et al. "Lipoproteins, Cardiovascular Disease, and Death: The Framingham Study." *Archives of Internal Medicine,* Vol. 141, Aug. 1981.

Habermann, Edward T. "Orthopaedic Aspects of the Lower Extremities," in *Clinical Geriatrics,* op. cit.

Hart, Ron, and Setlow, Richard. "Correlation between Deoxyribonucleic Acid Excision Repair and Lifespan in a Number of Mammalian Species." *Proceedings of the National Academy of Sciences,* Vol. 71, 1974.

Hayflick, Leonard. "The Cell Biology of Human Aging." *Scientific American,* Jan. 1980.

———. "The Cellular Basis for Biological Aging," in *Handbook of the Biology of Aging,* ed. Finch, Caleb E., and Hayflick, Leonard. New York: Van Nostrand Reinhold, 1977.

"Heart Facts, 1984." American Heart Association pamphlet, Dallas, 1984.

"Hold the Eggs and Butter," *Time,* March 26, 1984.

"How the Brain Works." *Newsweek,* Feb. 7, 1983.

Kripke, D., et al. "Short and Long Sleep and Sleeping Pills." *Archives of General Psychiatry,* Vol. 36, 1979.

Lakatta, Edward G., and Gerstenblith, Gary. "Cardiovascular System," in *Health and Disease in Old Age,* op. cit.

Leiblum, Sandra, and Bachmann, Gloria, et al. "Vaginal Atrophy in the Postmenopausal Woman." *Journal of the American Medical Association,* Vol. 249, April 22/29, 1983.

"A Long and Healthy Life," in *Nova, Adventures in Science.* Reading, Mass.: Addison-Wesley Publishing Co., 1983.

"The Melanoma Letter." The Skin Cancer Foundation, Vol. 2, 1984.

Orwell, Eric, and McClung, Michael R. "Disorders of Calcium and Mineral Metabolism," in *Geriatric Medicine,* Vol. 1, ed. Cassel, Christine K., and Walsh, John R. New York: Springer-Verlag, 1984.

Parker, Frank. "Dermatology," in *Geriatric Medicine,* op. cit.

"Pooling Project Research Group: Relationship of Blood Pressure, Serum Cholesterol, Smoking Habit, Relative Weight and ECG Abnormalities to Incidence of Major Coronary Events." *Journal of Chronic Disease,* Vol. 31, 1978.

Rich, Larry F. "Ophthalmology," in *Geriatric Medicine,"* op. cit.

Riddle, Matthew C. "Diabetes Mellitus," in *Geriatric Medicine,* op. cit.

Rose, Richard M., and Besdine, Richard W. "Immune System," in *Health and Disease in Old Age,* op. cit.

Rossman, Isadore. "The Anatomy of Aging," in *Clinical Geriatrics,* op. cit.

Schaie, K. Warner. "The Seattle Longitudinal Study: A 21-Year Exploration of Psychometric Intelligence in Adulthood," in *Longitudinal Studies of Adult Psychological Development,* ed. Schaie, K. Warner. New York: The Guilford Press, 1983.

Shock, Nathan W. "System Integration," in *Handbook of the Biology of Aging,* op. cit.

Strehler, Bernard L. "Fundamental Mechanisms of Neuronal Aging," in *Brain Aging: Neuropharmacology* (Aging, Vol. 21), ed. Cervos-Navarro, J., and Sarkander, H. I. New York: Raven Press, 1983.

Weitzman, Elliot D. "Sleep and Aging," in *The Neurology of Aging,* ed. Katzman, Robert, and Terry, Robert. Philadelphia: F. A. Davis Co., 1983.

Weksler, Marc. "A Search for Immunological Markers of Aging in Men," in *Biological Markers of Aging,* ed. Reff, Mitchell E., and Schneider, Edward L. National Institutes of Health, April 1982.

Zach, Leo. "The Oral Cavity," in *Clinical Geriatrics,* op. cit.

Chapter 3

Brody, Jane E. "Personal Health—Long Term Risks and Adverse Reactions from Cosmetics." *The New York Times,* Sept. 19, 1984.

"Consumer Expenditure Study." *Product Marketing,* Aug. 1984.

Franklin, Ben A. "Cosmetic Unit Aids Research." *The New York Times,* Sept. 23, 1981.

Goldman, Leon. "Look Better as You Grow Older," in *After-40 Health and Medical Guide,* ed. Cooley, Donald G. Des Moines: Meredith Corporation, 1980.

Heller, Linda, and Marano, Estroff. "What's Safe on Your Face." *American Health,* May/June 1983.

Ship, Arthur. Personal interviews.

Chapter 4

Ames, Bruce N. "Dietary Carcinogens and Anticarcinogens." *Science,* Vol. 221, 1983.

Applesweig, Norman. Personal interview and communications.

Balin, Arthur K. Personal interviews.

————. "Oxygen Modulates Growth of Human Cells at Physiologic

Partial Pressures." *Journal of Experimental Medicine,* Vol. 160, July 1984.

————. "Testing the Free Radical Theory of Aging," in *Testing the Theories of Aging,* ed. Adelman, R. C., and Roth, G. S. CRC Press, 1982.

Coleman, D., et al. "Therapeutic Effects of Dehydroepiandrosterone Metabolites in Diabetes Mutant Mice." *Endocrinology,* Vol. 115, 1984.

Cristofalo, Vincent J. Personal interviews and communications.

————. "The Destiny of Cells: Mechanisms and Implications of Senescence." Kleemeir Lecture presented to the Gerontological Society of America, San Francisco, Nov. 19, 1983.

————, and Stanulis, Betzbé M. "Cell Aging: A Model System Approach," in *The Biology of Aging,* ed. Behnke, John A., Finch, Caleb E., and Moment, Gairdner B. New York: Plenum Press, 1978.

Cutler, Richard G. Personal interview.

————. "Evolutionary Biology of Senescence," in *The Biology of Aging,* op. cit.

Finch, Caleb E. "The Brain and Aging," in *The Biology of Aging,* op. cit.

Fixx, James F. *The Complete Book of Running.* New York: Random House, 1977.

Hallowell, Christopher. "DHEA Backgrounder." Unpublished paper prepared for Progenics, Inc.

Harman, Denham. "The Aging Process." *Proceedings of the National Academy of Sciences,* Vol. 78, 1981.

Harman, S. Mitchell. "Aging, Sexual Activity and Sex Hormones in Healthy Men." *Generations,* Fall 1981.

Hayflick, Leonard. "The Cellular Basis for Biological Aging," in *Handbook of the Biology of Aging,* ed. Finch, Caleb E., and Hayflick, Leonard. New York: Van Nostrand Reinhold, 1977.

Rosenfeld, Albert. "Superpowder." *Omni,* Aug. 1982.

Sacher, George A. *Maturation and Longevity in Relation to Cranial Capacity in Hominid Evolution.* Vol. 1, ed. Tuttle, R. The Hague: Mouton, 1975.

Sohal, R. S., and Buchan, P. B. "Relationship Between Physical Activity and Lifespan in the Adult Housefly, Musca Domestica." *Experimental Gerontology,* Vol. 16, 1981.

————, and Donato, H. "Effects of Experimentally Altered Life Spans on the Accumulation of Fluorescent Age Pigment in the Housefly, Musca Domestica." *Experimental Gerontology,* Vol. 13, 1978.

Walford, Roy L. Personal interview.

————. "Immunology and Aging." *American Journal of Clinical Pathology,* Vol. 74, Sept. 1980.

————. *Maximum Life Span*. New York: W. W. Norton and Company, 1983.

————. "A Speculative Proposal about the Immemorial Ancestry of the MHC." *AACHTions News*, Vol. V., June, 1981.

Wang Associates. Unpublished material on DHEA and about Progenics, Inc.

Chapter 5

Abraham, Sidney, National Center for Health Statistics. Personal interview.

Altman, Lawrence K. "James Fixx: The Enigma of Heart Disease." *The New York Times*, July 24, 1984.

Barrows, Charles H., and Kokkonen, Gertrude C. "Relationship Between Nutrition and Aging," in *Advances in Nutritional Research*, Vol. 1, ed. Draper, Harold. New York: Plenum Press, 1977.

Blair, S. N., et al. "Physical Fitness and Evidence of Hypertension in Healthy Normotensive Men and Women." *Journal of the American Medical Association*, Vol. 252, July 27, 1984.

Bortz, Walter M. II. "Disuse and Aging." *Journal of the American Medical Association*, Vol. 248, Sept. 10, 1982.

Brody, Jane E. *Jane Brody's Nutrition Book*. New York: W. W. Norton & Co., 1981.

————. "Panel Finds Obesity a Major U.S. Killer Needing Top Priority." *The New York Times*, Feb. 14, 1985.

Fixx, James F. *The Complete Book of Running*. New York: Random House, 1977.

Goodrick, Charles L. "Effects of Long-Term Voluntary Wheel Exercise on Male and Female Wistar Rats." *Gerontology*, Vol. 26, 1980.

————, et. al. "Differential Effects of Intermittent Feeding and Voluntary Exercise on Body Weight and Lifespan in Adult Rats." *Journal of Gerontology*, Vol. 38, 1983.

Greenberg, Joel. "Exercise: A Matter of Life or Death?" *Science News*, Vol. 126, Sept. 1, 1984.

Gurin, Joel. "What's Your Natural Weight?" *American Health*, May, 1984.

"It's All in the Hips." *Science News*, Vol 127, Jan. 26, 1985.

Kent, Saul. "The Procaine 'Youth' Drugs." *Geriatrics*, Vol. 37, April, 1982.

Lew, Edward A., and Garfinkel, Lawrence. "Variations in Mortality by Weight Among 750,000 Men and Women." *Journal of Chronic Disease*, Vol. 32, 1979.

McCay, Clive, et al. "The Effects of Retarded Growth upon the Length of Life Span and Upon Ultimate Body Size." *Journal of Nutrition,* Vol. 10, 1935.

Masoro, Edward J. Personal interviews and communications.

———. "Nutrition as a Modulator of the Aging Process." Prepublication manuscript.

———, et al. "Nutritional Probe of the Aging Process." *Federation Proceedings,* Vol. 39, Dec. 1980.

"More Alcohol, Less Milk in U.S. Consumer's Diet." *The New York Times,* Nov. 27, 1984.

Neuberger, A., and Jukes, T. H. *Human Nutrition: Current Issues and Controversies.* Lancaster, England: MTT Press, 1982.

"Nutrition and Fitness Awareness and Behavior: The New Rochelle Report." Researched and published by Research and Forecasts under the auspices of the city of New Rochelle, 1983.

Overmann, Stephen R. "Dietary Self-Selection by Animals." *Psychological Bulletin,* Vol. 83, 1976.

Paffenbarger, R. S., Jr. "A Natural History of Athleticism and Cardiovascular Health." *Journal of the American Medical Association,* Vol. 252, July 27, 1984.

"The Perrier Study: Fitness in America." New York: Louis Harris and Associates, 1979.

"Recommended Dietary Allowances—Definitions and Applications." *Recommended Dietary Allowances,* 9th Edition. Washington, D.C.: National Academy Press, 1980.

Rigotti, Nancy A. "Exercise and Coronary Heart Disease." *Annual Review of Medicine,* Vol. 34, 1983.

Ross, Morris H. "Nutritional Regulation of Longevity," in *The Biology of Aging,* ed. Behnke, John A., Finch, Caleb E., and Moment, Gairdner B. New York: Plenum Press, 1978.

———, and Lustbader, E. "Dietary Practices and Growth Responses as Predictors of Longevity." *Nature,* Vol. 262, Aug. 12, 1976.

Sacher, George A. "Life Table Modification and Life Prolongation," in *Handbook of the Biology of Aging,* ed. Finch, Caleb E., and Hayflick, Leonard. New York: Van Nostrand Reinhold, 1977.

Shapiro, James E. *Meditations from the Breakdown Lane: Running Across America.* New York: Random House, 1982.

Thomas, Gregory S. "Fitness and Exercise for the Elderly." Prepublication manuscript.

———, et al. *Exercise and Health: The Evidence and the Implications.* Cambridge, Mass.: Oelgesschlager, Gunn and Hain Publishers, Inc., 1981.

Ward, Alex. "Athletes: Older but Fitter." *The New York Times Magazine,* Oct. 8, 1984.

Webb, James L. "Physiological Characteristics of a Champion Runner: Age 77." *Journal of Gerontology,* Vol. 32, 1977.

Weindruch, Richard H., et al. "Influence of Controlled Dietary Restriction on Immunologic Function and Aging." *Federation Proceedings,* Vol. 38, May, 1979.

Young, Eleanor A. "Nutrition, Aging and the Aged." *Medical Clinics of North America,* Vol. 67, March 1983.

Zohman, Lenore R. "Exercise Your Way to Fitness and Heart Health." Published by Mazola Corn Oil, 1981.

Chapter 6

Arcury, Thomas A. "Kentucky Longevity Project: A Preliminary Analysis of Demographic Structure and Longevity in a Rural Kentucky County." *Proceedings of the First Joint US–USSR Symposium on Aging and Longevity,* Vol. I. New York: International Research and Exchanges Board, 1981.

Benet, Sula. *Abkhasians: The Long Living People of the Caucasus.* New York: Holt, Rinehart and Winston, 1974.

———. "Abkhasians, the Long Living People of the Caucasus," in *Case Studies in Cultural Anthropology,* ed. Sindler, George, and Sindler, Louise. New York: Holt, Rinehart and Winston, 1974.

Bryant, Carol A., et al. "Nutrition." Unpublished manuscript, June, 1982.

Georgakas, Dan. *The Methuselah Factors.* New York: Simon and Schuster, 1980.

Kopeshavidze, G. G. "Notes on the Traditional Abkhasian Diet." *Proceedings of the First Joint US–USSR Symposium on Aging and Longevity,* Vol. I, op. cit.

Krupnik, I. I. "The Problem of Leadership in Abkhasian Social Organization from the Point of View of Longevity." *Proceedings of the First Joint US–USSR Symposium on Aging and Longevity,"* Vol. I, op. cit.

Leaf, Alexander. "Getting Old." *Scientific American,* Vol. 229, Sept. 1973.

———. "Long Lived Populations." *Journal of the American Geriatrics Society,* Vol. 30, August 1982.

———. *Youth in Old Age.* New York: McGraw-Hill, 1975.

Mazess, Richard B., and Forman, Sylvia H. "Longevity and Age Exaggeration in Vilcabamba, Ecuador." *Journal of Gerontology,* Vol. 34, 1979.

Medvedev, Zhores A. "Caucasus and Altay Longevity: A Biological or Social Problem?" *The Gerontologist,* Vol. 14, 1974.

Murray, John M. Personal interview.

"Nutritional Differences Among Elderly Residents of Robertson County, Kentucky." Anonymous unpublished manuscript.

Palmore, Erdman B. "Longevity in Abkhasia: A Reevaluation." *The Gerontologist,* Vol. 121, Feb. 1984.

Pelletier, Kenneth R. *Longevity, Fulfilling Our Biological Potential.* New York: Delacorte Press/Seymour Lawrence, 1981.

Rubin, Vera. Personal interviews and communications.

Sullivan, Walter. "Clues to Healthy Old Age Found in Soviet Villages." *The New York Times,* Nov. 30, 1982.

van Willigen, John G., and Bryant, Carol B. "Social Aging in a Rural American Community: Theory and Preliminary Results." Unpublished manuscript.

———, and Wolf, David J. *Progress Report, Kentucky Longevity Project: Ethnography,* July 1, 1979–April 15, 1980. Unpublished submission to National Institute on Aging.

·———. Untitled grant proposal to National Institute on Aging, 1976.

Wolf, David J. Personal interviews and communications.

Chapter 7

Ader, Robert, ed. *Psychoneuroimmunology,* New York: Academic Press, 1981.

———, and Cohen, N. "Behaviorally Conditioned Immunosuppression." *Psychosomatic Medicine,* Vol. 37, 1975.

Anderson, Alan. "How the Mind Heals." *Psychology Today,* December 1982.

Brody, Jane E. "Finding a Method to Reduce Stress." *The New York Times,* February 10, 1982.

Cobb, S., and Rose, R. M. "Hypertension, Peptic Ulcer, and Diabetes in Air Traffic Controllers." *Journal of the American Medical Association,* Vol. 224, 1973.

Cohen, J. B., and Brody, J. A. "The Epidemiologic Importance of Psychosocial Factors in Longevity." *American Journal of Epidemiology,* Vol. 114, 1981.

Colligan, M. J., et al. "An Investigation of Apparent Mass Psychogenic Illness in an Electronics Plant." *Journal of Behavioral Medicine,* Vol. 2, 1979.

Derogati, L. R., et al. "Psychological Coping Mechanisms and Survival Times in Metastatic Breast Cancer." *Journal of the American Medical Association,* Vol. 242, 1979.

Eckholm, Erik. "Value of Meditation Against Stress Now Questioned." *The New York Times,* July 24, 1984.

"Economic Woes May Harm Health Later." *Science News,* July 7, 1984.

Frankenhaeuser, M., and Gardell, B. "Underload and Overload in Working Life: Outline of a Multidisciplinary Approach." *Journal of Human Stress,* September, 1976.

Friedman, M., and Rosenman, R. H. *Type A Behavior and Your Heart.* New York: Knopf, 1974.

Gonzalez, Elizabeth R. "Stressed Whites Especially Prone to 'Trench Mouth,' Study Finds." *Journal of the American Medical Association,* Vol. 247, January 14, 1983.

Haynes, Suzanne E., et al. "Spouse Behavior and Coronary Heart Disease in Men: Prospective Results from the Framingham Heart Study." *Journal of Epidemiology,* Vol 118, July, 1983.

Herbert, W. "Depression: Too Much Vigilance?" *Science News,* Vol. 124, 1982.

Holmes, T. H. "Development and Application of a Quantitative Measure of Life Change Magnitude," in *Stress and Mental Disorder,* ed. Barrett, James E., et al. New York: Raven Press, 1979.

———, and Rahe, R. H. "The Social Readjustment Rating Scale." *Journal of Psychosomatic Research,* Vol. 11, 1967.

Holmes, T. S., and Holmes, T. H. "Short-Term Intrusions into Life Style Routine." *Journal of Psychosomatic Research,* Vol. 14, 1970.

Jemmott, John B. III, et al. "Academic Stress, Power Motivation, and Decrease in Secretion Rate of Salivary Immunoglobulin A." *The Lancet,* June 25, 1983.

Karasek, R. "Job Socialization and Job Strain; The Implications of Two Related Psychosocial Mechanisms for Job Design," in *Working Life: A Social Science Contribution to Work Reform,* ed. Gardell, B., and Johansson, G. London: Wiley, 1981.

Keller, Steven E., et al. "Suppression of Immunity by Stress: Effect of a Graded Series of Stressors in Lymphocyte Stimulation in the Rat." *Science,* Vol. 213, September 18, 1981.

Kobasa, Suzanne O. "How Much Stress Can You Survive?" *American Health,* September 1984.

Levy, Sandra M. "Emotions and the Progression of Cancer: A Review." *Advances,* Vol. 1, Winter 1984.

Lewis, Myrna I. "Stress of the Retirement Years." *Medical Aspects of Human Sexuality,* Vol. 18, May 1984.

McClean, A. A. *Work Stress.* Reading, Mass.: Addison-Wesley, 1979.

Murphy, L. R., and Colligan, M. J. "Mass Psychogenic Illness in a Shoe Factory, A Case Report." *International Archives of Occupational and Environmental Health,* Vol 44, 1979.

Nelson, Bryce. "Bosses Feel Less Risk than the Bossed." *The New York Times,* April 3, 1983.

Rahe, R. H., et al. "The Epidemiology of Illness in Naval Environments." *Military Medicine,* Vol. 135, 1970.

Rosch, Paul H. "Stress and Cardiovascular Disease." *Comprehensive Therapy,* Vol. 9, September, 1983.

Rose, R. M. *Air Traffic Controller Health Change Study.* Boston: Boston University Press, 1978.

Sapolsky, Robert. Personal interviews and communications.

Schleiffer, Steven J., et al. "Suppression of Lymphocyte Stimulation Following Bereavement." *Journal of the American Medical Association,* Vol. 250, July 15, 1983.

Selye, Hans. "The General Adaptation Syndrome and the Diseases of Adaptation." *Journal of Clinical Endocrinology,* Vol. 6, 1946.

———. *The Stress of Life,* Revised edition. New York: McGraw-Hill, 1976.

Singer, J. E., et al. "Stress on the Train: A Study of Urban Commuting," in *Advances in Environmental Psychology, Vol. 1; The Urban Environment,* ed. Baum, A., et al. Hillsdale, N.Y.: Lawrence Erlbaum Associates, 1978.

Taulbee, P. "Study Shows Stress Decreases Immunity." *Science News,* Vol. 124, July 2, 1983.

Chapter 8

Anonymous. "Effects of Sexual Activity on Beard Growth in Men." *Nature,* Vol. 226, May 30, 1970.

Boyer, Gerry, and Boyer, James. "Sexuality and Aging." *Nursing Clinics of North America,* Vol. 17, September 1982.

Brecher, Edward M. *Love, Sex and Aging.* Boston: Little, Brown and Co., 1984.

Butler, Robert N., and Lewis, Myrna I. *Sex After Sixty.* New York: Harper and Row, 1976.

Davidson, Julian M. "Sexuality and Aging." Prepublication manuscript.

———. Personal interview.

———, et al. "Effects of Androgen on Sexual Behavior in Hypogonadal Men." *Journal of Clinical Endocrinology and Metabolism,* Vol. 48, 1979.

Harman, S. Mitchell. "Aging, Sexual Activity and Sex Hormones in Healthy Men." *Generations,* Fall 1981.

———, et al. "Hormonal Changes and Sexual Function in Aging Men." *Journal of Endocrinology and Metabolism,* Vol. 57, July 1983.

Lieblum, Sandra; Bachman, Gloria, et al. "Vaginal Atrophy in the Postmenopausal Woman." *Journal of the American Medical Association,* Vol. 249, April 22/29, 1983.

Martin, Clyde E. "Factors Affecting Sexual Functioning in 60–79-Year-Old Married Males." *Archives of Sexual Behavior,* Vol. 10, 1981.

———. "Sexual Activity in the Aging Male," in *Handbook of Sexology,* ed. Money, J., and Musaph, H. New York: Elsevier/North Holland Biomedical Press, 1977.

Masters, William H., and Johnson, Virginia E. *Human Sexual Inadequacy.* Boston: Little, Brown and Co., 1970.

————. *Human Sexual Response.* Boston: Little, Brown and Co., 1966.

Pocs, Ollie. "The Value of Sexuality for the Elderly." Presentation before the Sixth World Congress of Sexology, Washington, D.C., May 24, 1983.

Ramey, Estelle. Personal interview.

Rose, Robert M., et al. "Plasma Testosterone Levels in the Male Rhesus: Influences of Sexual and Social Stimuli." *Science,* Vol. 178, Nov. 1972.

Rowand, A. "The (Anti-Cancer?) Pill." *Science News,* Vol. 125, June 30, 1984.

Sheehy, Gail. *Passages.* New York: E. P. Dutton and Company, 1976.

Solnick, Robert L. "Sexual Responsiveness, Age and Change: Facts and Potential," in *Sexuality and Aging,* ed. Solnick, Robert L. Los Angeles: University of California Press, 1978.

Tsitouras, Panayiotis D. "Relationship of Serum Testosterone to Sexual Activity in Healthy Elderly Men." *Journal of Gerontology,* Vol. 37, 1982.

Chapter 9

Davies, Peter. Personal interviews.

————. "An Update on the Neurochemistry of Alzheimer's Disease," in *The Dementias,* ed. Payeux, R., and Rosen, W. G. New York: Raven Press, 1983.

————. "The Neurochemistry of Alzheimer's Disease and Senile Dementia." *Medicinal Research Reviews,* Vol. 3, 1983.

————. "Neurotransmitters and Neuropeptides in Alzheimer's Disease," in *Banbury Report 15; Biological Aspects of Alzheimer's Disease,* ed. Katzman, Robert. Cold Spring Harbor Laboratory, 1983.

Davis, Kenneth. Personal interview.

Dickson, Alan G., et al. "The Relevance of Scrapie as an Experimental Model of Alzheimer's Disease," in *Banbury Report 15,* op. cit.

Epstein, Charles J. "Down's Syndrome and Alzheimer's Disease: Implications and Approaches," in *Banbury Report 15,* op. cit.

Gajdusek, D. Carlton. "Unconventional Viruses and the Origin and Disappearance of Kuru." *Science,* Vol. 197, September 2, 1977.

Goldsmith, Marsha F. "Attempts to Vanquish Alzheimer's Disease Intensify, Take New Paths." *Journal of the American Medical Association,* Vol. 251, April 13, 1984.

Heston, Leonard J. "Dementia of the Alzheimer's Type: A Perspective from Family Studies," in *Banbury Report 15,* op. cit.

Heyman, Albert. Personal interview.

————, et al. "Alzheimer's Disease: Genetic Aspects and Associated

Clinical Disorders." *Annals of Neurology*, Vol. 14, November 1983.

————. "Alzheimer's Disease: A Study of Epidemiological Aspects." *Annals of Neurology*, Vol. 15, 1984.

Hubbard, Linda. "The Alzheimer's Puzzle; Putting the Pieces Together." *Modern Maturity*, August-September 1984.

Hyman, B. T., et al. "Alzheimer's Disease: Cell-Specific Pathology Isolates the Hippocampal Formation." *Science*, Vol. 225, 1984.

Mace, Nancy L., and Rabins, Peter V. *The 36-Hour Day: A Family Guide to Caring for Persons with Alzheimer's Disease, Related Dementing Illnesses, and Memory Loss in Later Life*. Baltimore: Johns Hopkins University Press, 1981.

Miller, J. A. "For Want of an Inhibitor: Alzheimer's Disease." *Science News*, Vol. 126, 1984.

Perl, Daniel P. "Aluminum and Alzheimer's Disease: Intraneuronal X-Ray Spectrometry Studies," in *Banbury Report 15*, op. cit.

Powell, Lenore S., and Courtice, Katie. *Alzheimer's Disease: A Guide for Families*. Reading, Mass.: Addison-Wesley Publishing Co., 1983.

Prusiner, Stanley B. "Prions and Dementia," in *Banbury Report 15*, op. cit.

————. "Some Speculations about Prions, Amyloid, and Alzheimer's Disease." *The New England Journal of Medicine*, Vol. 310, March 8, 1984.

Reisberg, Barry. Personal interview.

————. *Brain Failure: An Introduction to the Current Principles of Senility*. New York: Free Press, 1983.

————. *A Guide to Alzheimer's Disease for Families, Spouses and Friends*. New York: Free Press, 1983.

————. "Stages of Cognitive Decline." *American Journal of Nursing*, February 1984.

Roach, Marion. "Another Name for Madness." *The New York Times Magazine*, January 16, 1983.

Silberner, J. "Cautious Optimism on Alzheimer's Finding." *Science News*, Vol. 126, October 27, 1984.

"A Slow Death of the Mind." *Newsweek*, December 3, 1983.

Chapter 10

Aging in the Eighties: America in Transition. A survey conducted by Louis Harris and Associates, Inc., for the National Council on the Aging, 1981.

"As More Firms Nudge Out Employees." *U.S. News and World Report*, February 28, 1983.

Bosse, Raymond, and Ekerdt, David J. "The Effect of Retirement on Physical Health." Prepublication manuscript.

Bradford, Leland P. "Can You Survive Your Retirement?" *Harvard Business Review*, November-December 1979.

Butler, Robert N. *Why Survive? Being Old in America*. New York: Harper & Row, 1975.

Casscells, W., et al. "Retirement and Coronary Mortality." *The Lancet*, Vol. 1, 1980.

Ekerdt, David J. Personal interview.

———, et al. "Claims That Retirement Improves Health." *Journal of Gerontology*, Vol. 38, 1983.

———, and Bosse, Raymond. "Change in Self-Reported Health with Retirement." *International Journal of Aging and Human Development*, Vol. 15, 1982.

———, et al. "The Effect of Retirement on Physical Health " *American Journal of Public Health*, Vol. 73, July 1983.

Keslar, Linda. "Executives in Retirement." *The New York Times*, August 5, 1984.

Palmore, Erdman B. Personal interview.

———, et al. "Consequences of Retirement." *Journal of Gerontology*, Vol. 39, 1984.

Perkins, Joseph S. Personal interview.

"Why Late Retirement Is Getting a Corporate Blessing." *Business Week*, January 16, 1984.

Chapter 11

Continuing Care Retirement Communities. Published jointly by the American Association of Homes for the Aging and the American Association of Retired Persons, 1984.

Continuing Care Retirement Communities: An Empirical, Financial and Legal Analysis. Published for the Wharton School, University of Pennsylvania, by Richard D. Irwin, Inc., 1984.

Constantinou, Marianne. "For Empty-Nesters, the Adult Village." *The New York Times*, May 15, 1983.

Ferretti, Fred. "Elderly Choose Retirement Community Living." *The New York Times*, April 5, 1984.

———. "Retirement Life Varies in Three Communities." *The New York Times*, April 12, 1984.

Fitzgerald, Frances. "A Reporter at Large: Interlude." *The New Yorker*, April 25, 1983.

Hinds, Michael deCourcy. "For Older People, Communal Living Has Its Rewards." *The New York Times*, January 31, 1985.

Janson, Donald. "Retirement Towns Flourish in Jersey's Fields." *The New York Times*, March 5, 1984.

Marans, Robert W. *Changing Properties of Retirement Communities*. Institute of Gerontology. Ann Arbor, Mich.: University of Michigan, 1984.

McPhee, John. *The Pine Barrens.* New York: Farrar, Straus & Giroux, 1967.

Chapter 12

Aging America, Trends and Projections. Prepared by the U.S. Senate Special Committee on Aging with the American Association of Retired Persons, 1984.

Butler, Robert N. *Why Survive? Being Old in America.* New York: Harper and Row, 1975.

Fries, James F. "Aging, Natural Death and the Compression of Morbidity." *The New England Journal of Medicine,* Vol. 303, July 17, 1980.

The U.S. Health Care System: A Look to the 1990s. Proceedings of the Cornell Conference on Health Policy, March 7–8, 1985. New York: Cornell University Medical College.

Index